LILLIAN HELLMAN

Lillian Hellman. (Billy Rose Theatre Collection. New York Public Library for the Performing Arts. Astor, Lenox and Tilden Foundations.)

LILLIAN HELLMAN

A Research and Production Sourcebook

Barbara Lee Horn

Modern Dramatists Research and Production Sourcebooks, Number 15
William W. Demastes, Series Adviser

GREENWOOD PRESS
Westport, Connecticut • London

Library of Congress Cataloging-in-Publication Data

Horn, Barbara Lee.
    Lillian Hellman : a research and production sourcebook / Barbara
Lee Horn.
       p.   cm.—(Modern dramatists research and production
sourcebooks, ISSN 1055–999X ; no. 15)
    Includes bibliographical references and index.
    ISBN 0–313–30264–2 (alk. paper)
    1. Hellman, Lillian, 1906– —Criticism and interpretation.
2. Hellman, Lillian, 1906– —Stage history. 3. Hellman, Lillian,
1906– —Bibliography. 4. Hellman, Lillian, 1906– —Plots.
I. Title. II. Series.
PS3515.E343Z72 1998
812′.52—dc21   98–21824

British Library Cataloguing in Publication Data is available.

Library of Congress Catalog Card Number: 98–21824
ISBN: 0–313–30264–2
ISSN: 1055–999X

First published in 1998

Greenwood Press, 88 Post Road West, Westport, CT 06881
An imprint of Greenwood Publishing Group, Inc.

Printed in the United States of America

The paper used in this book complies with the
Permanent Paper Standard issued by the National
Information Standards Organization (Z39.48–1984).

10 9 8 7 6 5 4 3 2 1

This book is for my sister
Gail Arden Gradowski

"It is very difficult to explain that one goes through a play with elation, depression, hope. That is the exact order. Hope sets in toward nightfall. That's when you tell yourself that you're going to be better the next time, so help you God. I am not special in this: I don't believe there ever was a writer who wanted to be a decent writer who was satisfied with what he had done and who wasn't willing to kid himself he'd be a Dostoyevsky the very next time."

"Back of Those Foxes." *New York Times* 26 Feb. 1939: X, 1-2.

Contents

Preface

Lillian Hellman's name will always be associated with the McCarthy era, if not for her memoir, *Scoundrel Time*, then for her response to the House Committee on Un-American Activities that has become a most memorable quotation: "I cannot and will not cut my conscience to fit this year's fashions." And her name will always be associated with the controversy that engulfed her career since the writing of her first play, *The Children's Hour* (1934), through the writing of her memoirs, a literary career that spanned five decades. During that time she wrote eight original plays and four adaptations for the Broadway stage, as well as three memoirs, *An Unfinished Woman* (1969), *Pentimento* (1973), *Scoundrel Time* (1976), and the novella, *Maybe.* (1980). She also wrote and adapted screenplays, adapting three of her own plays to film (*The Children's Hour*, as *These Three*, *The Little Foxes*, and *The Searching Wind*). She contributed to other literary activities, writing articles on diverse subjects for national magazines, and editing a selection of Chekhov's letters and a collection of Dashiell Hammett's mystery stories; her plays and memoirs providing others with material for plays, films, and an opera adaptation. The purpose of this study, however, is to document Hellman's contribution to dramatic literature.

Lillian Hellman: A Research and Production Sourcebook is a contribution to a series by Greenwood Press devoted to important figures in twentieth-century drama. This Research and Production Sourcebook has been planned to make Lillian Hellman and her work as accessible as possible to scholars and students interested for a variety of reasons in Hellman, including textual, theatrical, and performative. To those who are unfamiliar with Hellman's works, the play synopses and critical overviews should be useful. To scholars in the field, the opening essay, the critical overview sections, and the annotated bibliographies should be helpful. And while the secondary bibliography may not interest the theatre practitioner in general, the extensive summary of reviews in that section may provide staging insights; and the production credits may reveal insights into how a character was portrayed simply by revealing the actor originally cast in the role.

This volume is intended to serve as a quick reference guide as well as an exhaustive resource. It is divided into six sections. An overview of Hellman's life is provided, in chronology form, as well as in fuller essay form. The major section on the plays provides detailed plot summaries, stage histories, and critical overviews. The next section comprises an annotated bibliography of primary sources. This is followed by a secondary bibliography which has been divided into a review chapter and another on books, sections, and articles. Both secondary bibliographies are fully annotated chronologically and then alphabetically with the year of publication, affording the reader a fuller sense of Hellman's playwriting career. An author index and a general index are provided at the end of the book.

I would like to acknowledge my indebtedness to Mark Estrin, Katherine Lederer, Carl Rollyson, and William Wright, and all the patient scholarship that has preceded this study and on which I have built. My thanks go to St. John's University for the continued support of my research; and to the library staff at St. John's University, especially the interlibrary department.

A Note on Codes
and Numbering

"A"--A prefix identifying references to Lillian Hellman's writings, listed alphabetically, annotated, and arranged as: I. Plays; II. Articles and Essays on Drama and Theatre; and III. Other Works; located in the chapter "Primary Bibliography: Writings by Hellman."

"P"--A prefix identifying references to Lillian Hellman's productions, listed alphabetically and annotated in the chapter "The Plays: Summaries, Productions, and Critical Overviews."

"R"--A prefix identifying reviews, chronologically arranged according to year and annotated in the chapter "Secondary Bibliography: Reviews."

"S"--A prefix identifying other secondary materials, chronologically arranged in the chapter "Secondary Bibliography: Books, Articles, Sections."

LILLIAN HELLMAN

Chronology

1906 Born on June 20, 1906, in New Orleans, Louisiana, the only child of Julia Newhouse Hellman and Max Bernard Hellman, a shoe salesman.

1911 Moves with parents to New York; spends six months a year in New York with mother's family and six months with father's two sisters in New Orleans.

1922 Graduates from Wadleigh High School in New York.

1922-24 Attends New York University for two years; one semester at Columbia University in 1924.

1924-25 Works as a manuscript reader and an editorial assistant for Horace Liveright, Inc. Meets theatre press agent Arthur Kober whom she marries on 31 December 1925.

1925-29 Writes book reviews for the *New York Herald Tribune*; reads playscripts for Herman Shumlin; writes short stories of which most were unpublishable.

1926 Goes to Paris because of Kober's work; Kober writes for the *Paris Comet*, the magazine that publishes a couple of Hellman's short stories.

1929 Abandons plans to study for a year in Bonn, Germany, because of the anti-Semitism she experiences when she gets there.

1930 Goes with Kober to Hollywood where he works as a scriptwriter and she reads scripts for MGM.

1931 Moves back to New York with Dashiell Hammett whom she has met in Hollywood. Meets Dorothy Parker at a party.

1932 Divorces Kober. Collaborates with Louis Kronenberger on play, *Dear Queen* (unpublished/unproduced).

1933 Reads playscripts again for Shumlin.

1934   Hammett dedicates his last novel *The Thin Man* to Hellman (January). *The Children's Hour*, dedicated to D. Hammett, opens on Broadway at Maxine Elliot's Theatre (November 30).

1935   Returns to Hollywood to work for Samuel Goldwyn; writes first screenplay *The Dark Angel* with Mordaunt Shairp for United Artists (an adaptation from the play by Guy Bolton); begins writing the first screen adaptation of *The Children's Hour*, titled *These Three*, for Samuel Goldwyn-United Artists. Meets Parker again; they become lifelong friends.

1936   *These Three*, directed by William Wyler, premieres in New York (March 3). *The Children's Hour* is given a private performance at the Gate Theatre Studio in London (November). *Days to Come* opens on Broadway (December 15).

1937   Founds, with Archibald MacLeisch and Dorothy Parker, Contemporary Historians to back the antifascist film documentary, *The Spanish Earth*, to be shot by Joris Ivens (January). Goes to Hollywood to work on screen version of Sidney Kingsley's *Dead End* for Samuel Goldwyn-United Artists (Winter). Returns to New York (July 30). Sails to Europe with Dorothy Parker and Parker's husband, Alan Campbell; meets Ernest Hemingway on the crossing (August). Attends a theatre festival in Moscow. Goes to Spain to tour the Spanish Civil War zone, thereafter to become a militant anti-Fascist (October).

1939   *The Little Foxes* opens on Broadway at the National Theatre (February 15). Refuses to support the pro-Nazi Finnish resistance movement by declining to donate proceeds from a benefit performance against cast members' wishes. Buys Hardscrabble Farm, Pleasantville, NY, where she makes her home until 1952.

1940   Works on screenplay *The Little Foxes* (June).

1941   *Watch on the Rhine* opens on Broadway at the Martin Beck Theatre (April 1); receives the Drama Critics' Circle Award (April 27). Awarded an Honorary Master of Arts degree from Tufts University (June 15). The film *The Little Foxes* (screenplay by Hellman) opens at Radio City Music Hall, NYC (August 21). Lives at 5 East 83rd Street after *Watch on the Rhine* until Summer 1943.

1942   Contracts with Samuel Goldwyn to collaborate with William Wyler on the making of *The North Star*, an anti-Fascist documentary film of the war in Russia. Edits Hammett's film version of *Watch on the Rhine*. *Watch on the Rhine* is staged in London. An illustrated, limited edition of 349 copies of *Watch on the Rhine*, with special foreword by Parker, is privately published by the Joint Anti-Fascist Refugee Committee to raise general relief funds. Co-chairs dinner with Ernest Hemingway to raise money for release of noted anti-Fascists from French internment camps to Mexico.

1943   Buys townhouse at 63 East 82nd Street, NYC, where she lives until 1969. *Watch on the Rhine*, the Warner Bros. film (screenplay by Dashiell Hammett), opens at the Rialto Theatre, NYC (August 27). *The North Star* (screenplay by Hellman), a Crescent-RKO film release, premieres in two Broadway theatres simultaneously (November 4).

1944   *The Searching Wind* opens on Broadway at the Fulton Theatre (April 12).
        Hellman goes to Moscow on a cultural mission (September). Attends rehearsals
        of *The Little Foxes* and *Watch on the Rhine* in Moscow (September). Leaves
        from Kiev for the Polish front (December).

1945   Spends two weeks with the First White Russian Army on the Warsaw front
        (January). Returns from Moscow to New York (February).

1946   Inducted into the National Institute of Arts and Letters (May 17). The film
        version of *The Searching Wind* (screenplay by Hellman), written for Hal Wallis
        Productions-Paramount Pictures, premieres at the Paramount Theatre, NYC (June
        26). *Another Part of the Forest* opens on Broadway at the Fulton Theatre
        (November 20).

1947   Attends International Theatre Institute Conference in Paris (April).

1948   Goes to Hollywood; is denied work, as she has been blacklisted. Film adaptation
        of *Another Part of the Forest* (screenplay by Vladimir Pozner) is released by
        United Motion Pictures (May 18). Teaches a one-week course on playwriting at
        an Indiana University Writers' Conference (Summer). Becomes involved in
        Henry Wallace presidential campaign (July). Flies to Prague, Belgrade, and
        Paris, her principal mission to interview Marshall Tito in Belgrade for the New
        York *Star*; attends a performance of *The Little Foxes* in Belgrade (October).

1949   Speaks at Cultural and Scientific Congress for World Peace, sponsored by the
        National Council of the Arts, Sciences and Professions, NY (March). Named by
        Senator Jack B. Tenney as "having followed or appeased some of the Communist
        party-line programs." *Another Part of the Forest*, under the title of "*Ladies and
        Gentlemen*," is presented by the Moscow Drama Theatre (October). *Montserrat*
        opens on Broadway at the Fulton Theatre (October 29). *Regina*, the musical
        version of *The Little Foxes*, libretto and music by Marc Blitzstein, opens on
        Broadway at the Forty-Sixth Street Theatre (October 31).

1951   *The Autumn Garden* opens on Broadway at the Coronet Theatre (March 7).
        Hellman goes to Europe when Hammett is sentenced to six months in jail for
        refusing to provide names of contributors to the bailbond fund of the alleged pro-
        Communist Civil Rights Congress (April).

1952   *Montserrat* opens in London after a run in Hammersmith (May). Hellman receives
        a subpeona to appear before the House Committee on Un-American Activities
        (HUAC); sends a letter stating conditions under which she will testify (May).
        Meets with subcommittee in Washington, DC, and is dismissed without charges.
        Sells Hardscrabble Farm (May). Revival of *The Children's Hour* opens on
        Broadway at the Coronet Theatre.

1953   Hammett appears before Senator Joseph R. McCarthy Committee (March 26).

1954   Asked by Kermit Bloomgarden to adapt Jean Anouilh's *L'Alouette* for
        Broadway. Flies to London to see Christopher Fry's adaptation of *L'Alouette*,
        directed by Peter Brook (May).

1955   Edits and introduces *The Selected Letters of Anton Chekhov*, published by Farrar, Straus. Purchases summer home on Martha's Vineyard. *The Lark*, adapted from *L'Alouette*, opens on Broadway at the Longacre Theatre (November 17).

1956   *Candide, A Comic Operetta Based Upon Voltaire's Satire*, opens on Broadway at the Martin Beck Theatre (December 1).

1957   Goes abroad; visits London and Paris (Fall). *Autumn Garden* is presented in Moscow (1957-58 season).

1958   Returns to New York (February); lectures at University of Chicago (May).

1959   *Candide* opens in London (April 30).

1960   *Toys in the Attic* opens on Broadway at the Hudson Theatre (February 25); receives New York Drama Critics' Circle Award (May 19). Hellman is elected to the American Academy of Arts and Sciences (May). Supervises the London production of *Toys in the Attic* (November).

1961   Hammett dies (January 12). Hellman is appointed visiting lecturer in English at Harvard (Spring). Receives women's division of Albert Einstein College of Medicine of Yeshiva University Achievement Award (April); awarded honorary Litt.D. by Wheaton College (June 4); receives Brandeis University Creative Arts Medal in Theatre for Distinguished Contribution to the American Theatre (June 10).

1962   Elected Vice President of National Institute of Arts and Letters (February 13). The United Artists film adaptation of *The Children's Hour* (second film version with screenplay by John Michael Hayes) opens in New York (March 14); released in England under title *The Loudest Whisper*. Elected to American Academy of Arts and Letters (December 5).

1963   *My Mother, My Father and Me*, adapted from Burt Blechman's novel *How Much?*, opens on Broadway at the Plymouth Theatre (March 21). Hellman is inducted as a member of the American Academy of Arts and Letters (May 22). Receives an honorary Litt.D. from Douglass College, the women's division of Rutgers (June 5). The United Artist film adaptation of *Toys in the Attic* (screenplay by James Poe) premieres (July 31). Attends Edinburgh Festival and concurrent International Drama Conference sessions (Summer). Goes to Washington to cover Civil Rights March (August).

1964   Goes to Israel to cover Pope Paul's visit.

1965   Accepts John Hersey's invitation to conduct a seminar in literature and writing for a select group of Yale University freshmen.

1966   Edits and introduces *The Big Knockover: Selected Stories and Short Novels by Dashiell Hammett*, published by Random House (1966). Writes screenplay for *The Chase*, a United Artist film adapted from Horton Foote's novel and play.

1967   Attends reception for President of PEN in Budapest (May). Visits Soviet Union, Moscow, and Leningrad (May). Returns to New York for casting of *The Little Foxes* (May). Dorothy Parker dies (June 7). Hellman speaks at the memorial services (June 9). Goes abroad to Moscow, London, and Paris (October-November). Revival of *The Little Foxes* opens at the Vivian Beaumont Theatre at Lincoln Center, NYC (October 26).

1968   Gives spring seminar at Harvard University. Receives first Jackson Award of Distinction of Jackson College, the women's division of Tufts University; and the students of Jackson College endow a Chair in her name at the Elma Lewis School of Fine Arts in Roxbury, MS. Joins "100 Notables" for a seminar at Princeton, sponsored by the Institute for Advanced Study and the Paris-based International Association for Cultural Freedom for Intellectuals to share their view on "The United States, Its Problems, Impact and Image in the World."

1969   *An Unfinished Woman: A Memoir*, the first of her three memoirs, is published by Little, Brown.

1970   Receives the National Book Award for *An Unfinished Woman* (March 4). Appointed Regents Professor, University of California, Berkeley (Spring). Sells townhouse on East 82nd Street, NY, and moves into a tenth-floor co-op apartment at 695 Park Avenue at 65th Street. Founds the Committee for Public Justice, setting up well-attended meetings across the country that report on the calculated erosion of First Amendment rights by the CIA and FBI.

1971   Gives writing seminar at Berkeley (February); teaches at the Massachusetts Institute of Technology for month (Spring).

1972   Named Distinguished Professor, Hunter College, NY (September 26). First critical biography, Richard Moody's *Lillian Hellman*, is published.

1973   *Pentimento: A Book of Portraits*, her second memoir, is published by Little, Brown. Named to Theatre Hall of Fame (November 19). Receives first Woman of the Year Award from New York University Alumnae Club.

1974   Receives an honorary Doctor of Letters from Smith College and an honorary Doctor of Letters from Yale University. Guest speaker at Bryn Mawr College (October 29); and at Smithsonian's Baird Auditorium (November 11).

1975   Selected to join the editorial board of *The American Scholar*, through April 1978. Lectures at Boston College (November 13). Honored for her contributions to theatre, to literature, and to the protection of civil liberties at Circle in the Square celebration to benefit the Committee for Public Justice.

1976   *Scoundrel Time*, her third memoir, is published by Little, Brown. *Three*, the collected memoirs, is also published by Little, Brown. Revival of *The Autumn Garden* is presented at the Long Wharf Theatre, New Haven. Awarded an honorary Doctor of Letters by Columbia University (May 12). Speaks at luncheon meeting of Council of New York Law Associates, Association of the Bar of the City of New York (May 26). Gives commencement address, Mount

Holyoke College (May 30). Receives the Edward MacDowell Medal for contribution to literature (August 15); and the Actors' Equity Association third annual Paul Robeson Award (October 8).

1977   *Julia* (screenplay by Alvin Sargent), based on a segment from *Pentimento*, opens at Cinema 1, NYC (October 2).

1978   Participates in Rutgers' Conference on "Women and the Arts in the 1920s in Paris and New York" (April). Serves as consultant for authorized biography of Hammett by Diane Johnson.

1980   *Maybe: A Story*, a novel, is published by Little, Brown.

1984   Publishes her last book, *Eating Together: Recipes and Recollections*, with coauthor Peter Feibleman (Little, Brown). Dies of cardiac arrest on Martha's Vineyard (June 30).

1986   William Luce's *Lillian*, a one-woman play based on Hellman's autobiographical works opens at the Barrymore Theatre, NYC, starring Zoe Caldwell (January).

1996   Peter Feibleman's *Cakewalk*, a play based on the 20-year Hellman-Feibleman relationship, opens at the Variety Arts Theatre, off-Broadway, NYC, starring Linda Lavin and Michael Knight (October). The play was originally produced by the American Repertory Theatre, Cambridge, MA.

Life and Career

Lillian Hellman has been widely acclaimed as one of America's most distinguished female playwrights. She made an entrance into a predominantly male-dominated field in 1934 with *The Children's Hour*, a drama that rocked the literary establishment with its frank treatment of lesbianism while calling attention to her writing talents. Krutch (R33) noted, "So far as sheer power and originality are concerned the play is not merely the best of the year but the best of many years past." Written between 1934 and 1963, Hellman's dramatic canon includes eight original plays and four adaptations. Two of these received Drama Critics' Circle Awards: *Watch on the Rhine* (1941) and *Toys in the Attic* (1960). *The Little Foxes* (1939), about a family of predatory entrepreneurs who at the turn of the twentieth century pursue industrial fortune on the ruins of the old South, is perhaps her best remembered play and generally considered her finest. Hellman wrote well-made plays involving significant sociological and psychological issues in the tradition of Ibsen, creating clearcut characters and memorable female figures such as Regina Giddens of *The Little Foxes* and *Another Part of the Forest* (1946). In her last two original plays, *The Autumn Garden* (1951) and *Toys in the Attic*, Chekhov's influence took prominence. The use of multiple characters and novelist structure, however, can be traced to her earlier plays, *Watch on the Rhine*, *The Searching Wind* (1944), and *Another Part of the Forest*, "where leisurely discursiveness resembling Jamesian (*Watch on the Rhine*) or Jonsonian (*Forest*) comedies of manners alternates with tight dramaturgy" (S256, 4). After Tennessee Williams, Hellman is considered the most important dramatist writing about the South. Four of her best plays deal directly with Southerners, *The Little Foxes*, 1939; *Another Part of the Forest*, 1946; *The Autumn Garden*, 1951; and *Toys in the Attic*, 1960. Along with Clifford Odets and other writers of the 1930s, she showed a strong interest in Marxist theory, exploring the relationship between the nuclear family and capitalism; and employing Brechtian gestures before she had even heard of his anti-empathetic theories.

Lillian Florence Hellman was born in New Orleans, Louisiana, on 20 June 1906, the only daughter of Julia Newhouse Hellman and Max Bernard Hellman. Her mother was a Newhouse from Demopolis, Alabama, a member of a wealthy family presided over by her grandmother Sophie Marx Newhouse who had come from long-established family of bankers and shopkeepers in drygoods, bringing her own riches to her Newhouse marriage. Sophie's brother, Jake Marx, was a successful banker in Demopolis and New York. The grandmother's side of the family, the Marxes, were the dominant family in Lillian's mind when she described the Newhouses as the rich, powerful, and greedy "banking and storekeeping" clan contemptuous of her father's poor prospects (S249, 16). Julia's family had moved from Demopolis to Cincinnati and then to New Orleans many years before her birth. She was educated at Sophie Newcomb College in New Orleans. Max Bernard Hellman, Lillian's father, was a self-educated man of lower class who had advanced from being a bookkeeper to opening his own shoe manufacturing business with the help of his wife's dowry. His Hellman Shoe Company was located on Canal Street in New Orleans, the city of his birth. The Newhouses, the Marxes, and the Hellmans were all German Jews of the 1840s immigration.

When Lillian was six years old, her father moved the family to New York City, where members of the Newhouse/Marx family had relocated. The shoe enterprise had failed, and he was attempting to start over "as a travelling salesman for a clothing firm" (S31, 221). From that time through age sixteen, Lillian spent half the year in New York with her mother's wealthy family--the Hellman apartment was on Manhattan's Upper West Side at West Ninety-fifth Street between Riverside Drive and West End Avenue--and the other half in New Orleans with her father's two unmarried aunts, Jenny and Hannah, at the Hellman tawdry boarding house at 1718 [and later at number 4631] Prytania Street in the frayed edges of the fashionable Garden District; "with an absent father; a black maid whose presence both frightened and comforted; school systems so divergent that she could skip class in the South and then struggle to catch up in her New York semester; and the paradoxical invisibility and spectacle of being an only child" (S285, 207). Lillian was a frightened, shy, and rebellious child. Unable to understand the world of grownups, she fled from reality, taking refuge in her books and sketching into her "writing book" a portrait gallery of adults who would later serve as models for the characters in her plays and memoirs. Her memoirs confirm the use of her mother's family as models for the Hubbards of *The Little Foxes* and *Another Part of the Forest*, her father's family for *The Autumn Garden* and *Toys in the Attic*.

According to Hellman's childhood recollections, her mother was small and delicately made, a charming woman of simple tastes who complacently endured the financial hardships of her marriage, as well as her husband's infidelities. So far apart were mother and daughter in temperaments that only after her mother had been dead for five years did she realize how much she loved her. She described her father as humorous, earthy, impulsive, and outspoken; someone she idealized, yet resented for his betrayal to her mother. Her father's talent for blunt, direct talk seems to explain the writing style that she was to develop (as well as her attraction to Dashiell Hammett). Lillian adored the colorful Hellmans, her unmarried Aunts Hannah and Jenny and their motley, eccentric boardinghouse acquaintances, describing her father's family as "intellectual, energetic Jews" (S238, 17). She disliked the wealthy, upper-middle classed Newhouses who made her feel socially inferior, their ponderous dinners and constant talk of money, but who never referred to their Jewishness. The assumption is that the family was "gentile, an assumption reinforced by the common knowledge that the non-Jewish Hubbard family in Hellman's play *The Little Foxes* was based on her mother's relatives" (S238, 17).

Hellman graduated from Wadleigh High School, NYC, in 1922. Though indifferent to her studies, her best subjects (1921-22), according to Rollyson (S249), were grammar (95), English (89), and history (88). From 1922 to 1924, she attended New York University, taking courses in Kant, Hegel, Marx, and Engels with the same indifference, confessing that she would cut classes by a famous, well-bred editor, slamming her seat and leaving in the middle of the lectures given by Alexander Woollcott "whenever he paraded the gibe-wit and shabby literary taste of his world" (A24, 41). After a summer semester at Columbia University in 1924, and an enjoyable exposure to Dostoevsky, Dante, Melville, and Lewis Carroll, she lost interest in college.

While living at home at age nineteen, she begin working for the legendary publisher Horace Liveright as a copywriter in the advertising department and as a manuscript reader. With time on her hands, she began to write short stories that were submitted, but returned with discouraging regularity. In *An Unfinished Woman*, Hellman recalled the "plum" position at Horace Liveright, Inc., the "party" atmosphere, the writers discovered by the firm, "Faulkner, Freud, Hemingway, O'Neill, Hart Crane, Sherwood Anderson, Dreiser, e.e. cummings, and many other less talented but remarkable people . . ." (A24, 43). The exposure to the adventurous, glamorous, and often reckless life of the literary world of the 1920s seems to have appealed to and influenced her own career and lifestyle.

In 1925 Hellman married budding playwright, Arthur Kober, who was at the time a press agent for Jed Harris. In 1926 the Kobers went to Paris, plunging into the intellectual stream of embryonic artists of the Left Bank. He edited *The Paris Comet*, an English-language magazine which published two of her "lady-writer" short stories, as she later described them, while she wandered aimlessly throughout Europe. From 1925-1932, she wrote book reviews for the *New York Herald Tribune*, read playscripts, did the publicity for a Broadway revue and a stock company in Rochester, and wrote several unpublished short stories. In 1929, she abandoned vague plans to study in at the university in Bonn, Germany, where she quite innocently became involved with a Nazi youth movement, an experience carried over to her anti-Fascist war plays, *Watch on the Rhine* (1941) and *The Searching Wind* (1944). In 1930, she followed Kober to Hollywood, taking a position that he secured for her, writing story synopses of books, magazines, and newspapers, and other potential film material for Sam Marx at Metro-Goldwyn-Mayer. Her position was terminated when Marx realized Hellman's perpetual state of indignation: she was full of causes and attempting to start a union. While in Hollywood, she met Dashiell Hammett, an ex-Pinkerton detective and celebrated crime fiction novelist (*The Maltese Falcon*, 1930), who was to become her mentor and lifelong companion. In 1931, Hellman returned to New York, her relationship with Hammett precipitating an amicable divorce from Kober in 1932. Hellman and Hammett lived together on and off until his death in 1961. They never married.

Hellman was twenty-five and Hammett thirty-six, when they met. Under his tutelage, her playwriting potential as a creative artist was realized, her political nature unleashed, "and a rebelliousness that threatened as much havoc in her emotional life as in her professional one was brought under control" (S238, 61). Mellen (S229) describes their relationship as "something unspoken but profound" (39). Hammett, who was at the end of his career, recognized in Hellman the energy to carry on his writing, style, persona, and politics. Hellman, on the other hand, saw in him a persona to take as her own; and she began to imitate him, his tough talk, his bravado, his drinking, his smoking, and his life without constraints. His writing style was similar to his character: "direct, blunt, brutally honest, and rudely impatient with pretension" (S299, 24).

Hammett was a respected Knopf author; and for two years after their meeting, Hellman would be known only as "Hammett's girl." During this time he wrote his last novel, *The Thin Man* (1934), modeling Nora, the loyal wife of Nick Charles, the detective-hero, after Hellman who had inspired him, dedicating the book to her. During this same time she collaborated with Kronenberger on *Dear Queen*, a comedy about a royal family who wanted to be bourgeois that was neither published or produced; she published two short stories; and, in 1933, began reading plays for Herman Shumlin who would produce her first five plays. As theatrical mentor, and lover for a short period (after the success of *The Children's Hour*), Shumlin played an important role in Hellman's career, though Hammett's contribution was paramount. A very dedicated man about writing, Hammett was to work very painstakingly on Hellman's writing--to become her severest and most sensitive critic. Energized by his love for her, he was ready to pass on his ideas; and his endpoint--a concern with corruption--served to spark her career (S299).

In the spring of 1933, Hammett came across a collection of British court cases in William Roughead's *Bad Companions*. The book was not one that Hellman would have read, but it was one that appealed to Hammett as a former Pinkerton operative and writer of detective fiction. One chapter in particular caught his interest: "Closed Doors, or The Great Drumsheugh Case" about two headmistresses of a girl's boarding school in Scotland who were accused of having a lesbian relationship by a troublesome student and the ensuing scandal that forced them to close the school. Hammett thought it would make a good play and suggested the project to "Lilly." On 29 November 1934, fourteen rewrites later, all supervised by Hammett, *The Children's Hour* opened on Broadway where it ran for 691 performances, the longest of Hellman's Broadway runs, establishing her career as a major Broadway playwright at age 29. Rollyson (S249) reports that she profited $125,000 from the production.) She had dedicated the play to Hammett. Years later she told her playwriting class at Harvard how fortunate she'd been to have had Hammett's suggestion. Given the ready-made plot, she had been able to concentrate on dialogue, character development, and pacing of scenes.

Critics praised the powerful dialogue, the characters, and the writing, despite the melodrama (the revenge, suicide, blackmail, secrets concealed and revealed), and the mettlesome third act, insisting, for the most part, that the play should have ended with Martha's suicide. Hellman agreed, commenting later, "I am a moral writer, often too moral a writer, and I cannot avoid, it seems, that last summing-up" (A15, ix). In the play, lives are destroyed by a big lie, which people believe more readily than a little lie. Interestingly enough, "In 1933, while Hellman wrote the play, Hitler published *Mein Kampf*, which states: 'The great masses of people [. . .] will more easily fall victim to a big lie than to a small one'" (S215, 144). As Triesch (S124) notes, *The Children's Hour* remains a study of the destructive power of evil, a subtle protest against society and its treatment of the individual. Hellman never again would "create a true tragic fate as she did in the character of Martha" (13).

In 1935, Hellman returned to Hollywood to work, as a screenwriter for $2500 a week, for Sam Goldwyn. She had been hired on the strength of *The Children's Hour*'s Broadway reception. After collaborating with Mordaunt Shairp on a remake of *The Dark Angel* (1935), an adaptation of the play by Guy Bolton, she turned to the screen adaptation of *The Children's Hour*, titled *These Three* (1936), censoring the lesbianism in accordance with the Hays Commission and the Hollywood moral code. The film was a critical and commercial success, establishing her career in Hollywood where she wrote seven screenplays from 1935-46. *The Chase* in 1966 was her eighth and final film. From 1934-1963, however, her reputation rested primarily on her dramatic writing--the eight original plays and four adaptations.

In *An Unfinished Woman* (A21) Hellman wrote of her need for a mentor, a need expressed in the dialogue that she gave to the heroine of her second play, *Days to Come*, which opened on Broadway on 15 December 1936. Bearing a resemblance to Hellman, Julie says, "When I was young, I guess I was looking for something I could do. Then for something I could be. Finally, just for something to want, or to think, or to believe in. I always wanted somebody to show me the way . . . I decided a long time ago there were people who had to learn from other people. I'm one of them" (Act II, 2). The play concerned a strike in a brush factory and its social manifestations, and reflected Hellman's organizing experience in Hollywood and labor-management relations during the Depression. The theme again, Hellman stated, was good and evil, but this time the evil was in the hands of innocent people on both sides drawn into circumstances beyond their understanding (A15). The production received negative press and closed after seven performances, the playwright's only critical failure. On opening night, Hellman rushed to Hammett's side, calling him an "SOB" and asking him why he hadn't told her that the play was so bad. He replied that he had changed his mind after seeing it staged (S238, 124). The conception of the play seems influenced by her screenwriting; thus the film medium might have served better to accommodate the scope of the piece. In his opening night review, Atkinson (A39) noted an elliptical writing style that tapered off in bizarre direction, a mixture of a crime play with an analysis of female neuroticism which seemed tangentially connected with the basic subject of labor trouble.

Hellman later acknowledged that she had made the amateur's mistake of trying to say too much. "I knew a woman like Cora and I hated her, and *that* hate had to go into the play; I knew a woman like Julie, I pitied her, and *that* pity had to go in the play . . ." (A15, ix). Elsewhere she had this to say of the play: "it is crowded and overwrought, but it is a good report of rich liberals in the 1930s, of a labor leader who saw through them, of a modern lost lady, and has in it a correct prediction of how conservative the American labor movement was to become" (A19, 163). Cora, the factory owner's spinster sister, had shades of the self-concerned aunt in *The Children's Hour*--her mean spirit and her inability to comprehend anything beyond the dividends from the factory--yet looked forward to the despicable characteristics of Regina and the Hubbards of *The Little Foxes*.

Before writing that next play, Hellman returned to Hollywood to write the screenplay for Kingsley's *Dead End*. With this project completed, Hellman began a tour of Europe which included visits to Russia, France, and Spain where she became interested in the Loyalist cause. During her career, she would make several trips to Russia and Europe, including her alleged visit to Nazi Germany to take money to the underground at the request of her friend, Julia.

While in Spain, Hellman began to think of her next play, *The Little Foxes*, which opened on Broadway on 15 February 1939. It had taken Hellman two years to get over the failure of *Days to Come*. In *Pentimento*, she confessed to nine rewrites--her future as a playwright was on the line and she was scared--and to tremendous dependence upon the support of "Dash" (A19, 162). Some of the problems came from the material's "distant connection" to the Newhouses and to the tripping over tangled roots. The title of the play had been suggested by her friend, Dorothy Parker, taken from the biblical reference in the Song of Solomon, II, xv, wherein the little foxes "spoil the vines; for our vines have tender grapes." The symbolic "foxes" of the play are the Hubbards who, at the turn of the twentieth century, are determined to attain wealth from the rise of industrialism in the South. They are the "new rich," who have acquired wealth by "cheating niggers on a pound of bacon," and who seal their dominance of a community by building cotton mills and exploiting cheap labor; a family who takes vindictive "pleasure in the destruction and parodying of the old values, appropriating the public forms of a decaying system as a conscious cover for rapacity" (S208, 280). The play was designed to be a drama of morality, first and last, Hellman told Beebe (S14). Dukore (S215) noted that the parable was "as much about the potential despoilers of the world in 1939 as those of the American south in 1900" (153).

Critics praised vivid characters, shrewd writing, and expert technique, much of which seemed taken from Ibsen, yet found the work occasionally more melodramatic than necessary. An improvement over the first two plays, however, Hellman had learned how to handle the interplay between her highly individualized characters and their environment (S193). The role of Regina--originally played by Tallulah Bankhead--, who icily looks away as her husband suffers a fatal heart attack and who outmaneuvers her equally greedy brothers in a major business coup, became a favorite vehicle for female actresses. The play ran on

Broadway for 410 performances, its success establishing Hellman's career as one of America's leading playwrights.

Commenting later on the play's reception, Hellman wrote, "I had meant to half-mock my own youthful high-class innocence in Alexandra, the young girl in the play; I had meant people to smile at, and to sympathize with, the sad, weak Birdie, certainly I had not meant them to cry; I had meant the audience to recognize some part of themselves in the money-dominated Hubbards: I had not meant people to think of them as villains to whom they had no connection" (A19, 180). She agreed that the play was a melodrama, but that the genre had a corrupted modern meaning. "It used to be a good word. For many centuries of writers a good way to write. If you believe, as the Greeks did, that man is at the mercy of the gods he might offend and who will punish him for the offense, then you write tragedy. The end is inevitable from the beginning. But if you believe that man can solve his own problems and is at nobody's mercy, then you will probably write melodrama" (A14, 2).

During the 1940s, Hellman divided her time between Broadway and Hollywood. Perhaps her greatest success of this period was *Watch on the Rhine*, which premiered on Broadway on 1 April 1941. The play concerns a rich, liberal Washington family who meet, for the first time, their anti-Fascist German son-in-law. When the son-in-law is forced to kill a Romanian count for fear of exposure, support comes from his American in-laws; bringing up an issue that had been important to Hellman's art since *The Children's Hour*: "[t]he actions, the reactions, and the responsibilities of those engaged in or witnessing political actions" (S285, 213.) Hailed as one of the most effective dramas to come out of the war years, the play won the Drama Critics' Circle Award, confirming Hellman's place among America's leading playwrights. Critics observed an increased humanness in Hellman's writing, likable characters and humorous and affectionate scenes, defending the melodramatics, for the most part, as a reflection of what was going on in real life. In 1942 an illustrated, limited edition of the play with special foreword by Parker was privately published to raise funds for the Joint Anti-Fascist Refugee Committee.

After editing Hammett's film adaptation of *Watch on the Rhine* (1943), and completing the film *The North Star* (1943) about the heroism of the Russian people in face of the German invasion, Hellman wrote her second war play, *The Searching Wind* which opened on Broadway on 12 April 1944. The play chronicles the appeasing diplomacy of the twenties and thirties that facilitated the growth of Fascism, and is considered Hellman's most politically overt work. The plot concerns an American diplomat, an attaché in Rome who follows an isolationist policy during the rise of Mussolini and Hitler in order to escape from the ugly reality. His political philosophy is carried over from his unresolved emotional life, which he also avoids facing. Produced in 1944 when the Allies were on the point of annihilating the offenders, play's message was anticlimactic; and the run was short. A contender for the Drama Critics' Circle Award, *The Searching Wind* fell one vote short; and the prize went unclaimed.

In 1945, Hellman made a second trip to Russia, this time traveling as "a kind of cultural emissary" and honored guest of the Soviets--perhaps because they were producing *Watch on the Rhine* and *The Little Foxes* in Moscow. In *An Unfinished Woman*, she describes the highlights of her adventures which include two weeks on the Warsaw front with the Russian's freely discussing the war and their battle plans. Back home again, after completing the screen adaptation of *The Searching Wind* (1946), she turned her attention to the writing of her sixth play.

Another Part of the Forest opened on Broadway on 20 November 1946. Hellman had always planned *The Little Foxes* as a trilogy: the first part going back to the post-Civil War years of the Hubbards' youth; *The Little Foxes* as the middle part; and the third part, which was never written, going forward some twenty years to show Regina in Europe, her daughter perhaps as an angry and disappointed, spinsterish social worker. With the writing of *Another Part of the Forest* Hellman chose the early period, hoping this time to make clear the play's satirical intent. Once again, as with *The Little Foxes*, she was forced to concede that, "What I had thought was bite they thought sad, touching, or plotty and melodramatic" (A19, 197). In the final analysis, the weaknesses of the former play were exaggerated in the latter; and the play came no closer in explaining the family's destructive egotism or placing them in terms of an historical process. Though respectfully received by the critics, the play did not evoke as much enthusiasm as *The Little Foxes*, perhaps because it was more analytic and less concentrated in its picture of evil. Krutch (R158) declared the piece, "a Marxian study of the decline of the Southern feudal aristocracy and the rise of the capitalist exploiter," without admirable characters because, by antecedent premise, there were none (671). Kermit Bloomgarden produced the play, replacing Shumlin who had produced and directed her first five plays; and Hellman made her directorial debut, "not because I wanted to, but because I was tired of arguments and knew no director I thought was right for me" (A19, 197). While first class actors covered directorial deficiencies, Hellman still could not control the tone of the play. *Another Part of the Forest*, perhaps the most melodramatic of her works, garnered mixed reviews and ran for a modest 182 performances.

In 1946 Hellman completed the film script for *The Searching Wind*. Prepared to make a movie with William Wyler of Theodore Dreiser's *Sister Carrie* in 1948, she learned, quite by accident, that she had been under surveillance and blacklisted by Hollywood. Her FBI file was detailed with years of leftist activities which included "her sponsorship of numerous events, organizations, and petitions under the governance or the influence of the Soviet Union, of the American Communist party, or of party sympathizers" (S249, 183). The unwritten, unofficial, powerful blacklist stayed in effect until 1960. In Hellman's words, "I couldn't do movies which I had not only liked but had made a living, a steady living" (S133, 121).

Despite the threat of the infamous House Committee on Un-American Activities hearings, Hellman continued in her leftist causes. In 1948 she took a prominent position in the Presidential campaign supporting Henry Wallace on the ultra-liberal Progressive party ticket. In March 1949, she helped to sponsor a dinner for the Cultural and Scientific Conference on World Peace, though the State Department had declared the meeting "inimical to the country's interests," and several scheduled guests had declined invitations to attend. In October of the previous year, she had flown to Prague, Belgrade, and Paris, her principal mission to interview Marshall Tito in Belgrade for a series of six articles that appeared in the New York *Star*, 4-10 November 1948. (Yugoslavia had just been expelled from the Cominform, an association of Communist parties, for challenging Soviet supremacy.) She stopped first in Prague to meet with the vice premier of Czechoslovakia. After her stay in Belgrade she flew to Paris to see Emmanuel Robles's *Montserrat*, a French play that Norman Mailer recommended. She became interested, arranging immediately to acquire American rights for an adaptation.

Hellman's *Montserrat* opened on Broadway, 29 October 1949 for 65 performances. Once again she directed the play. The critics found the play a workmanlike melodrama, intellectually arresting; yet rarely deeply moving, identifying flaws in Hellman's writing and direction. Harold Clurman (S180), who took over at some point as director, asserted that Hellman had made the piece into a revolutionary documentary, misinterpreting Robles's existential point of view. In her memoirs, Hellman admitted to directing the play "in a fumbling, frightened way" that intimidated the actors and contributed to the failure of the play (A19, 198).

In *The Autumn Garden*, which opened on Broadway 7 March 1951, Hellman concentrated on a group of characters and the theme of middle-age despair in the brooding tradition of Chekhov. Gathered together in a shabby-genteel summer boarding house in the South, the characters are moral failures who search to fill the emptiness of their lives; their personal unhappiness unrelated to the social problems of the time. The play received a mixed critical reception and ran for 102 performances. In many ways, it was considered Hellman's most mature and probing play, her most psychoanalytic play. Hammett thought it was her best; and she considered it her favorite. Clurman (R204), who directed the production, praised the deft construction, but felt that the playwright had failed, despite her probing, to reveal the warmth of Chekhov's portrayals. Hammett had written General Griggs's speech of self-insight in the last act, summarizing the play's theme of missed opportunities; and the play's dedication read, "For Dash."

The fifties were disturbing times for Hellman and Hammett. Hammett, a trustee of the Civil Rights Congress, was imprisoned for six months; and after his release interrogated by the McCarthy committee, taking the Fifth Amendment in response. When Hellman was subpoenaed to appear before the HUAC in 1952, her letter response stated that she would testify about herself but no one else. The letter contained her famous proclamation, "I cannot and will not cut my conscience to fit this year's fashions" (A24, 659). At the hearing, Hellman resorted to the Fifth Amendment, but was never prosecuted. Although she maintained that she was never a party member--that she never had strong enough convictions to belong to any party--, an earlier draft of her letter admits that she was a Communist party member between 1938 and 1940" (S249, 319). In *Scoundrel Time*, she explains "The middle and the late thirties were a time when many people were turning toward radical political solutions, and he [Hammett] was one of them, with me trailing behind . . ." (A24, 609). "In any case," she continues, "whether I signed a Party card or didn't was of little importance to me. I couldn't have known then what importance would be attached to it a few years later" (A24, 611).

The results of the investigations were devastating. First of all there was the bad press. And then there was the financial hardship. With the Hollywood income a thing of the past, and the Internal Revenue Service pressing both writers for unpaid taxes, the Pleasantville farm that Hellman owned and shared with Hammett had to be sold. Hammett became ill soon after his release from prison--never to regain his comfortable life style--; and she would take care of him until his death in 1961.

Unable to concentrate on a new play with all the turmoil, Hellman was urged by Bloomgarden to revive *The Children's Hour* which opened on Broadway in 1952, Hellman directing the production. Through minor rewriting and editing, the analogy between the destructive character assassination of the play with that of the McCarthy investigations was stressed. Atkinson (R225) thought the political overtones fitting of the slander of the day. Hewes (R250) suggested that the play should be called "The McCarthyites' Hour." Next, at the suggestion of Kronenberger, who was the general editor of the "Great Letters Series, Hellman edited a volume of Chekhov's letters for Farrar, Straus and Cudahy, 1955. Her introductory essay praised the playwright's common sense, social ideals, and workmanship which reflected her own views. She "seems to have found in him justification for her own political state of mind" (S238, 262). In any case, she greatly admired Chekhov whom she had come across when in search of nonmelodramatic playwrights. This project was followed by *The Lark*, an adaptation of Jean Anouilh's *L'Alouette*, which opened successfully on Broadway, 17 November 1955, for 229 performances, setting her finances once again in the black. Bloomgarden had seen the original play in Paris and acquired the American rights, prodding Hellman's interest in Joan of Arc's feminist qualities (S155). Joan (Julie Harris) took on the qualities of a down-to-earth woman, much like the playwright herself. Brantley (1993) observed that the play was unquestionably self-referential, "as much about the mood of the McCarthy era as it [was] about a medieval French peasant hero" (183). The incidental music had been written by Hellman's good friend Leonard Bernstein. Since September 1950, she had been discussing with him an idea for the adaptation of Voltaire's *Candide*. She wanted him to compose some incidental music, as he had done for *The Lark*.

Candide: A Comic Operetta opened at the Martin Beck Theatre on 1 December 1956, for 73 performances, Bernstein's musical score dominating the production. Director Tyrone Guthrie (S87) recalled the artistic skirmishes and the unconscious acquiescence to "the diamond quality of Bernstein's brilliance" (241). Hellman, who had never written for musical theatre, was unaccustomed to the brisk telegraphic style. "With her text radically reduced," Moody (S155) noted, "her satiric thrusts seemed too dull, cumbersome, and serious for the mocking lyricism of Bernstein's score and the verbal playfulness of Wilbur's lyrics" (283). And while there was much that was brilliant about the production in the way of musical excellence, visual beauty, and boldness of design, the show had book problems and closed an artistic and financial failure. Only Bernstein's sophisticated score emerged with credit.

The material for Hellman's last original play *Toys in the Attic* (1960) had been suggested by Hammett. His storyline concerned a man who people loved and who wanted to do good; but when he became successful, they didn't like him that way, so he "fucked" things up, and came out worse than before (A19, 206). Hellman said she couldn't write a play that centered on a man. Instead, she made the play about the women around the man, two maiden aunts who sacrificed their lives for their brother in a story that resembled the relationship of her own two aunts, Hannah and Jenny, to her father (A19, A21). In the writing, Hellman abandoned the loose, reflective style of *The Autumn Garden*, moving into the murky areas of Southern gothicism and melodramatic devices that resembled the plays of Tennessee Williams; the new flirtation with Freud, influenced no doubt by her own psychoanalysis. Reviewers welcomed the production which opened on 25 February 1960 for 556 performances. Hailed by some as Hellman's most mature work, the play garnered the New York Drama Critics' Circle Award as the best American drama of the year. On 10 January 1961, Hammett died at age sixty-six. She never wrote another original play.

During the 1960s Hellman secured her position as a literary figure. In May 1960, she was elected a fellow of the American Academy of Arts and Sciences. Shortly thereafter, Harvard's Faculty Committee on Dramatics invited her to give the Theodore Spencer Memorial Lecture on Drama. In Spring 1961, she was brought back as a visiting lecturer in English. In 1961, she received the Brandeis University Creative Arts Medal in Theatre and an achievement award from the women's division of the Albert Einstein College of Medicine of Yeshiva University; and she was honored by Wheaton College with an honorary Litt.D. In 1962, she was elected vice president of the National Institute of Arts and Letters.

Hellman's last play, *My Mother, My Father and Me*, was an adaptation of Burt Blechman's novel *How Much?*. The novel had come to her attention while she was teaching at Harvard. The satire on Jewish American life reminded her of her own family: the father whose shoe business fails; the ditsy mother who "carries common sense to nonsensical extremes," and the 26-year-old son who gropes to find his way. *My Mother, My Father and Me* opened on Broadway 2 March 1963 for 17 performances. A departure in setting and subject matter from her other works, the experimentation with the Albeeish absurdist style failed, and Hellman vowed never to write another play. "It isn't that I minded the form," she told Meras (S205) in an interview, "that isn't why I stopped, but I minded what the theatre had become. I got tired of talking about money all the time and I got tired of the idea that a play could be ruined by one or two critics in just a day or two" (285). The truth is that she really didn't like the theatre--except for the times when she was alone in a room putting the plays on paper. Her disillusionment with theatre had begun with the production of *Candide*, when she realized that she was not a collaborator.

Hellman continued her teaching, conducting writing seminars at Yale University (1965), Harvard University (1968), the University of California at Berkeley (1970 and 1971), the Massachusetts Institute of Technology (1971), and Hunter College, NY (1972); speaking also at other major universities. In 1963, she received an honorary doctorate from Douglass College, the women's division of Rutgers; in 1974, from Smith College and from Yale; and in 1976, from Columbia University. Among various other distinguished awards, she was named to the Theatre Hall of Fame in 1973.

In 1969 Hellman published *An Unfinished Woman*, the first of her three memoirs, for which she won the National Book Award. Her second memoir *Pentimento: A Book of Portraits* (1973), was even more highly regarded, continuing on the best seller list for more than four months. *Julia* (1977), the film release of the Julia section--with seventies radicals Vanessa Regrave and Jane Fonda--, added to Hellman's enduring fame while perpetuating the myth of legendary stature. Her third memoir *Scoundrel Time* (1976) recounted the events surrounding her HUAC encounter twenty years earlier, resurfacing charges of betrayal against other liberals such as Clifford Odets and Elia Kazan. In 1980 she published *Maybe: A Story*, which contains biographical material, but is considered a work of fiction, corresponding with the style of the book (S238). Her last work with Peter Feibleman, *Eating Together: Recipes and Recollections* (1982), is a cookbook with reminiscences. Her redirected career as a memoirist brought both renewed distinction, yet controversy centering on charges of profound misrepresentations and distortions having to do with *Scoundrel Time*, and other issues such as the "Julia" story which was actually based on the anti-Fascist experiences of Muriel Gardiner, that continued until her death (S217, S219).

Hellman's political activities continued through the Seventies. In 1970, during the Nixon administration, she called together a group of prominent inner circle friends to found the Committee for Public Justice, setting up well-attended meetings across the country that reported on the calculated erosion of First Amendment rights by the FBI and the CIA. Times seemed perilously close to McCarthyism again, she thought. Vietnam war dissenters were being harassed, and then the Watergate scandal emerged in the summer of 1972. In *Scoundrel Time*, published two years after Nixon's resignation from the presidency, Hellman described the capers of the McCarthy era as a step "straight into the Vietnam War the days of Nixon" (A24, 721). Throughout this period her plays continued in revivals, but she never returned to writing for the stage.

On 30 June 1984, at age seventy-eight and after a long bout with emphysema and failing eyesight, Hellman died on Martha's Vineyard, MA, where she was buried. She left an estate of four-million dollars, much of which was divided between the Dashiell Hammett Fund to be guided by the political, social and economic beliefs "of the late Dashiell Hammett, who was a believer in the doctrines of Karl Marx;" and the Lillian Hellman Fund to promote "educational, literary, or scientific purposes and to aid writers regardless of their national origin, age, sex, or political beliefs" (S249, 547). At the Chilmark Cemetery grave site where friends gathered, John Hersey spoke of the anger that had informed Hellman's art, concluding that she was "a finished woman now. I mean 'finished' in its better sense. You shone with a finish of integrity, decency, uprightness . . . We thank you, we honor you, and we all say goodbye to you now with a love that should calm that anger of yours forever" (S248, 361-62). Robert Brustein spoke of Hellman's legacy to the theatre. Before abandoning the theatre, she had written eight original plays and four adaptations. "Not all were of quality; at least three, I believe, will live as long as there is an American theater: *Toys in the Attic*, *The Autumn Garden* and of course, her classic, *Little Foxes* [sic]" (S248, 359).

The dramatic characteristics for which Hellman is best remembered can be found in her very first play, *The Children's Hour*: "crisp, forceful, realistic dialogue; clear character construction and analysis; a clear-cut plot line in the tradition of the well-made play, with fast movement and adroitly handled suspense which kept audiences enthralled," though these are handled more skillfully in subsequent works (S286, 1140). The absence of inflated rhetoric, another of her artistic traits, "is not stylistic idiosyncrasy; it is a form of moral control (almost a repression) which instructs her not to say more than what she thinks is true, precise, just. This characteristic leads to a notable scrupulousness in dramatic diction and meticulous logic of dramatic construction" (S155 xii). As Clurman noted, she had vanishingly little patience for sentimentality, exorcising it frequently by humorous contempt as witnessed in *The Autumn Garden* and *Toys in the Attic*; and the brutal honesty of her work might have been mistaken for a lack of feeling "were it not for her no-nonsense humor and, more especially for her only half-declared but unmistakable admiration for every kind of excellence: self-discipline, loyalty . . . and, most important, that unselfish pursuit of humanly valid ideals" (S155, xiii).

Created largely in the manner of Ibsen in his middle period, Hellman's early plays are vehicles for social and psychological commentary with powerful characters and convincing dramatic dialogue that transcend the limitations of plot contrivance and rigid plot symmetry. Like Ibsen, her characters include memorable female figures such as Regina Giddens of *The Little Foxes* and *Another Part of the Forest*, perhaps modeled after Hedda Gabler. Unlike Ibsen, "her issues are cut-and-dried and her discussions confirm, not challenge our judgements" (S215, 143). The hidden character of her plays is money, functioning symbolically but tangibly, as in *Toys in the Attic* where "money is stroked as if it were a domestic animal" (Brustein, S248, 359). Blackmail plays another notable role; linking the features of money and power that define her major theatrical preoccupations, and taking prominence in all but one of her original plays, *Toys in the Attic* and an adaptation of *Montserrat* (S252).

For the most part, Hellman's plays are melodramatic well-made plays, constructed according to mechanical formulae and sensational effects; "parables, sometimes obvious, sometimes not" (S215, 142). She freely admitted to the use of melodramatic devices, blackmail, suspense, and violence, and to other contrivances of the well-made play, which she defended as "tricks" of the theatre (A15). Her plays, however, were never pure melodrama which would by definition exclude due consideration for well-drawn characters, significant themes, logic of situation, and inconclusive endings. To critics who found her dramaturgy too melodramatic or violent, she answered that there was evil in the world and that it was her right to expose it. "I think the word melodrama, in our time," she wrote in the preface to her plays, "has come to be used in an almost illiterate manner. By definition it is a violent dramatic piece, with a happy ending. But I think we can add that it uses its violence for no purpose, to point no moral, to say nothing, in say-nothing's worse sense" (A15, xi). Later in her career Hellman turned to the "indirect and plotless techniques of Chekhov, but she never wavered in her conviction that theatre could be a force for change in an unethical, unjust, essentially venal world" (Brustein in S248, 359).

In her last two original plays, *The Autumn Garden* and *Toys in the Attic*, Chekhov's influence took prominence, though Estrin points out that Ibsenite and Chekhovian strains are neither conflicting or sequential, but complementary to her plays, tracing the use of multiple characters and novelist structure to her earlier plays, *Watch on the Rhine*, *The Searching Wind* and *Another Part of the Forest*, "where leisurely discursiveness resembling Jamesian (*Watch on the Rhine*) or Jonsonian (*Forest*) comedies of manners alternates with tight dramaturgy" (S256, 4).

Categorizing the plays in terms of "well-made play," "melodrama," Ibsen and/or Chekhov, of course, is to dismiss the complexities of "form and genre that Hellman consistently and consciously stretched beyond her influences and often beyond her contemporaries" (S294, 137). While *The Children's Hour* is influenced by Ibsen, Lederer (S193) labels the treatment "*stylized realism*," a technique perfected in *The Little Foxes* and *Toys in the Attic*. As Hayes (R249) writes of the 1952 revival, "What I should like to underline . . . is the immense theatricality of the work--the sheer, exhilarating sense it conveys of a positive dramatic talent, of a playwright who is not afraid to calculate her exits and entrances, to drop her curtains at a provocative moment, or to expose her characters to passion and violence. It is this imaginative boldness which has carried Miss Hellman past the failures of realism to secure and irreproachable ground" (377)

The later plays, Lederer argues, grow from the tradition of the novel and use the techniques of dramatic irony. Hellman's masterpiece, *The Little Foxes*, is "dark satiric comedy" that uses "melodramatic devices to make its point" (S193, 49). In a similar mode, Kronenberger (R157), Gassner (S170), and Brown (S152) equate *Another Part of the Forest* with somber Elizabethan comedy; and in a later analysis, Wiles sees Hellman attempting a Jonsonian comedy of humours, creating "a sociohistorical satire" carried forward to her adaptations, *Candide* and *My Mother, My Father and Me*--which reveal continued experimentation with dramatic form, musical theatre in the former, absurdist theatre in the latter.

In study of Hellman's political plays, Wiles (S264) leads to greater speculation about genre, underscoring Hellman's kinship with Brecht--as early as *Days to Come*--, techniques that she intuited before she had ever heard of the theories. "For all her use of suspense, representational narrative, and the well-knit plot, she bears several significant resemblances to this antinaturalist; in terms of influence, the parallel development is accidental, but the two writers shared the same politics, even to the matter of their unhappy protracted loyalty to Stalin . . ." (S264, 95). In terms of the length of career, coherence of politics, and willingness to experiment with form and fable, Wiles finds Hellman comparable to Miller; though Adler (S223) considers her second to Arthur Miller as an American Ibsenian.

Hellman's interest in Marxist theory also draws comparisons with her major theatrical contemporary Odets, though her views are more ambiguous, her antagonists at times innately malicious. Goldstein (S130) finds Hellman "the more impressive dramatist, by virtue of her avoidance of the easy answer;" and her plays had a life outside the context of the Thirties, and her art continued "to develop in admirable though infrequent contributions to the stage" (36).

Four of Hellman's best plays deal directly with Southerners (*The Little Foxes*, *Another Part of the Forest*, *The Autumn Garden*, and *Toys in the Attic*) though all of the original plays except the first two, *The Children's Hour* and *Days to Come*, are set in the South. In his studies of Modern Southern Drama, Adler (S94, S223) cites useful contrasts and parallels, yet concludes that Williams is the more profound playwright due to a wider variety of technique and his "far greater ability to make characters function both as characters and as multiple symbols" (S94, 375). After Williams, Hellman is placed as one of the most important dramatists writing about the South, though her approach to character is more cosmopolitan.

A number of studies have investigated Hellman's reputation as a precursor of feminism, examining the roles and status of the women of her plays, though Hellman seemed amazed at being considered as a standard bearer for the cause. When asked her thoughts about the women's movement, she answered, "Of course I believe in women's liberation, but it seems to make very little sense in the way it's going. Until women can earn their own living, there's no point in talking about brassieres and lesbianism. While I agree with the women's liberation and ecology and all the other good liberal causes, I think at this minute they're diversionary--they keep your eye off the problems implicit in our capitalist society. As a matter of fact, they're implicit in socialist society, too, I guess" (S163, 132). She reinforces her position in an interview with Bill Moyers, saying, "I think it all comes down to whether or not you can support yourself as well as a man can support himself and whether there's enough money to make certain decisions for yourself rather than dependence" (S171, 149).

Asked why playwriting had remained primarily a man's profession, Hellman responded that there had been a few women playwrights, none of them very good. "I don't think many women write with the vigor of men, whether they are novelists or playwrights or poets." (S132, 85). She was the exception. She smoked cigars, drank whiskey, played poker, thought and talked like a man, never giving up her fondness for cooking, gardening, and hosting parties. And she wrote with such power, zeal, and conviction, that Jed Harris called her America's "most virile" dramatist (S299, 80). She learned the craft of writing from Hammett who patiently and persistently endeavored to pass on the "style of bare-boned lucidity, that he had developed independently of Hemingway," where sparse "language granted force to complex ideas" (S299, 67). But even as she learned and conquered the field, her temper would flair if referred to as "one of our leading women playwrights;" yet she would be equally perturbed if you insisted that she wrote like a man. She simply wanted to be recognized for her work. Writing at the height of her career in 1947, Howard Lindsay had this to say of her reputation. "She can think and reason like a man . . . she has to my mind, no superior in the playwriting field, man or woman" (S299, 80).

Lillian Hellman's name will always be associated with the McCarthy era, if not for her memoir, *Scoundrel Time*, then for her response to the House Committee on Un-American Activities that has become a memorable quotation, "I cannot and will not cut my conscience to fit this year's fashions." Her name will always be associated with the controversy that engulfed her career since the writing of her first play, *The Children's Hour* (1934), through the writing of her memoirs, a literary career that spanned five decades. But most importantly she will be remembered for boldly forging a niche in an art world heretofore dominated by men; as one of the most influential and controversial women of the 20th century who, in the end, paved the way for other women playwrights.

The Plays:
Summaries, Productions,
and Critical Overviews

The following is a collection of summaries and overviews of Hellman's dramatic canon which includes eight original plays and four adaptations. The summaries provide brief outlines of the significant events of the play. The productions and credits are of major productions and include cast lists when available as well as additional information, such as length of the production's run. A list of reviews cited in the Secondary Bibliography follows the production information. The overviews provide sketches of critical responses and ensuing scholarly discussions. Citations are keyed to the relevant entry in the Secondary Bibliography section of this volume, followed by a page number when appropriate.

I. ORIGINAL PLAYS

Another Part of the Forest (1946). P1

Plot Summary--Set in the small town of Bowden, Alabama, the play goes back twenty years to the summer of 1880 to explore the earlier lives of the Hubbards of *The Little Foxes*. Marcus Hubbard has amassed a family fortune, started during the Civil War in illegal deals with the Union army, the secret of which has driven his genteel, fervently religious wife to near insanity. The autocratic Marcus treats his sons with contempt, but lavishes attention on his cold and manipulative daughter, Regina. Regina is in love with John Bagtry, Birdie's cousin, who wants to go to Brazil to preserve the institution of slavery. Oscar, Regina's weaker brother, wants to marry the town whore and live idly in New Orleans, while Ben, her clever older brother, is driven only to power and money. When Birdie asks Ben for money to save her family's plantation, he manipulates the loan, sending Bagtry off to war in Brazil, and leaving Regina free to marry a richer prospect. Ben coaxes the secret of his father's criminal past from his mother, promising her that she will be able to go back to her hometown to start a school for black children. He then blackmails his father into giving him control of the family estate. At the play's end, the Hubbards regroup with Ben in command. Regina, adopting the same air of adolescent sensuousness that she used on her father, moves to her brother's side.

Production and Credits--P1.1 Fulton Theatre, New York City, 20 Nov. 1946. 182 Performances. Produced by Hermit Bloomgarden; directed by Hellman; settings by Jo Mielziner; costumes by Lucinda Ballard; original music by Mark Blitzstein.

Cast:
Regina Hubbard--Particia Neal
John Bagtry--Bartlett Robinson
Lavinia Hubbard--Mildred Dunnock
Coralee--Beatrice Thompson
Marcus Hubbard--Percy Waram
Benjamin Hubbard--Leo Glenn
Jacob--Stanley Greene
Oscar Hubbard--Scott Mc Kay
Simon Isham--Owen Coll
Birdie Bagtry--Margaret Phillips
Harold Penniman--Paul Ford
Gilbert Jugger--Gene O'Donnell
Laurette Sincee--Jean Hagen

Reviews: R148-72

P1.2 *Another Part of the Forest*, under the title of *Ladies and Gentlemen*, Moscow Drama Theatre, Moscow, Oct. 1949.

Reviews: R187, R188, R194

P1.3 Liverpool Playhouse, Liverpool, Sept. 1953.

Review: R244, R253

P1.4 Lenox Hill Playhouse, Off Broadway, New York City, 1956.

P1.5 Goodman Memorial Theatre, Chicago, 1957.

P1.6 Booth Tarkington Civic Theatre, Indianapolis, 1961.

P1.7 Denver Civic Theatre, Denver, 1961.

P1.8 Trinity Square Repertory Company, Providence, RI, 1975-76 season.

P1.9 Seattle Repertory Theatre, 1981. With Kate Mulgrew, Kim Hunter, John Kellogg, Keith Carradine, John Procaccino.

P1.10 Ahamson Theatre, Los Angeles, CA, 1982. With Tovah Feldshuh, Dorothy McGuire.

P1.11 Equity Theatre Library, Off Broadway, New York City, 1985.

Critical Overview--Written almost eight years after *The Little Foxes*, *Another Part of the Forest* explores an earlier period in the life of the Hubbard family. Both plays are based largely on the Newhouses, Hellman's mother's banking/storekeeping family from Alabama, and were intended as satire and as parts of a trilogy that was never realized (A19). Daily papers indicate that the title of *Another Part of the Forest* is derived from a notation of scene changes in Shakespeare's *As You Like It* (S53, 163). Triesch (S124) suggests, however, that the title comes from the stage directions of Shakespeare's *Titus Andronicus*, II, iv, arguing also that the two central characters share the same names, Marcus and Lavinia, and that both Lavinias are agents of revenge who bring about defeat by making secrets known. The play marked Hellman's directorial debut, opening to mixed critical reception.

Of the daily reviewers, Atkinson (R148) praises individual scenes of great intensity like Birdie's pathetic farewell scene in the second act, yet finds the work an overwritten, gaudy melodrama. Kronenberger (R157) is impressed by the power and tension of the play, the vigorous characterizations, criticizing the dramatically inadequate Act III, however, wherein melodrama gets the upper hand and "the operations of villainy crowd out the inner nature of villains." Krutch (R158) believes the play more expertly written than Hellman's previous works, yet his enthusiasm is also lessened by the overly melodramatic last scene with its unbelievable, unrelieved villainy. Young (R166) complains of raging violence and lurid vehemence which seem insufficiently motivated. Phelan (R161) faults melodramatic excess, especially the final action which "sprawls in an attempt to provide farce and sentiment where only character should be necessary" (202). Gassner (R169) praises well-rounded, morally appalling but engrossing, characters; yet criticizes the mechanical aid of incriminating papers and testimonies in the third-act resolution which should come through character. Gibbs (R155) is disappointed by melodramatic ornamentation which renders the play "an untidy sequel to an infinitely superior play [*The Little Foxes*]." Barnes (R151) finds the play marred by "lurid" melodramatics, noting that moments of solid impact are "few and far between." Beyer (R168) and Nathan (R160) add to complaints of excessive melodramatic contrivance. Watts (R165), on the other hand, sets aside melodramatic criticism to consider the play superior to Hellman's earlier efforts and one of the most fascinating works of modern theatre.

Kronenberger (R157) suggests that the play "has more than a little in common with those somber Elizabethan 'comedies' swarming with cheats and knaves and evildoers," though lacking their simple emotions. Gassner (R170) similarly observes a "joyless comedy" in the spirit of the Elizabethans. Brown (R152) equates the "venomous 'witches' broth" to that of Shakespeare, cites Ibsen and Webster's *The Duchess of Malfi* as spiritual parents of the work; and finds the "guignol" interesting, yet detracting from serious intent. Bentley (R167) calls *Another Part of the Forest*, like *The Little Foxes*, grand guignol in the guise of realism; commenting that: "Despite the outward trappings of seriousness, the spirit of Broadway carries the day."

In the first extended study of Hellman's plays, Adler (S135) categorizes the work as "straight" melodrama; applauds the Ibsenian technique of the end-play, the tight, tense construction, and reinforces earlier opinions that consider Marcus Hubbard to be one of Hellman's most believable/interesting characters (See also, Atkinson (R149), Kronenberger (R157), Watts (R165). In an earlier work, Adler (S94) explores the relationship of Lavinia to Blanche of William's *Streetcar Named Desire*. In his study, Falk (S184) considers the resemblance of Marcus Hubbard to Shakespeare's Marcus Aurelius, and Lavinia to O'Neill's Electra of *Mourning Becomes Electra* (63).

Bigsby (S208) observes greed and egotism raised to the level of social strategy, though never penetrated; suggesting, more importantly, that a lack of objectivity prevented Hellman from projecting the broken spirit of the old South in the comic light of her intent. Holditch (S241) analyzes southern elements and themes that indelibly underlie and unify the play. In his study, Erbin (S239) examines a reliance on O'Neill's *Mourning Becomes Electra* trilogy, the almost parallel plots, settings, and characters. Wiles (S264) notes the "trying out" of a Jonsonian comedy of humours, developed later and more overtly in the sociohistorical satires, *Candide*, and *My Mother, My Father and Me*; yet sees the play as "genteel cliché," repeating "the superficial forms of Chekhov without his hard-edged irony or his universal reduction of our interaction to absurdity" (95). In a 1984 study of feminist themes, Friedman (S216) explores conditions in the characters lives which "lead to manipulating, passive and 'emasculating' behavior" (83). In 1990, Austin (S265) applies feminist theories to an analysis of the five female characters of the play, who struggle within circumscribed roles only to be overpowered in the end.

The play (screenplay by Vladimir) was successfully transferred to film in 1948. The cast included Fredric March (Marcus Hubbard), Florence Eldridge (Lavinia), Dan Duryea (Oscar), Edmond O'Brien (Ben), Ann Blyth (Regina), and John Dall (John Bagtry).

The Autumn Garden (1951). P2

Plot Summary--The action is set in September of 1949 in an elegant summer mansion on the gulf of Mexico, one hundred miles from New Orleans, where every summer since her father's death, Constance Tuckerman has filled the family home with paying guests. During this particular summer the well-bred spinster has the help of young Sophie, her half-French niece, who serves as a maid but yearns to return to Europe where she was born. Sophie is engaged to young Ellis, though neither is genuinely committed, and he would rather go to Europe with an unsavory off-stage character named Payson. Ellis' mother and grandmother are old family friends and rich paying guests. Among the effete, middle-aged group is the quiet, retired army general Benjamin Griggs who is attempting to persuade his flirtatious, pathetically foolish wife, Rose, to give him a divorce so that he can follow some unrealized romantic adventure. There is also the intellectual bachelor/banker Ed Crossman, a cynical drinker who harbors the illusion that he still loves Constance since their youth. Between the two has been the shadow of artist Nick Denery who jilted Constance many years ago. Into the languorous vacation setting the artist returns for the first time in twenty-three years, bringing with him his rich wife Nina who is attracted to her husband, as an artist and a bohemian, for his sense of adventure. Although Nick once showed promise, he now does more philandering and meddling in others' lives than painting. In a drunken state, he involves the French girl in a compromising situation, which, in the end, forces all of the characters to face their inadequacies: that they are the sum of their small acts and impervious to change.

Production and Credits--P2.1 Coronet Theatre, New York City, 7 Mar. 1951. 101 Performances. Produced by Hermit Bloomgarden; directed by Harold Clurman; settings by Howard Bay; costumes by Anna Hill Johnstone.

Cast:
Rose Griggs--Florence Eldridge
Mrs. Mary Ellis--Ethel Griffies
General Benjamin Griggs--Colin Keith-Johnston
Edward Crossman--Kent Smith
Frederick Ellis--James Lipton
Carrie Ellis--Margaret Barker
Sophie Tuckerman--Joan Lorring
Leon--Maxwell Glanville
Constance Tuckerman--Carol Goodner
Nicholas Denery--Fredric March

Nina Denery--Jane Wyatt
Hilda--Lois Holmes

Reviews: R200-19, R221-23

P2.2 Lenox Hill Playhouse, Off Broadway, New York City, 3 May 1956.

P2.3. Moscow Arts Theatre, 1957-58 season.

P2.4. Charles Playhouse, Boston, 1962.

P2.5 Long Wharf Theatre, New Haven, CT, Nov. 1976. With Joyce Ebert, Carmen Matthews, John McMartin, Victor Garber.

Reviews: R363-64

P2.6 Arena Stage, Washington, D.C., 1977. With Laurie Kennedy, Leslie Cass, Richard Bauer, Leora Dana.

Critical Overview--Hellman's own favorite play, *The Autumn Garden* is based upon biographical material of her father's family, and marks a departure from the well-made structures of her earlier plays. Most of the critics invoke the distinct dramatic shade of Chekhov in the story of middle-age despair and the emphasis on character and mood. Hellman's advance in technique and style is viewed as the logical development in view of her lifelong study of Chekhov, "a devotion which culminated in her edition of *The Selected Letters of Chekhov,* published in 1955" (S90, 53). General Griggs's speech of self-insight in the last act was written by Dashiell Hammett. It summarizes the play's theme of missed opportunities. *The Autumn Garden* opened to mixed critical reception and ran for 102 performances.

Of the daily reviewers, Watts (R222) describes the brooding introspection as a mature deliberation from the febrile intensity of Hellman's early plays, criticizing its lack of excitement. Hawkins (R212), Lardner (R214), and Marshall (R215), and others recognize a mellowing in Hellman's attitude toward her characters. Atkinson (R200)ranks Hellman at the peak of her talents--observant, sympathetic, honest, and alert--, praises brilliantly drawn characters, yet concludes that the play is "boneless and torpid." McClain (R216) applauds realistic characterizations, and pardons the playwright for attempting to say too many things at once. Marshall (R216) commends the "shrewd and ruthless humor," applied to the characters, but complains that the action is dull and unconvincing. Kerr (R213) finds the play interesting, but not exhilarating; criticizing a lack of variety in the loosely related characters who are too unconvincingly trapped in precisely the same stalemate. Brown (R202) observes a Chekhovian strain without the lyricism, yet praises shrewd and penetrating observations made "by a wise woman who is writing a play which, in spite of its faults, is in many ways the most mature and probing to have come from her gifted pen" (29). *Time* magazine (R219) reports of characters that mingle but never merge, noting a Chekhovian method without the poetic quality. Hawkins (R212) considers the tapestry of personal narratives favorably woven, but suggests deleting the European niece's "windup" story. Coleman complains of dull mazes, diffused action, and characters that do not successfully embody theme. Nathan

(S68) finds the theme elusive, the characters illuminated "gratuitously, with a small pocket flashlight" (242).

Clurman (R204) praises the work as Hellman's most lucid and probing play, but regrets the lack Chekhov's warm embrace in the characters that have been drawn with a "certain smiling asperity, an astringent, almost cruel clarity" (48.) Gassner (S91) praises perceptively drawn characters and penetrating dialogue, noting that Chekhov's oblique style and bizarre humor are missing, that the indictment against the characters is too generalized, that the tough-minded resolution is too dubious.

Though many reviewers describe the work as the comedy of Hellman intent, Felheim (S90) argues that it is modern tragedy in the Chekhovian sense, observing that no American play was so completely Chekhovian as her recent contribution. Adler (S135) praises newfound techniques, successful dialogue and characterization; suggests that Chekhov is a tough act to follow, concluding that the work lacks the power and drive of Hellman's best. Downer (S63) notes "an almost Chekhovian image of society," calling *The Autumn Garden*, "the most promising play of the year" (140-41). Lederer (S193) argues that Hellman never intended to write in the manner of Chekhov; she sees the play as the culmination of earlier attempts at the novelistic techniques, "walking away from the big scene and giving us only the emotional effects of it" (89). Sievers (S144) praises profound psychoanalytic perceptions, noting weak plot development.

Strasberg (S103) blames the show's failure on the acting style which was inhibited by the confining set. The set did not accurately approximate a Chekhovian environment, and thereby interfered with the portrayal of humaneness of character. Clurman (S205) expresses similar reservations: the set was too literal; it "had been designed in consultation with the author before I had been engaged as director--a sign of artistic disorganization and ignorance of the director's function" (47). In an interview with Funke (S132), Hellman regrets that the play was badly cast, and that "for some reason it never came to life and it droned rather than moved" (103). In *An Unfinished Woman* (A21), she reflects upon the cheerfulness that was lost during rehearsals, "which can and does happen on the stage and once started can seldom be changed" (268).

Holditch (S241) examines Southern elements and themes that underlie and unify the play. In a 1989 assessment, Wiles (S264) considers the play a genteel cliché, mirroring "the superficial forms of Chekhov without his hard-edged irony or his universal reduction of our interaction to absurdity" (95).

The Children's Hour (1934). P3

Plot Summary--Karen Wright and Martha Dobie are headmistresses of a girls' boarding school, a converted farmhouse which is set in a small New England town. Classmates in college, they'd worked eight long years to save enough money to buy the farm and start the school which means to them self-respect and honest work. In an attempt to frustrate the discipline of the headmistresses, a spoiled, malevolent young girl runs away from the school, convincing her wealthy, aged grandmother, the main pillar of the school's support, that the headmistresses have engaged in lesbian acts. Although one of the teachers is engaged to her grandson, the grandmother withdraws the child (Mary) from the school and encourages other parents to do the same. The teachers sue for libel, but lose when Martha's ex-actress aunt does not appear to clear their names. Karen calls off her engagement. The grandmother learns that her granddaughter has lied. She comes to make amends to the teachers who have been ruined financially and morally; but

Martha, having realized, in the end, that she does have unnatural affections for Karen, has already committed suicide.

Production and Credits--P3.3 Maxine Elliot's Theatre, New York City, 20 Nov. 1934. 691 Performances. Produced and directed by Herman Shumlin; settings by Aline Bernstein.

Cast:
Peggy Rogers--Eugenia Rawls
Mrs. Lily Mortar--Aline Mc Dermott
Evelyn Munn--Elizabeth Seckel
Helen Burton--Lynne Fisher
Lois Fisher--Jacqueline Rusling
Catherine--Barbara Leeds
Rosalie Wells--Barbara Beals
Mary Tilford--Florence Mc Gee
Karen Wright--Katherine Emery
Martha Dobie--Anne Revere
Doctor Joseph Cardin--Robert Keith
Agatha--Edmonia Nolley
Mrs. Amelia Tilford--Katherine Emmet
A Grocery Boy--Jack Tyler

Reviews: R1-37, R41-45

P3.2 New York Library production, Dec. 1936.

P3.4 Gate Theatre (private theatre), London, Nov. 1936. Produced by Messrs. Norman Marshall and Reginald Beckwith. With Mavis Edwards (Mary), Pamela Standish (Rosalie), Mary Merrall (Mrs. Ameila Tilford), Ursala Jeans (Karen Wright), Valerie Taylor (Mary Tilford).

Reviews: R49, R53, R54, R58

P3.5 Copenhagen, 1936.

P3.6 Paris, under the title of *The Innocents*, 1936.

P3.7 Werba's Theatre, Brooklyn, NY, 28 Mar. 1938.

P3.8 Shubert Theatre Production, Brooklyn, NY, 8 Nov. 1938.

Review: R62

P3.9 Seattle Repertory Playhouse, Seattle, 1939. With Esther Tate and Marion Litonius.

P3.10 Actors Company of Chicago, 1941-42 season. Directed by Minnie Galatzer.

P3.11 New York Public Library, May 1945.

Reviews: R145-46

P3.12 Alley Theatre, Houston, 1948.

P3.13 New Bolton's Theatre, London, 1950-51 season.

Reviews: R198, R220

P3.14 Coronet Theatre, New York City, 18 Dec. 1952. 189 Performances. Produced by Kermit Bloomgarden; directed by Hellman; settings by Howard Bay; costumes by Anna Hill Johnstone.

Cast:
Peggy Rogers--Sandra March
Catherine--Nancy Plehn
Lois Fisher--Carolyn King
Mrs. Lily Mortar--Mary Finney
Evelyn Munn--Denise Alexander
Helen Burton--Toni Hallaran
Rosalie Wells--Janet Parker
Janet--June Connelly
Leslie--Sandee Preston
Mary Tilford--Iris Mann
Karen Wright--Kim Hunter
Martha Dobie--Patricia Neal
Dr. Joseph Cardin--Robert Pastene
Agatha--Leora Thatcher
Mrs. Amelia Tilford--Katherine Emmet
A Grocery Boy--Gordon Russell

Reviews: R224-28, R230-32, R236-38, R240, R242-43, R245-52, R254-55

P3.15 Cleveland Arena Theatre of the Karamu Theatre, Cleveland, OH, 1956.

P3.16 Arts Theatre, London, 1956.

Review: R272

P3.17 New Paltz Summer Repertory Theatre, New Paltz, NY, 1988. With Missy Alexander, Jennifer Evans.

P3.18 Lyttelton Theatre, London. Oct. 1994. Directed by Howard Davies. Setting by Ashley Martin-Davies.

Review: R378

P3.19 Off Off Broadway, New York City, 1996.

Critical Overview--The first and most successful of Hellman's plays, *The Children's Hour* was banned in Boston, Chicago, and London, its diversionary theme of lesbianism turning the study of good and evil into one the most controversial plays of the 1930s. Hellman insisted that play had nothing to do with lesbianism, "just the charge of the young girl, that's all" (S171, 167). As Mantle (S8) observed, the central issue is the "scandalmongering and the whispering campaign, the kind of vicious lying that may easily wreck the lives of innocent persons" (33). The production opened without tryouts or advance publicity for fear of censorship or police interference, neither of which transpired. The play was taken from a famous nineteenth century Scottish law report, "Closed Doors; or, The Great Drumsheugh Case," from William Roughead's *Bad Companions*, the source transformed into an original piece with contemporary characters and New England setting. As Williams (S210) notes, "the dynamics of the action and the denouement of the drama are the creation of her [Hellman's] imagination" (99). The show was an astounding success, running on Broadway for 691 performances, then touring the United States and abroad for another year; even though the Pulitzer Prize Committee had rejected it as a contender for the prize because of its unsavory theme. William Lyon Phelps, one of the judges on the Pulitzer Committee, refused to see the play, and the prize that year ironically went to *The Old Maid*, a tepid study by Zoe Akins.

The daily critics praise the dramatic intensity and psychological insight of the piece, despite the weakness of the third act. Atkinson (R2) hails the work as one of the most straightforward, driving dramas of the season, distinguished chiefly for its characterization of the child, yet criticizes the mettlesome conclusion that should have ended with the suicide. Krutch (R12) finds the first two acts tense and gripping, but complains that Mary, the central interest of the play, is missing from the conclusion. Similarly, Isaacs (R32) observes that Mary's appallingly strong characterization guides the course of the plot, her absence leading both the play and the actors to a dull and perplexed third act. Carven (R29) criticizes the confused ending, in which Hellman proves the innocence of the accused women--the excuse for the play's existence--, then concludes "by trying to convict them of the charges which, in lying mouths, caused all the trouble." Brown (R5) notes big moments of undeniable tension that rise above "slightly threadbare hokum," yet argues that the third act is in need of drastic cutting. Benchley (R4) calls the play "the season's dramatic high-water mark," praising the tight, brave writing until the last act which has "two too many endings"(34). And in the introduction to *Four Plays*, published in 1942, Hellman responds to the criticism, acknowledging that the play should have ended with Martha's suicide: "I am a moral writer, often too moral a writer, and I cannot avoid, it seems, that last summing-up" (A15, x, xi).

In a 1936 study Lawson (S17) pinpoints the climax (Martha's suicide) as the crux of the problem, for it "exposes the conceptual confusion which splits the play into a dual system" (223); if one were to correctly select the suicide as the climax, Martha's confession would occur in the exposition, not in the conclusion, thus unifying the development of psychological and social conflicts, while strengthening both lines of action. In a critique that follows, Lawson (S20) again blames the lack of unity on Hellman's failure to dramatize the social roots of the action, stating: "We are not shown the conditions in the environment which explains the little girls' demoniac hatred and the suffering of the two school teachers" (15). Nonetheless, Block (S22) praises the breakthrough directness of the subject matter, the tragic conflict of everyday characters, and the social implications. Triesch (S124) calls the play a "subtle protest against society and its treatment of the individual," observing that Hellman would never again would "create a true tragic fate as she did in the character of Martha" (13).

In his 1944 study, Clark (S40) commends the tension and tight construction, but thinks the "summing up" is not integral to the action. To the contrary, Nathan (S18) finds the grandmother's apologies and the explanation of the child's malfeasance absolutely essential. Miller (S99) argues that the third act turns the play from a sub-Ibsen account of integrity into simple melodrama, calling the ironic reductivism, "a piece of calculated posing" (275). Adler (S135) justifies the ending. In the manner of Ibsen's *The Wild Duck*, it concludes "not with the suicide but with a brief discussion pinning down the issues" (8). Lederer (S193) argues similarly that the summing up is "necessary to a play written in the tradition of the Ibsen realistic drama" (31). Moody (S155), however, is less intrigued with the last act, directing attention to particular weaknesses, such as the boyfriend's silence, the child's absence, and the anticlimactic closing scene. Sievers (S144) applies a Freudian interpretation to the characters, concluding that the play successfully takes "a daring step forward in the theatre's humanizing power to create understanding and empathy for unconscious deviation as a tragic flaw rather than a loathsome anomaly" (28-81). Armato (S160) examines the perverse structure of victim-victimizer relations within the play and sees the ending as structurally necessary to the resolution.

Falk (S184) calls attention in Act I to the careful preparation of Martha's final confession, to her high strung and nervous appearance, to the aunt's comment on her "unnatural" fondness for Karen; comments on the irony of the opening lines from *The Merchant of Venice*, read by the school girls, which refer to mercy "singularly lacking in those who implement the destruction of others" (45); asserting that the theme of lesbian is used as a metaphor. Williams (S210) argues that homosexual love was deliberately chosen as a theme, since Hellman "had been close to this subject in her own life and saw not only the consequences for the lovers but also--and even more--the evil responses aroused in the minds of the unloving outsiders" (104). Reynolds (S235) reasons that the issue is neither lesbianism nor homosexuality among school teachers or in the abstract: "the issue is the 'big lie' . . . the smear that remains from the accusation" (134). Tufts (S263) proposes that "big lie" of the play is neither Mary's devious tale nor Martha's denial of it, but Hellman's insistence that the play has "nothing to do with lesbianism" (64). Similarly, Titus (S277) argues that suggestions of lesbian desire are diffused throughout the text, touching every character but Karen Wright (Miss "Right"); and that, "The violence against Martha Dobie and the diffusion of desire among almost all of the female characters reflect both the energy of Hellman's public denial of sexual deviance and a private struggle to understand her own personal desires" (226).

The Children's Hour returned to Broadway in 1952. The revival was directed by Hellman, and, through minor rewriting and editing, stressed the analogy between the destructive character assassination of the play and the McCarthy investigations. Of the revival, Atkinson (R224) once again observed an excessive summing up in the last act, yet a taut and pertinent play with political overtones that accurately fit the slander of the day. Bentley (R246) criticized the "clumsy" ending, the mechanical inversion of stock melodramatic characters, the weak political analogy, and the direction; and pronounced the play a failure. Gassner (R247), however, dismissed flaws; and praised the power of the play, especially the "throbbing" second act which he saw as a rare occurrence in the theatre of recent years. In a later evaluation, Estrin (S256) endorses the play as "one of the most compelling works to emerge from the serious American theater before Blanche DuBois and Willy Loman arrived on Broadway in the late 1940s" (2).

The first motion picture adaptation with Merle Oberon (Karen Wright), Miriam Hopkins (Martha Dobie), Joel McCrea (Dr. Joe Cardin), and screenplay by Hellman was released in 1936, as *These Three*. In accordance with the Hays Commission and the Hollywood moral code, the lesbianism was censored, the plot centering on a love triangle The child says she saw Martha in bed with Karen's fiancee. The 1962 film, with Audrey Hepburn (Karen Wright), Shirley MacLaine (Martha Dobie), James Garner (Dr. Joe Cardin), and screenplay by John Michael Hayes, restored the original title and plot. Hellman preferred the censored version.

Days to Come (1936). P4

Plot Summary--Arthur Rodman, the head of a paternalistic brush factory in Ohio, has been forced to cut salaries during the Depression in order to maintain the family business. The workers strike; and after three weeks of a work stoppage, Rodman reluctantly calls in professional strikebreakers. He has been advised to do so by an attorney/best friend to whom he is heavily in debt, because of his wife's extravagant lifestyle. The labor union leader, a decent and peaceful organizer/negotiator foresees problems, since the strikebreakers are actually gangsters/agitators. One of the gangsters kills another of the gangster/strikebreakers during a gambling quarrel. The body is dumped in an alley in an attempt to frame the union leader, but this is witnessed by Rodman's intellectually frustrated, promiscuous wife when she goes to the union leader's office to offer herself (unsuccessfully) to him. The union leader is taken to jail; and the foreman's daughter is killed during a riot that erupts. When the strike is brought to an end, there are losses on both sides, especially for Rodman. He loses his wife (who admits to having had an affair with the attorney) as well as the tradition of caring for his workers, their friendship, and their respect.

Production and Credits--P4.1 Vanderbilt Theatre, New York City, 15 Dec. 1936. 7 Performances. Produced and directed by Herman Shumlin; settings by Aline Bernstein.

Cast:
Hannah--Clare Woodbury
Lucy--Muriel Gallick
Cora Rodman--Frieda Altman
Henry Ellicott--Ned Wever
Andrew Rodman--William Harrigan
Julie Rodman--Florence Eldridge
Thomas Firth--Joseph Sweeney
Leo Whalen--Ben Smith
Sam Wilkie--Charles Dingle
Mossie Dowel--Jack Carr
Joe Easter--Thomas Fisher

Reviews: R38-40, R44, R46-48, R50-52, R55-57, R59-61

P4.2 WPA Theatre, Marymount Manhattan Theatre, Off Off Broadway, New York City, 19 Oct. 1978.

Reviews: R365, R366

Critical Overview--The most political of Hellman's early plays, the theme is clearly derived from Marxian thought. Early manuscripts indicate references to *Ecclesiastes* and *Isaiah* and the relationship between capital and labor, references also to Hellman's visit to a brush factory in Ohio where she gathered background material (S256). The action deals primarily with labor relations/unionization, and contains a secondary plot about family greed and degeneracy. In an interview with Beebe (1936), Hellman insists, "It's the family I'm interested in principally; the strike and social manifestations are just backgrounds. It's a story of innocent people on both sides who are drawn into conflict and events far beyond their comprehension" (5). The production was not well-received and withdrawn after six performances.

Of the daily reviewers, Atkinson (R39) criticizes the elliptical writing style that tapers off in bizarre direction, the mixture of a crime play with an analysis of female neuroticism which seems tangentially connected with the basic subject of labor trouble. Gabriel (R47) observes an awkward mix of a socialism and sex. Brown (R40) calls it "an embarrassing failure," noting material for several plays: (1) one about the strike from the striker's point of view; (2) one about the strike from the employer's point of view; (3) another about the inexcusable tactics of the strikebreakers; (4) still another about the attraction of the rich man's wife for the labor agitator; (5) and finally, one about the complicated relationships in the rich man's unhappy home. Comparing the play to *The Children's Hour*, Krutch (R50) observes the same unresolved discords, sultry hates, murderous impulses, and below decorous lives; and of the similarity of dual plots comments, "one is not sure just where its center lies" (769). Watts (59) also finds much of the play confused and ineffective. Young (R60) applauds the subject matter, yet dismisses the work as "an overwhelming stylistic hurdle." Lawson (S20) observes structural weaknesses, a final act that is retrospective and futile (similar to *The Children's Hour*), and concludes that Hellman has struggled "with psychological and technical problems which go beyond the present scope of her social thinking" (16). Taylor (R57) finds the play "rather absorbing" despite inherent defects, such as duality of focus; yet agrees with Dexter (R46) that more emphasis should have been placed on the working class.

Of the later considerations, Clark (S40) criticizes the love scene, its late introduction at the climax of the action. Pollock (R55) suggests that the "ponderous" piece is written with something of the austerity of Galsworthy's *Strife*. Adler (S135) complains that the play "fails to keep its focus on its prime material [labor problems]" (10). Moody (S155) argues that confused audiences were asked to invest with the good guys and decry the bad, uncertain in the end "about where to stake their allegiance" (65). Sievers (S144) observes a mixture of socioeconomic themes with psychoanalytic treatment, yet concludes that the play fails in terms of labor relations, of psychological analysis, and of theatre. Confirming the incompatibility plots, Bigsby (S208) argues that the central concern is the family, and "identifying a moral failure in the class from which she [Hellman] herself derived" (278). Wiles (S264) observes flaws, but considers the play far truer than the strike plays produced by thirties counterparts; suggesting, more importantly, that the work deserves recognition as an anthology of 1930s gestures and as working out of ideas to be perfected in *The Little Foxes*, and calling attention as well to Brechtian theories of political art that Hellman intuited.

Of the 1978 Off Off Broadway revival, Clurman (R365) defends the play despite its weaknesses, observing that the play is about the strike for the first two act--even though Hellman maintains that the strike was not her main concern; and that the plot "does not wholly convey its intended meaning or creative impulse" (588). In the introduction to

Four Plays in 1942, Hellman admits that she ruined a good play, believing that every thought must be written into the work. "I am only sorry that the confusion in the script confused the best director in the theatre, who, in turn managed to confuse one of the most inadequate casts" (A15, ix).

The Little Foxes (1939). P5

Plot Summary--The action takes place in 1900 in a small Southern town in Alabama, where Oscar and Benjamin Hubbard with their sister Regina Giddens arrange to get Northern capital to finance a cotton mill. One-third of the investment money is to come from Horace, Regina's husband, who has been at a hospital in Baltimore with a heart condition for several months. Since he refuses to answer his wife's correspondence, Regina sends their daughter Alexandra to fetch him. He arrives home weakened from the journey and ill-disposed to finance that which his wife has negotiated. In their eagerness to bring the deal to fruition, Oscar and Benjamin arrange for the theft of securities from Horace's safety deposit box, cutting Regina out of her share of the deal. Horace discovers the missing bonds and tells his wife that he plans to revise his will, leaving only the stolen securities to her. She becomes enraged, causing Horace to have a fatal heart attack as she mercilessly refuses to help him. In the end, Regina blackmails her brothers into a seventy-five percent share of the new venture; Ben retaliates with the suggestion that he will expose her for murder, and Alexandra announces that she will go off on her own.

Production and Credits--P5.1 National Theatre, New York City, 15 February. 1939. 410 Performances. Produced and directed by Herman Shumlin; settings by Howard Bay; costumes by Aline Bernstein.

Cast:
Addie--Abbie Mitchell
Cal--John Marriott
Birdie Hubbard--Patricia Collinge
Oscar Hubbard--Carl Benton Reid
Leo Hubbard--Dan Duryea
Regina Giddens--Tallulah Bankhead
William Marshall--Lee Baker
Benjamin Hubbard--Charles Dingle
Alexandra Giddens--Florence Williams
Horace Giddens--Frank Conroy

Reviews: R63-87, R89

P5.2 Pasadena Playhouse, Pasadena, CA, 1942.

P5.3 Piccadilly Theatre, London, Oct. 1942. Directed by Emlyn Williams; with Fay Compton (Regina).

Reviews: R112, R113, R115, R117

P5.4 Oxford Repertory Theatre, Oxford, England, 1943.

P5.5 National Theatre, Belgrade, Yugoslavia, 1948. Directed by Dr. Klein.

P5.6 Paris production, 1962. Translated to French by Simone Signoret, who also played Regina.

P5.7 Studio Arena Theatre, Buffalo, NY, 1966. With Colleen Dewhurst, Gerald Richards, Bette Henritze.

P5.8 Vivian Beaumont Theatre, the Repertory Theatre of Lincoln Center under the direction of Jules Irving, New York City, 26 Oct. 1967; limited run of 60 performances; moved to Ethel Barrymore Theatre (Saint-Subber and Katzka-Berne Productions), 19 Dec. 1967, for an additional 40 performances. Directed by Mike Nichols; setting and lighting by Howard Bay; costumes by Patricia Zipprodt.

Cast:
Addie--Beah Richards
Cal--Andre Womble
Birdie Hubbard--Margaret Leighton
Oscar Hubbard--E.G. Marshall
Leo Hubbard--Austin Pendleton
Regina Giddens--Anne Bancroft
William Marshall--William Prince
Benjamin Hubbard--George C. Scott
Alexandra Giddens--Marcia Tucci
Horace Giddens--Richard A. Dysart

Reviews: R341-58

P5.9 The Lamb's Club, Off Broadway, New York City, 1969.

P5.10 St. Martin's Theatre, Melbourne, Australia, 1969.

P5.11 Seattle Repertory Theatre, Seattle, Feb. 1970.

Reviews: R359, R360

P5.12 Zweibrücken Entertainment Center, Germany, Mar. 1971.

P5.13 American College Theatre Festival, Washington, DC, 1972.

P5.14 Walnut Street Theatre, Philadelphia, 1974. With Geraldine Page, Rip Torn.

P5.15 University of California, Santa Barbara, 1975.

Review: R362

P5.16 Trinity Square Repertory Company, Providence, RI, 1975-76 season. With Zina Jaspar, Ricardo Wiley.

P5.17 Culbreth Theatre, Charlottesville, VA, 1976. With Celia Howard, David Cupp.

P5.18 Cincinnati Playhouse in the Park, Cincinnati, OH, 1976. With Jan Farrand, Jo Henderson.

P5.19 Meadowbrook Theatre, Rockland, MI, 1976. With Polly Holliday, Nancy Coleman.

P5.20 Old Globe Theatre, San Diego, CA, 1976. With Jenifer Henn.

P5.21 Missouri Repertory Theatre, Kansas City, MO, 1978-79 season. With Robin Humphrey, John Cothran, Jr.

P5.22 American Conservatory Theatre, San Francisco, CA, 1979. With Elizabeth Huddle.

P5.23 Hartman Theatre Company, Stamford, CT, 1979.

P5.24 Berkshire Playhouse, Stockbridge, MA, 1980. With Kim Hunter, John McMartin.

P5.25 Martin Beck Theatre, New York City, 7 May 1981. Directed by Austin Pendleton; settings by Andrew Jackness; lighting by Paul Gallo; costumes by Florence Klotz.

Cast:
Regina--Elizabeth Taylor
Addie--Novella Nelson
Cal--Joe Seneca
Birdie Hubbard--Maureen Stapleton
Oscar Hubbard--Joe Ponazechi
Leo Hubbard--Dennis Christopher
William Marshall--Humbert Allan Astredo
Benjamin Hubbard--Anthony Zerbe
Alexandra Giddens--Ann Talman
Horace Giddens--Tom Aldredge

Reviews: R368-77

P5.26 London, 1982. With Elizabeth Taylor, Sada Thompson.

P5.27 Equity Theatre Library, Off Broadway, New York City, 12 Feb. 1987.

P5.28 Vivian Beaumont Theatre at Lincoln Center, New York City, previews 3 Apr. 1997, opens 27 Apr. 1997. Directed by Jack O'Brien; settings by John Lee Beatty, costumes by Jane Greenwood; lighting by Kenneth Posner. With Stockard Channing

(Regina), Ethel Ayler, Frances Conroy, Richard E. Council, Jennifer Dundas, Brian Kerwin, Brian Murray, Charles Turner, Frederick Weller, Kenneth Welsh.

Reviews: R379-84

Critical Overview--The title of the play was suggested by Dorothy Parker and taken from the biblical reference in the Song of Solomon, II, xv, in which the little foxes "spoil the vines; for our vines have tender grapes." The "little foxes" of the play are the Hubbards, a Southern family drawn largely from Hellman's maternal side, a banking/storekeeping family from Alabama, who are determined to attain wealth from the rise of industrialism. Early manuscripts reveal Hellman's method of dramatic composition, giving evidence to painstaking research of the history of the South from 1880 to 1900, the minutest of details that were worked into her script (S124). The play ran on Broadway for 410 performances, then toured the country for two years. It was translated into German, and strongly supported on the stages of Vienna, Frankfurt, and Hamburg. Generally considered Hellman's finest, and by the playwright's admission the most difficult to write--she rewrote it nine times, *The Little Foxes* remains a classic of the American theatre, the most frequently revived of her plays. Its success established Hellman's career as one of America's leading playwrights.

The daily critical fraternity evoke the power of the piece, by implication important and provocative, despite shortcomings. Atkinson (R64) observes a vibrant theatre piece with viable roles for the actors, though second to *The Children's Hour*, "melodramatic rather than tragic, none too fastidious in its manipulation of the stage and presided over by a Pinero frown of fustian morality." Lockridge (R75) notes shrewd characters, touches of melodrama effectively executed, last act trouble as with *The Children's Hour* --the movement falters taking Regina slightly out of focus--, concluding that the play is "steadily interesting and almost, but never quite, more." Mantle (R77) praises a feeling of impending tragedy that overshadows the action and keeps the audience interested, and the taut writing--until the last act which falters with an indecisive ending. Watts (R86) is all praise for the important and convincing play which is told with an Ibsen-like directness. Brown (R67) finds the play a pretense to sociological significance, "superlatively 'good theatre'" despite excessive contrivances and writing that "is too expert in the worst manner of Ibsen, which is only another way of saying in the best manner of Pinero." Krutch (R74) praises vivid characters, shrewd writing, and expert technique, much of which seems taken from Ibsen; yet considers the play less perfect than *The Children's Hour*, "less inevitable in its development and occasionally more melodramatic in its action than it should be" (244). Nathan (R80) approves of strong characters and the integrity of the play," rare among her playwriting sex;" notes shades of Ibsen, Pinero, and Strindberg, yet criticizes the monotony of emotional drive and the "periodic confusion of melodramatic bitterness with suggestive tragedy." Gassner (R71) commends the power of the piece, the forceful dialogue, despite melodramatic underpinnings and ineffective declamation of idealism at the end; since there is no indication that daughter Alexandra understands "the social forces or the complex society that she now intends to defy" (748-49). Kronenberger (R73) praises the power and significance of the play and the overwhelming moral sense that has direct social meaning; underscoring Hellman's vision that "our age is not one of personal tragedy but one of social confusion and dislocation;" and concluding that, *The Little Foxes* comes through as the most effective kind of protest, sending its audiences out of the theatre "not purged, not released, but still aroused and indignant" (55). Anderson (R63) finds the play slightly over-plotted and occasionally melodramatic, but containing the advantages of sharp observation and incisive character drawing, the action stemming "directly from the characters as they reveal themselves to make an absorbing drama" (15). Fergusson (R70) harshly criticizes melodramatic aspects, the inclusiveness of the piece, and much of the cast, including Bankhead's "baritone register," concluding that the play an "evening of diversion . . . a thing of some keen edges and no point." Most of the critics call attention to an outstanding performance by Tallulah Bankhead, later to be recalled as one of her most popular starring roles. Bette Davis starred in the role of Regina in the 1941 film version that reached the screen "with no diminution of power" (S209).

Of the play's later studies, Clark (S40) praises a rhythmical quality that never intrudes, a surface reality that masks "the work of a conscious and determined and scrupulous writer" (130), calling attention to the sparsely and beautifully sketched "Negro" maid who effectively speaks her piece. In an introduction to the play, Gassner (S97) considers the real theme "'original sin' in a modern sense" . . . bringing Hellman "closer to such contemporary Catholic writers as Mauriac than to Bernard Shaw or Karl Marx" (984). Miller (S99) considers the work a fine example of the craft of playmaking combined with the qualities of excellent realistic drama: characters talk and behave in a realistic fashion, depicting a tale of social degradation and moral decay, and everything happening on stage is a direct contribution to plot character and theme. Lewis (S114) is impressed by the masterpiece of Ibsen-influenced theatre, "almost flawless in economy and structure, realization of character, and pertinence of dialogue" (107), ranking the "powerful human drama" alongside Gorky's *Yegor Bulitchev* and Becques's *Les Corbeaux.*

Adler (S135) examines the play in terms of melodrama and well-made play structure to determine that: (1) the melodramatic aspects are used legitimately "toward character and meaning" (15), and (2) the tight and complex construction does not involve unfair or obvious trickery, nor does it interfere with honest characterization, motivation, or ideas (19). In another study, he (S94) compares Hellman to Williams, though he concludes that Hellman's characters are less complex, that her portrayals do "not, in their central acquisitive 'foxiness,' seem typically of the South," that they are too depraved to be typical of anything (367). Of the character portrayals, Sievers (S144) observes unmistakable psychoanalytic overtones, yet finds Hellman "more concerned with describing and dramatizing evil than explaining it" (282).

Moody's critical overview (S155) confirms an Ibsen-like precision in the ordering of characters and events. Eatman (S162) traces the moral perspective to sources outside the period of the play, such as the social realism of Ibsen's plays, the intellectual skepticism of the 1930s, and Zola's spirit of objectivity; concluding that Hellman's synthesis of rational formulation and moral commitment casts "an image of American destiny--the continuing dialectic of the privileges versus the responsibilities of liberal democracy" (73). Heilman (S142) notes a line of continuity from Jonson's *The Fox* in the theme of dishonor among thieves, the irony, and the hint of black comedy, as "the play seems less to evoke the divided response of the best melodrama than to give us some comforting reassurance that sooner or later the bad guys will have their troubles, if only at the hands of each other" (28). Dick (S209) senses another fox in the making at the play's end, as Alexandra becomes her mother's tormentor by refusing to spend the night with her.

Lederer (S193) examines the irony of the piece; calling the work "a dark satiric comedy" that uses "melodramatic devices to make its point" (49), and suggesting that critics have confused the device of dramatic irony with the artificial trickeries of the well-made play. Bigsby (S208) argues that the moral scope of the play extends beyond the simplicities of mechanical plotting, noting resemblances to Chekhov's *The Cherry Orchard*. Wiles (S264) examines the politics of the play in terms of Marxist social analysis and through its embodiment in the women, calling attention Brechtian-like techniques used before Hellman had ever heard of such theories. A later study by Holditch (S241) gives focus to Southern elements and themes which underlie and unify the play.

Higdon (S225) points out that Chapter XXII of Henry James's *The Americans* seems to have shaped the celebrated scene in which Regina withholds her husband's medicine. And in a study of feminist themes, Friedman (S216) finds in the creation of Regina, "one of the most destructive women characters in the history of the theatre" (81).

The Searching Wind (1944). P6

Plot Summary--The play covers twenty-two years in turbulent world history and in the lives of its three principal characters--Alex Hazen, a career diplomat who is an ambassador in Rome during the rise of Mussolini and Hitler, and the two women who vie for his love, Emily Hazen, his wealthy wife and daughter of the liberal newspaper publisher, Moses Taney; and Cassie Bowman, a college professor, his mistress, and his wife's closest friend since childhood. Emily is depicted as an apolitical social butterfly/facilitator of Fascism; Cassie as a politically involved anti-Fascist; and Alex, as Fascist appeaser/appeaser of both women. Emily married Alex on the rebound and knows about his continuing affair with Cassie that began twenty-years ago when he was attached to the American Embassy in Rome. The play's personal story is intertwined with the passing of world events, from the beginning of Fascism in Rome and Berlin to the time of the Munich pact.

Act I begins in the with Cassie's arrival at the Hazens' Washington, DC, home on a spring evening in 1944. She has been invited to dinner for the first time in twenty-one years by Emily who insists that it is time to talk. Sam Hazen, the Hazen's son, who was gravely wounded during the war, listens as his family's history is revealed. The action flashes back to Rome in 1922 with Mussolini's marching into the city, returning to Washington for the last scene.

Act II takes the characters to Berlin during the pogrom of 1923, and to Paris in 1938 at the time of the Munich appeasement. The final scene is set again in Hazens' Washington, DC home where after twenty-two years of world upheaval and evasions and unresolved lives, the romantic triangle is made to face the truth of their frivolous lives. At the play's end, Sam expresses the heartbreak that has made him ashamed of his family, his father's appeasement policy, his mother and her rich pro-Nazi-friends, his grandfather's liberalism and inactivity, all of whom were partially responsible for the rise of Fascism and the loss of his leg.

Production and Credits--Fulton Theatre, New York City, 12 Apr. 1944. 318 Performances. Produced and directed by Herman Shumlin; settings by Howard Bay; costumes by Aline Bernstein.

Cast:
Moses Taney--Dudley Digges
Samuel Hazel--Montgomery Clift
Ponette--Alfred Hesse
Sophronia--Mercedes Gilbert
Emily Hazen--Cornelia Otis Skinner
Alexander Hazen--Dennis King
Catherine (Cassie) Bowman--Barbara O'Neil
Elderly Italian Waiter--Edgar Andrews
Young Italian Waiter--Joseph de Santis
Hotel Manager--Walter Kohler
Eppler--William F. Schoeller
Edward Halsey--Eric Latham
James Sears--Eugene Earl
Count Max von Stammer--Arnold Korff

Reviews: R119-44, R147

Critical Overview---The second of Hellman's war plays, *The Searching Wind* chronicles the appeasing diplomacy that facilitated the growth of Fascism. Hailed as Hellman's most politically overt work, the play was a contender for the Drama Critics' Circle Award, but fell one vote short; and the prize went unclaimed. The play was generally well-received due to the powerful writing and the distinguished staging of the piece, but not without expressed reservations.

Of the daily critics, Morehouse (R130) informs his readers that Hellman and the New York theatre should be proud of the play, yet criticizes the distractions and disadvantages of the flashback techniques as well as the unsuccessful dovetailing of the political and personal plots. Kronenberger (R128) notes "striking" merits, yet palpable faults, as the unintegrated parallel plots and the lack of development in the women of the personal plot. Barnes (R119) commends the eloquence and passion of "the outstanding drama of the season," its lack of propagandist bombast; yet faults the dislocated theme, lives, and actions represented. Chapman (R120) asserts that sexual affairs and affairs of international fate should not be given equal importance. Gibbs (R123) and Nichols (R132) find the issues of love and politics confused. Fleishman (S47) argues for stronger integration of romantic and historical plots. Nathan (R131) and Young (R144) complain of pretentious writing. Contrarily, Rascoe (R137) commends the perceptive depiction of feminine psychology, labeling the play Hellman's finest.

Of the later evaluations, Clark (S40) faults the awkward revelation and its implications, yet approves of Hellman's reliance on characterization and attitude. Gassner (S91) considers the play improperly fused, the triangle labored, the resolution forced; yet grants that "no serious drama of the season had so much intensity of heart-searching and so much challenge for the future" (136). Downer (S63) observes an over-concern with contemporary issues that weakens structure and impact; and attempts to relate the love triangle to changes in American foreign policy that confuse and dehumanize the lovers, while trivializing international problems. Adler (S135) attributes the success of the play partly to Hellman's skill in spite of unmanageable material and partly to its relevancy. Sievers (S144) gives a Freudian interpretation to the characters, making reference to defense mechanisms and rationalizations that create "ostrich-like" national and foreign policy; concedes to the weak plot, while suggesting that weak and charming characters are more difficult for Hellman to treat dramatically than "willfully sadistic ones" (287).

Moody (S155) sets aside incisive dialogue and provocative ideas to criticize the strained commingling of politics and personal, observing that the love machinations of the trio in the second act seem silly, "their problems too glib" (156). Lederer (S193) faults deficiencies in characterizations: we are interested in Cassie whose story remains untold; and the son's character is not developed--his ending speech is "superfluous" (61). Bigsby (S208) calls the play, "a mechanical thesis drama;" its characters, "simple exemplars dragged from one historical nodal point to another, lacking conviction and force" (290).

The 1946 film adaptation, directed by the eminent William Dieterle, was less successful than the play. The cast included Robert Young (Alex Hazen), Sylvia Sidney (Cassie Bowman), and Ann Richards (Emily).

Toys in the Attic (1960). P7

Plot Summary--Two doting spinster sisters have worked for years to support their improvident younger brother. After years of failure, the brother comes home with a young heiress-bride and $150,000 in cash which he has earned honestly through a married ex-mistress. He joyously lavishes the sisters with boxes of gaudy clothes, a paid-up mortgage on their home, and tickets for the grand tour of Europe of their dreams. Feeling wonderfully successful for the first time in his life, he is making repayment to his sisters for the sacrifices that they have made on his behalf. His good fortune, however, makes no one happy. Hate and mistrust begin to grow. The elder sister accuses the young one of repressed incestuous desires for the brother, the accusation striking a cruel but accurate blow. The younger sister sets about to destroy the brother through his feather-brained wife, thus keeping him tied to her. The brother is mercilessly slashed and robbed, and, at play's end, the *status quo ante* is restored.

Production and Credits--P7.1 Hudson Theatre, New York City, 25 Feb. 1960. 556 Performances. Produced by Kermit Bloomgarden; directed by Arthur Penn; setting and lighting by Howard Bay; costumes by Ruth Morely.

Cast:
Carrie Berniers--Maureen Stapleton
Anna Berniers--Anne Revere
Gus--Charles McRae
Albertine Prine--Irene Worth
Henry Simpson--Percy Rodriquez
Julian Berniers--Jason Robards, Jr.
Lily Berniers--Rochelle Oliver
Taxi Driver--William Hawley
Three Moving Men--Clifford Cothren, Tom Manley, Maurice Ellis

Reviews: R298-305, R307-20

P7.2 Piccadilly Theatre, London, 1960. Produced by John Dexter. With Diana Wynyard, Wendy Hiller, Ian Bannen, Coral Browne.

Review: R306

P7.3 New Theatre, Oxford, England, 1960.

P7.4 Nixon Theatre, Pittsburgh, PA, 1961.

P7.5 National Theatre, Washington, DC, 1961.

P7.6 Alley Theatre, Houston, TX, 1962.

P7.7 Cecilwood Theatre, Fishkill, NY, 25 Feb. 1962.

P7.8 Thalia Theatre, Hamburg, Germany, 1963. Translated into German.

P7.9 Baltimore Center Stage, Baltimore, MD, 1977.

P7.10 Palace Theatre, Watford, England, 1985.

Critical Overview--Hailed by some as her most mature work, Hellman's last original play met with remarkable success and was honored with the Drama Critics' Award. The idea for the play had come from Dashiell Hammett, though much of the thought was derived from biographical material of Hellman's father's family. Lederer's study examines the ironic theme of self-deception, life-lies begun during childhood, "their origins forgotten like toys in an attic," but still controlling behaviors (S193, 94).

Of the daily reviews, the praise is unanimous, though some critics express reservations. Watts (R319) voices the majority reaction, calling the play: "stunning in its frank theatrical power, disturbing in its ugly candor, and brutally alive;" highlighting the shrewdly deceptive manner of attack, the ironic title, and the brilliantly defined characters. Ashton (R298) praises Hellman's increasingly brilliant skill, her most "hellishly hypnotic" characters. Atkinson (R299) praises intelligently conceived characters, yet criticizes the "rigid" holding back of secrets until the second act. McClain commends tight construction and powerful writing, but wonders why all of the characters have to be so monstrously neurotic. Kerr (R311, R312) applauds uncompromisingly shaped language that defines characters, yet faults sections that are allusive and indirect, and the audience's degree of detachment from the characters. In the end, the brother is destroyed, but the play "does not offers us the alarm and troubled sympathy of regret" (R312, 3).

Clurman (R303) faults confused narrative structure, jumbled themes, and irrelevant melodramatic "turns of plot, implausibilities and jabs of lurid violence:" yet praises the dialogue, the "combination of selective realism and subtly rhetorical phrasing" (261). Brustein (R301) praises the tight form, yet thinks it may be "too corseted"; complains of contrivances, of characters other than the Southern mother that have little life beyond "dramatic function," and of Hellman's new flirtation with Freud (23). Tynan (R318) applauds the razor-edged dialogue and the tightly intertwined events, but criticizes the thematic shift from materialism to abnormal psychology. Gassner (R308) sets aside weaknesses; commending the absorbing play for its excellent and mature dialogue, its revealing and varied characterizations, and concluding that it is distinctly superior to other works of the 1959-60 season. Laufe (S122) applauds vigorous dialogue and action and interesting characters, commenting also on the weak characters. Lewis (S114) faults lengthy preparation time that weakens Act I, yet praises the explosive and artfully contrived final resolution, noting a striving towards Chekhov's complex of frustrated and unhappy people, though more in kinship to Williams in the use of violence and sexuality (108). Excluding plot construction, Adler (S104, S135) expounds resemblances to Chekhov's *The Three Sisters* in situation, character, dialogue, and theme; arguing, however, that the play is predictable and that it suffers by comparison to the Southern vernacular of Williams (S94, S135). Moody (S155) contends that the story had not been taken from Chekhov: the notion "never crossed her mind" (306). Holditch (S241) explores Southern elements and themes that underlie and unify the play. Bigsby (S208) observes a linguistic and dramatic reticence seldom achieved by Hellman in the past, yet certain facts and relationships that might have remained unstated. Wiles (S264) concludes that the play is a genteel cliché which mirrors "the superficial forms of Chekhov without his hard-edged irony or his universal reduction of our interaction to absurdity" (95).

The 1963 film adaptation was a failure. The cast included Dean Martin (Julian) and Geraldine Page (Carrie).

Watch on the Rhine (1941). P8

Plot Summary--In a gracious country mansion near Washington, DC, during the spring of 1940, Fanny Farrelly, widow of an American diplomat, anxiously awaits the arrival of her daughter, Sara, whom she has not seen in twenty years, her daughter's German husband, Kurt, and her three grandchildren. She does not know that Kurt is a leader of the anti-Nazi underground and that Sara and the children have lived a dangerous and impoverished life in the countries bordering the Reich. The daughter of a close friend and her Romanian count/ex-diplomat/husband are house guests at the same time. The count suspects, then discovers Kurt's identity, threatening to report him to the Nazi Embassy unless paid $10,000. In an attempt to protect her son-in-law, Fanny goes with her lawyer-son David to get the money. At play's end Kurt kills the count and returns to his underground activities, leaving his family until they can be reunited again in Germany.

Production and Credits--P8.1 Martin Beck Theatre, New York City, 1 Apr. 1941. 378 Performances. Produced and directed by Herman Shumlin; setting by Jo Mielziner; costumes by Helen Pons.

Cast:
Anise--Eda Heinemann
Joseph--Frank Wilson
Fanny Farrelly--Lucile Watson
David Farrelly--John Lodge
Marthe de Brancovis--Helen Trenholme
Teck de Brancovis--George Coulouris
Sara Müller--Mady Christians
Joshua Müller--Peter Fernandez
Bodo Müller--Eric Roberts
Babette Müller--Anne Blyth
Kurt Müller--Paul Lukas

Reviews: A88-109, R116

P8.2 Command performance before President Franklin Delano Roosevelt for the benefit of the Infantile Paralysis Fund, Washington, DC, Jan. 1942.

P8.3 Aldwych Theatre, London, April-May 1942. Directed by Emlyn Williams. With Athene Seyler (Fanny Farrell), Peter Murray Hill (David Farrelly), Charles Goldner (Teck de Brancovis), Judy Campbell (Marthe de Brancovis), Ivan Deley (Bodo Müller), Anton Walbrook (Kurt Müller), Diana Wynyard (Sara Müller), Betty Hardy (Anise).

Reviews: R110, R111, R114, R118

P8.4 Toronto, Canada, 1943.

P8.5 Intimate Theatre, London, 1944.

P8.6 Moscow, Nov. 1944.

P8.7 Vienna, 1947.

P8.8 Little Theatre, Florence, SC, 1954.

P8.9 London, Nov. 1960.

P8.10 Long Wharf Theatre, New Haven, CT, Oct. 1979. With Jan Miner, George Hearn, Joyce Ebert. Moved to John Golden Theatre, New York City, Jan. 1980.

Review: R367

P8.11 Center Stage, Baltimore, MD, 1980. With Carmen Mathews, Jana Hicken, Richard Kavanaugh.

Critical Overview--Written in response to World War II in Europe and at a time that America's neutrality was much debated, *Watch on the Rhine* revealed that the war was already being fought in the activities of foreign agents in this country. The play opened in the spring of 1941, about eight months before Pearl Harbor, enjoyed a successful Broadway run of 378 performances, received the Drama Critics' Circle Award, and was considered by many critics one of the most powerfully written war plays of its time. As Dick (S209) observes, "*Watch on the Rhine* had the kind of drawing-room nobility one might expect of an anti-isolationist drama written by an antifascist" (82). Hellman's memoirs later acknowledge an indebtedness to Henry James's *The American* and *The Europeans* (A19, 185). Reporting of the University of Texas manuscript collection, Triesch (S124) finds no major changes from the first draft to printed version.

The daily critical fraternity fault structural weaknesses, the slow beginning (Anderson (R88), Atkinson (R89), Brown (R92), Lockridge (R99), Watts (R106), Young (R109) and the protracted ending (Anderson, Brown, Young), yet praise the compelling dramatic impression: the vivid contrast of the American family and its unawakened innocence and the European family who had grown accustomed to tragic necessities, the oblique but forceful anti-Nazi references. Atkinson (R89) observes an increased humanness in Hellman's writing, likable characters and humorous and affectionate scenes, concluding that *Watch on the Rhine* is "incomparably her best." Brown (R92) defends the melodramatic plot and praises the careful avoidance of over-contrivance. Watts (R106) argues that the melodramatic aspects accurately reflect current events; approving of the quiet and orderly work which rarely raises its voice and spends scant time on political lecture, and of the full-bodied characters engaged in significant activities. Similarly, Krutch (R98) commends the determined avoidance of flat didacticism and thinness of character, yet faults artificial contrivances, suggesting that "the artist must see to it that his fiction does not seem as strange as truth." Kronenberger (R97) calls the work a "melodrama with meaning," enthusiastically endorsing the play "about human beings and their ideological ghosts; a play dedicated to the deeds they are called upon to perform, not the words they are moved to utter . . . " Gibbs (R95) praises the timeliness of the piece, concluding that fundamental issue has been treated "with dignity, insight, and sound theatrical intelligence." And Mantle (R100) proclaims the work the most convincing of the season's anti-Nazi war plays.

Atkinson (R89) hails Hellman's creation of a truly heroic modern man, and the elegant performance by Lukas, "one of the greatest performances in recent years." Gassner (R94)) praises the "modern hero," extending his approval to the entire roster of flesh-and-blood characters. Vernon (R104) voices disappointment with the reviews of many of his fellow critics; faulting the structure, much of the dialogue, many of the characters, and severely criticizing Hellman's use of the term "fascist", since the play is really about anti-Nazi propaganda. He clarifies that melodrama occurs only in the last act, and suggests that "the scenes before are probably supposed to be comedy of manners" (16).

In a 1944 study, Clark (S40) dismisses melodramatic underpinnings to consider the play the warmest, most human, and most understanding of Hellman's works. Of the later considerations, Sievers (S144) gives a Freudian interpretation to the characters, applauding precise characterizations, and noting "for the first time a warm emotional feeling within the family which makes *Watch on the Rhine* one of the finest plays to come out of the war years" (285). Adler (S135) confirms the comedy of manners form which he deems appropriate, since, in the end, the play exposes "the inadequacy of the comedy-of-manners approach to life" (23). Falk (S184) points out that Hellman's work quantitatively more comic and romantic, highlighting the children's comic relationship with their gruff, but sentimental grandmother, as well as the warmth of the Müller family, and the budding romance of Marthe and David. Lederer (S193) finds the charming, Washington, DC, country house setting a fitting choice. "Hellman's concern with ethical choices has caused her to study the behavior of the well-to-do because their money gives them the freedom to make moral choices, to deal with moral responsibilities" (57).

In his 1982 overview, Bigsby (S208) finds the story improbable, the plot revealing Hellman's worst instincts for melodrama, the language filled with clichés. Similarly, Wright (S238) concludes that *Watch on the Rhine* in later years was to be considered, "one of Hellman's most overrated plays; out of the context of the period, it seemed breathlessly jingoistic and too elementary in its good-guys-bad-guys delineations" (176). In Dick's opinion (S209), the play worked better as drama than as theatre and, thus, will be remembered more for its ideas than its theatricality. In still a later study, Patraka (S181) examines the intertextual relationship between *Watch on the Rhine* and the "Julia" section of *Pentimento*, Hellman having disclosed that Kurt was a form her antifascist female friend.

In the 1943 film version Lukas repeated his Broadway role, this time winning an Academy Award as best actor. Bette Davis starred in the portrayal of his wife, Sara. The screenplay was adapted by Hammett, the film directed by Shumlin.

II. ADAPTATIONS

Candide (with music by Leonard Bernstein, 1956). P9

Plot Summary--Under the tutelage of Dr. Pangloss, the idealistic philosopher who believes that "everything is for the best in this best of all possible worlds," Candide becomes an optimist. He falls in love with the beautiful Cunegonde, but loses her repeatedly through his travels from Westphalia, Lisbon, Paris, Buenos Aires, and Venice, only to marry her when she is grown old and ugly. Beaten, tortured, and cheated during his 80-day journey, Candide concludes that the hope of mankind rests not on philosophical speculation, but on a reliance of work and doing's one's best. Back in Westphalia, he settles down with Cunegonde to cultivate a garden.

Production and Credits--P9.1 Martin Beck Theatre, New York City, 1 Dec. 1956. 73 Performances. Comic operetta adapted from Voltaire's novel; libretto by Hellman; music by Bernstein; lyrics by Richard Wilbur, John Latouche, and Dorothy Parker; produced by Ethel Linder Reiner, in association with Lester Osterman, Jr.; directed by Tyrone Guthrie; settings by Oliver Smith; costumes by Irene Sharaff, lighting by Paul Morrison.

Cast:
Dr. Pangloss--Max Adrian
Cunegonde--Barbara Cooke
Candide--Robert Rounseville
Baron--Robert Mesrobian
Maximillian--Louis Edmonds
King of Hesse--Conrad Bain
Hesse's General--Norman Roland
Man--Boris Aplon
Woman--Doris Okerson
Dutch Lady--Margaret Roy
Dutch Man--Tony Drake
Atheist--Robert Rue
Arab Conjurer--Robert Barry
Infant Casmira--Maria Novotna
Lawyer--William Chapman
Very, Very Old Inquisitor--Conrad Bain
Very Old Inquisitor--Charles Aschmann
Beggars--Margaret Roy, Robert Cosden, Thomas Pyle
French Lady--Maud Scheerer
Old Lady--Irra Petina
Marquis Milton--Boris Aplon
Sultan Milton--Joseph Bernard
Pilgrim Father--Robert Rue
Pilgrim Mother--Dorothy Krebill
Captain--Conrad Bain
Martin--Max Adrian
Governor of Buenos Aires--William Olvis
Officers--George Blackwell, Tony Drake, Thomas Pyle
Ferone--William Chapman

Madame Sofronia--Irra Petina
Duchess--Maud Scheerer
Prefect of Police--Norman Roland
Prince Ivan (Fat Man)--Robert Mesrobian

Reviews: R273-75, R277-82, R284-87, R290, R292-97

P9.2 London, 30 Apr. 1959.

P9.3 Philharmonic Hall, New York City, 10 Nov. 1968. Concert version, adapted by
Michael Stewart. With Robert Rounseville, Irra Petina.

Critical Overview--Three of theatre's most talented people were involved in the musical
adaptation of Voltaire's masterpiece: Hellman, Bernstein, and Guthrie; and while there
was much that was brilliant about the production in the way of musical excellence,
visual beauty and boldness of design, the show had book problems and closed an
artistic and financial failure. Only Bernstein's sophisticated score emerged with credit.

Of the daily critical fraternity, Atkinson (R273) respects the "admirable" enterprise,
yet finds the plotlessness and repetitiveness ill-suited to the theatre, noting also that
Candide has been transformed into a disillusioned hero of the modern spirit. McClain
(R286) commends the brilliantly ambitious show, yet criticizes the leaden book.
Donnelly (R279) praises the score, but finds the book vague and meandering. Watts
(R290) comments on distinguishing features, yet finds the libretto "not satirically
powerful or dramatically striking." Mannes (R296) finds the satirical edge blunted, and
is surprised that Hellman's sense of timing has faltered in the adaptation. McCarthy
(R285) misses the satire, the folly, the negativism, and the sexual frankness--censored
perhaps so as not to assault the Church --, yet concludes that a *Candide* without
"daredeviltry" is foredoomed to failure. Hewes (R282) suggests that a musical version
of Voltaire's masterpiece would "be well-advised to stress the fact that it is optimistic
metaphysical philosophy which is being satirized, not the broad and familiar "target the
way of the world'" (34); adding that the deletion of toughminded unpleasantries has
weakened the spine and turned Candide from absurd and gullible into a romantic figure.
Hayes (R281) disparages the irrefrangibly moral tone that "wrenches Candide
irrevocably out of context (333). Chapman (276) alone is favorably impressed by
Hellman's "strong, clear and humorous libretto." He labels the work an artistic triumph,
"the best light opera since *Der Rosenkavalier*."

Clurman (R277) suggests that a sharp, polished, spare, economic Brechtian
treatment might have been more appropriate; criticizing the music, and, most
importantly, reminding the individually talented people who fashioned the operetta that
"the theatre is a collective art, which is not the same thing as an accumulation of artistic
contributions." In *Pentimento* (A19), Hellman recounts taking suggestions from the
experts in musical theatre, making changes though she really did not believe in them.
According to Triesch (S124), numerous revisions comprise the largest section of the
archival collection at the University of Texas, offering an excellent opportunity to review
Hellman's writing methods. In his opinion, the adaptation is far superior in its
avoidance of tiresome repetition, though it did sacrifice Voltaire's originality and
subtlety.

Commenting on the unhappy collaboration, director Guthrie (S87) recalls the
artistic skirmishes and the unconscious acquiescence to "the diamond quality of
Bernstein's brilliance" (241). None of Hellman's qualities as a writer showed to

advantage. "This was no medium for hard-hitting argument, shrewd, humorous characterization, the slow revelation of true values, and the exposure of false ones" (241). As lyricist Wilbur reflects, "Lenny's music got more and more pretentious. The audience forgot what was happening to the characters. Lillian's book got to be mere connective tissue. And I was inclined to be too literary and stubborn." (S155, 283.)

Of the later studies, Adler (S135) considers the book shrewd and workmanlike, though devoid of Hellman's characteristic style. And Moody (S155) argues that Hellman's style was handicapped by the musical's brisk telegraphic style, that her satiric thrust too dull for "the mocking lyricism of Bernstein's score and the verbal playfulness of Wilbur's lyrics" (283). On the otherhand, Lewis (S114) praises Hellman's versatility, underscoring the delightfully witty and sophisticated book which he believes is superior to most musicals (106). Wiles (S264) examines the exploitation of gestures and techniques, codified by Brecht, and used by Hellman before the Brechtian influence was registered among American playwrights; strongly praising her lyrics to "Eldorado" which encapsulate her social vision for the future.

Of the 1972 Kennedy Center revival, Hellman refused any connection to the "sad and wasteful" production (A19). She also played no part in the 1973 successfully revised production, which was mounted by Harold Prince as a total theatre piece with new book by Hugh Wheeler.

The Lark (1955). P10

Plot Summary--The drama tells the story of the trial of Joan of Arc. It is played on a bare stage, on different levels, against a soft, misty gray fog into which courtroom characters dissolve as Joan recalls the story of her life. Scenes are reenacted as they occur in testimony, comments from the courtroom interrupting, episodes recapturing the well-known events that lead to the trial with the one exception of her riding out to battle with La Hire. Joan is tempted to give in to her enemies at one point, but holds true to her beliefs, going to a heroic death for the love of Man.

Production and Credits--P10.1 Longacre Theatre, New York City, 17 Nov. 1955. 229 Performances. Adapted from Jean Anouilh's *L'Alouette*; produced by Kermit Bloomgarden; directed by Joseph Anthony, setting and lighting by Jo Mielziner, costumes by Alvin Colt; incidental music by Leonard Bernstein.

Cast:
Warwick--Christopher Plummer
Cauchon--Boris Karloff
Joan--Julie Harris
Joan's Father--Ward Costello
Joan's Mother--Lois Holmes
Joan's Brother--John Reese
The Promoter--Roger De Koven
The Inquisitor--Joseph Wiseman
Brother Ladvenu--Michael Higgins
Robert De Beaudricourt--Theodore Bikel
Agnes Sorel--Ann Hillary
The Little Queen--Joan Elan
The Dauphin--Paul Roebling

Queen Yolande--Rita Vale
Monsieur de la Tremouille--Bruce Gordon
Archbishop of Reims--Richard Nicholls
Captain La Hire--Bruce Gordon
Executioner--Ralph Roberts
English Soldier--Edward Knight
Scribe--Joe Bernard

Reviews: R257-71, R283, R288, R289, R291

P10.2 Lyric Theatre, Hammersmith, London, 1955.

P10.3 Playmakers Theatre, Chapel Hill, NC, 1957.

P10.4 Peoria Plays Experimental Theatre Group, Peoria, IL, 1961.

P10.5 Goodman Memorial Theatre, Chicago, IL, 1961.

P10.6 All India Fine Arts Theatre, New Delhi, 1961.

P10.7 Honolulu Community Theatre, Honolulu, 1964. With Diane Ewing.

P10.8 The New York Theatre Company, Church of the Heavenly Rest, Off Off Broadway, New York City, 19 May 1989.

Critical Overview--The critics unanimously praise the adaptation which "tightened the action and simplified the language, turning the play into exciting theater, with a first-rate part for Julie Harris as Joan" (S184, 83). Watts (R271) commends the adaptation that "stand[s] in its own right and power. Without sacrificing eloquence or lyric exultation, she [Hellman] has added the dramatic impact and conciseness of her personal quality, making her the perfect collaborator with Anouilh's Gallic intelligence and understanding." In accord, Atkinson (R257) praises the adaptation which has "solid strength in the theatre." Kerr (R268) applauds the hard-headed candor of this Joan, suggesting that it took a female dramatist to create the character's clever determination. Gassner (R308) praises the energetic adaptation which improves on the original version, counteracting Anouilh's sophisticated skepticism; yet finds himself in retrospect "longing for Ibsen's old-fashioned grip on experience or for Shaw's only slightly less old-fashioned hold on reality in *Saint Joan*" (S91, 249 footnote). Adler (S135) praises Hellman's characteristic ability at dialogue, adding his belief that *The Lark* could have been a great play, had not Shaw written his version.

Triesch's chronicle (S124) reveals Hellman's choice of translation, translation differences, and her own adaptation differences. Moody (S155) describes incisive alterations and deviations that improved upon Anouilh and Fry, the religious overtones, and incidental music composed by Leonard Bernstein. In 1993, Brantley (S283) observes that the play "is as much about the mood of the McCarthy era as it is about a medieval French peasant hero. Though the play is working with Anouilh's material, the play is undeniable self-referential" (183).

Montserrat (1949). P11

Plot Summary--The play deals with the uprising of Simon Bolivar and his South American patriots against the Spanish during their occupation of Venezuela in 1812. Spanish Captain Montserrat, who has gone to the side of the liberation, is trapped into the deaths of six innocent South Americans. Izquierdo vows to shoot the innocents, one by one, unless junior officer Montserrat reveals Bolivar's hiding place. The wealthy merchant pleads for his life in the face of death. He is followed by the artistically inspired woodcarver who cries for his right to life, and the strolling player who cringes with fear. The peasant boy goes willingly to his death, but the mother, who follows, shouts out for her two babies. Montserrat wavers, and is about to reveal the secret, when the young girl patriot begs him to remain true to the cause. She goes bravely to her death. When word comes that Bolivar has fled to safety, Montserrat is taken to the courtyard and shot.

Production and Credits--P11.1 Fulton Theatre, New York City, 29 Oct. 1949. 65 Performances. Adapted from Emmanuel Robles's play; produced by Kermit Bloomgarden and Gilbert Miller; directed by Hellman; settings by Howard Bay; costumes by Irene Sharaff.

Cast:
Zavala--Richard Malek
Antonanzas--Nehemiah Persoff
Soldier--Stefan Gierasch
Montserrat--William Redfield
Morales--Gregory Morton
Izquierdo--Emlyn Williams
Father Coronil--Francis Compton
Salas Ina--Reinhold Schunzel
Luhan--William Hansen
Matilde--Vivian Nathan
Juan Salcedo Alvarez--John Abbott
Felisa--Julie Harris
Ricardo--George Bartenieff
Monk--Edward Groag
Monk--Kurt Kasznar
Soldier--Robert Crawley
Lieutenant--Stephen Lawrence

Reviews: R173-86, R189-93, R195-97, R199

P11.2 Lyric Theatre, Hammersmith, England, 1952.

Reviews: R229, R233-35, R239, R241

P11.3 Lenox Hill Playhouse, Off Broadway, New York, 7 Apr. 1954. Equity Library Theatre production.

P11.4 Barbizon-Plaza Theatre, Off Broadway, New York, 25 May 1954. Equity Library Theatre production.

Reviews: R256

P11.5 Gate Theatre, Off Broadway, New York City, 8 Jan. 1961. Repertory Company production; directed by Boris Tumarin; scenery by Herbert Senn and Helen Pond; lighting by Richard Nelson.

Cast:
Zavala--Jay Lanin
Antonanzas--Frank Echols
Soldier--Robert Vandergriff
Montserrat--John Heidabrand
Morales--Rick Colitti
Izquierdo--Leonard Cimino
Father Coronil--John Leighton
Salas Ina--John Armstrong
Luhan--Maurice Shrog
Matilde--Dina Paisner
Juan Salcedo Alvarez--Albert Ackel
Felisa--Anne Fielding
Ricardo--Roy Scott
Monk--John Miranda
Guard--Michael Fischetti

Reviews: R321, R323-24

P11.6 Benton Hall , Minneapolis, MN, 1966. Theatre In the Round Players production.

Critical Overview--A study of tyranny versus idealism, the play was carefully adapted from the French original with minor changes, but not well-received. The daily critics found the play intellectually arresting, yet rarely deeply moving, identifying flaws in Hellman's writing and in her direction. Harold Clurman (R179), who took over at some point as director, asserted that Hellman misinterpreted Robles's existential point of view. The play went on to win the Vernon Rice Award for direction.

Expressing the views of the critical majority, Watts (R195) writes,"[O]f striking philosophical interest, it is oddly less powerful in its emotional impact than its deeply tragic theme would have suggested, and its strength is curiously hampered by a monotony that has crept into it." Brown (R177) criticizes the dominating portrayal of the complex, cynical, coldly intelligent Izquierdo which renders the idealist, Montserrat, pallid and ineffectual. *Theatre Arts* (R199) criticizes the unfairly weighted situation that bears scant relevance to actual moral dilemmas, the casting, and the direction. Atkinson (R173) finds the writing barren, the horror contrived, and the direction monotonous. Coleman (R180) complains of the uneven and insufficiently motivated script, of the villain (Izquierdo) who is the object of the audience's fascination, and of the performance which is overly melodramatic. Morehouse (R186) is sharply disappointed by the monotony that creeps in despite the gunfire, violence, and philosophy. Wyatt (R196) blames the failure on the original play, and thinks Hellman has wasted her time on the adaptation. Barnes (R174), Chapman (R178), Hawkins (R184), and Marshall (R185) stand together in their praise.

Of the later consideration, Gassner (S309) calls attention to the Existentialist concerns that Hellman brought to the adaptation. Adler (S135) praises Hellman's characteristic ability at dialogue, calls the piece a workmanlike melodrama, but finds the ending incompatible with "American audience's natural sympathy for the underdog" (39). In comparing the play to the original, Moody (S155) argues that Hellman "sought a stronger base in believable reality by tempering the melodramatic commitments of the principals," conceding, however, that the play is too discursive, and that its major weakness is that "we never know Bolivar" (197-98). In her memoirs, Hellman (A19) admits to directing the play "in a fumbling, frightened way" that intimidated the actors and contributed to the failure of the play (198).

In March 1971, a Hollywood Television Theatre production aired on educational television stations throughout the country.

My Mother, My Father, and Me (1963). P12

Plot Summary--The story of a neurotic New York Jewish family is narrated by the "Me" of the title, the 26-year-old beatnik son who consumes his time, as he gropes to find his way, with guitar, camera, transistor radio, drums, and a yearning to join an Indian tribe. His shoe manufacturer father complains continually about bankruptcy, about his wife's compulsive shopping, and about his college-educated son's inadequacies. The grandmother, a penniless widow, moves into the family's apartment, only to be shunted off to a nursing home. In the end the grandmother gives the beatnik grandson a small amount of money that she has saved for the burial she no longer wants when she dies. The son goes out West to live with the Indians, where he dons poncho and headdress, sells cheap Indian souvenirs to tourists, and writes a book which he dedicates to his grandmother.

Production and Credits--P12.1 Plymouth Theatre, New York City, 12 Mar. 1963. 17 Performances. Adapted from Burt Blechman's novel *How Much?*; directed by Gower Champion; sets and lights by Howard Bay; costumes by Dorothy Jeakins.

Cast:
Bernard Halpern--Anthony Holland
Rona Halpern--Ruth Gordon
Herman Halpern--Walter Matthau
Hannah--Helen Martin
Filene--Barbara Mostel
Mrs. Jenny Stern--Lili Darvas
Mrs. Parker--Elaine Swann
Waiter--Don Billett
Butler--Harry Smith
Dr. O'Hare--Leonard Hicks
Mr. Parker--Milo Boulton
Mrs. Lamb--Dorothy Greener
Binkie-Pie--Henry Gibson
Mrs. Compton--Leona Powers
Mrs. Lazar--Sudie Bond
Mrs. Kaufman--Eda Heinemann
Miss Evelyn--Avril Gentles
Mr. Lazar--Joe E. Marks
Dr. Zachary Katz--Mark Lenard

Tonio Crazzo--Tom Pedi
Mr. Kelly--Heywood Hale Broun
Mrs. Knopf--Dorothy Greener
Styron--Melvin Stewart
Negro Woman--Royce Wallace
Doorman--Don Billett
Girl--Jane Laughlin
Woman--Virginia Maddocks
Man--Harry Smith

Reviews: R325-40

P12.2 WPA Theatre, Off Off Broadway, New York City, 3 Jan. 1980.

Critical Overview--The show opened during a newspaper strike, met with negative
television reviews, delayed negative press, closing after 17 performances. Watts (R340)
observes, "while most of its individual interludes are devastatingly comic and merciless,
its central story lacks focus, giving it a frequent air of wandering about a little
uncertainly." Complaining also of the diffuseness, Chapman (R325) calls the play "a
flimsy whimsy; in its second and more desperate half it falls completely apart and . . .
gallops madly off in all directions." Kerr (R331) faults the unsuccessful attempt to
merge "the extravagant satirical incoherence of the theatre of the Absurd with the
homier, milder, and more plausible nonsense of something like *You Can't Take It With
You* [Kaufman and Hart]. In a terse pan, Coleman (R327) quotes Samuel Goldwyn:
"Include me out." Taubman (R338) and Nadel (R335) agree that work is dismal and
dull. McClain (R334) thinks the play a far cry from the usual Hellman work, yet a
worthy example of her talent in the field of comedy. Gottfried (R329) calls the work a
foolhardy attempt at comedy by a playwright who has no sense of comedy. Lewis
(S114) alone finds merit in the piece, yet thinks the direction would be better served in
the exaggerated, stylized fashion of the Comedie Francaise.

In an interview with Phillips and Hollander (S115), Hellman hoped for a revival off
Broadway, where she wanted the piece staged in the first place. She calls it "a cult
show. Oddly enough mostly with jazz musicians. The last week the audience was filled
with jazz musicians. Stan Getz had come to see it and liked it, and he must have told his
friends about it" (59).

Adler (S135) ranks the play as one of the two worst, the other being *Days to Come*,
observing that the piece is fraught with clichés and almost plotless, that the abrupt shifts
and unmotivated oddities border on the techniques of expressionism. Wiles (S264)
thinks the play would be better appreciated if considered "not as a would-be American
dream but as a continuation of the loosely structured social vaudeville stemming from
the thirties political musicals and living newspaper satires" (109). Moody (S155)
describes changes in the adaptation, the added characters and incidents that focus on
middle-class corruptions, rather than on Beckman's Golden Age Society Nursing
Home, attributing to Hellman the sardonic assault on the corruption of family life, the
beatniks, psychiatrists, hyperbolic consumers, and the "shysters" who run nursing
homes. Yet, the pursuit of pretension and fraud, the jumping from target to target, is so
intense that it defeats its purpose. Wright (S238) observes a resemblance to Albee's
absurdist dramatic style. Dick (S209) calls attention to the fact that, "It was one of the
first plays on Broadway to use *fuck*, surpassing another Hellman first--*vagina* in *Toys
in the Attic* " (125). And Rollyson (S249) notes that the black humor, the attack on

several targets at once, resembles the treatment of *The Dear Queen*, the unproduced comedy that Hellman and Kronenberger later disowned.

Primary Bibliography:
Writings by Hellman

This chapter provides listings of Hellman's writings arranged as: I. Plays: Original Plays and Adaptations; II. Articles and Essays on Drama and Theatre; III. Other Works: Memoirs, Fiction, and Works Edited by Hellman; and IV. Archival Sources.

I. PLAYS
The following is a list of Hellman's plays. It includes individual volumes, collections, and anthologies.

Original Plays:

A1   ANOTHER PART OF THE FOREST

Another Part of the Forest. New York: Viking, 1947.
Another Part of the Forest (Acting edition). *New York:* Dramatists Play Service, 1953.
The Little Foxes and Another Part of the Forest. New York: Viking Press, 1973; Penguin Books, 1976.
The Collected Plays. Boston: Little, Brown, 1972.
Six Plays by Lillian Hellman. With an introduction by Hellman. New York: Modern Library, 1960; Vintage, 1979.

Anthology:
Contemporary Drama: 11 Plays. Ed. E. Bradlee Watson and Benfield Pressey. New York: Charles Scribner's Sons, 1956.

A2   THE AUTUMN GARDEN

The Autumn Garden. Boston: Little, Brown, 1951.
The Autumn Garden (Revised acting edition). New York: Dramatists Play Service, 1952. Reprinted 1973, 1974.
The Collected Plays. Boston: Little, Brown, 1972.

Six Plays by Lillian Hellman. With an introduction by Hellman. New York: Modern
   Library, 1960; Vintage, 1979.

Anthologies:
Best American Plays: Third Series, 1945-1951. New York: Crown, 1952. New
   Crown, 1987. Second Series, titled *Best Plays of American Modern Theatre,
   1947.*
Contemporary Drama: Thirteen Plays, American, English, European. Ed. Stanley A.
   Clayes and David G. Spencer. New York: Charles Scribner's Sons, 1962.
Famous American Plays of the 1950s. Ed. Lee Strasberg. New York: Dell, 1962.
   Reprinted 1967+.

A3   THE CHILDREN'S HOUR

The Children's Hour. New York: Knopf, 1934.
The Children's Hour (Acting edition). New York: Dramatists Play Service, 1953.
   Reprinted, 1981, 1988.
The Collected Plays. Boston: Little, Brown, 1972.
Four Plays by Lillian Hellman. With an introduction by Hellman. New York: Modern
   Library, 1942.
Six Plays by Lillian Hellman. With an introduction by Hellman. New York: Modern
   Library, 1960; Vintage, 1979.

Anthologies:
Plays by and about Women. Eds. Victoria Sullivan and James Hatch. New York:
   Random House, 1973.
Twenty Best Plays of the Modern American Theatre: 1930-1939. Ed. John Gassner.
   New York: Crown, 1939.

A4   DAYS TO COME

Days to Come. New York: Knopf, 1936.
The Collected Plays. Boston: Little, Brown, 1972.
Four Plays by Lillian Hellman. With an introduction by Hellman. New York: Modern
   Library, 1942.
Six Plays by Lillian Hellman. With an introduction by Hellman. New York: Modern
   Library, 1960; Vintage, 1979.

A 5   THE LITTLE FOXES

The Little Foxes. New York: Random House, 1939.
The Little Foxes (Acting edition). New York: Dramatists Play Service, 1942.
   Reprinted 1986.
The Little Foxes and Another Part of the Forest. New York: Viking Press, 1973;
   Penguin Books, 1976.
The Collected Plays. Boston: Little, Brown, 1972.

Four Plays by Lillian Hellman. With an introduction by Hellman. New York: Modern Library, 1942.

Six Plays by Lillian Hellman. With an introduction by Hellman. New York: Modern Library, 1960; Vintage, 1979.

Anthologies:

American Dramatic Literature: Ten Modern Plays in Historical Perspective. Ed. Jordan Y. Miller. New York: McGraw-Hill, 1961.

The American Experience: Drama. Ed. Marjorie Wescott Barrows et al. New York: Macmillan, 1984.

Six Modern American Plays. Ed. Allan Halline New York; Random House, 1951.

Sixteen Famous American Plays. Eds. Bennett Cerf and Van H. Cartmell. New York: Garden City Publishing Company, 1941. Reprinted as Modern Library edition, 1942.

Modern Drama. Ed. Harlan Hatcher. New York Harcourt, Brace, 1941.

Patterns in Modern Drama. Ed. Lodvick C. Hartley and Arthur Ladu. Englewood Cliffs, NJ: Prentice-Hall, Inc., 1948.

A Treasury of the Theatre. From Henrik Ibsen to Eugene Ionesco. Ed. John Gassner. New York: Simon and Schuster, 1960.

A Treasury of the Theatre, Vol. 3. From Oscar Wilde to Eugene Ionesco. Ed. John Gassner. New York: Simon and Schuster, 1963.

A6   THE SEARCHING WIND

The Searching Wind. New York: Viking, 1944.
The Collected Plays. Boston: Little, Brown, 1972.

A7   TOYS IN THE ATTIC

Toys in the Attic. New York: Random House, 1960.
Toys in the Attic (Acting edition). New York: Samuel French, 1960.
The Collected Plays. Boston: Little, Brown, 1972.

A8   WATCH ON THE RHINE

Watch on the Rhine. New York: Random House, 1941.

Watch on the Rhine (Acting edition). New York: Dramatists Play Service, 1942. Reprinted 1986.

Watch on the Rhine. With foreword by Dorothy Parker. New York: Privately Published by the Joint Anti-Fascist Committee in cooperation with Random House, 1942. A limited edition of 349 copies. Copies 1-50, leather bound.

The Collected Plays. Boston: Little, Brown, 1972.

Four Plays by Lillian Hellman. With an introduction by Hellman. New York: Modern Library, 1942.

Six Plays by Lillian Hellman. With an introduction by Hellman. New York: Modern Library, 1960; Vintage, 1979.

Anthologies:

Best American Plays: Third Series, 1945-1951. *New York: Crown, 1952. New Crown, 1987.* Second Series, titled *Best Plays of American Modern Theatre, 1947.*

Critics' Choice: New York Drama Critics' Circle Prize Plays. Ed. Jack Gaver. London: Arco Publications, 1956.

Drama of Our Time. Ed. Munjon Moses Nagelberg. New York: Harcourt, Brace & World, Inc., 1948. 31-96.

Sixteen Famous American Plays. Eds. Bennett Cerf and Van H. Cartmell. New York: Garden City, 1941. Reprinted as Modern Library edition, 1942.

Adaptations:

A9   CANDIDE. Musical score by Leonard Bernstein. Lyrics by Richard Wilbur, John Latouche, and Dorothy Parker. New York: Random House, 1960.

      The Collected Plays. Boston: Little, Brown, 1972.

A10   THE LARK (1955).

      The Lark (Acting edition). New York: Dramatists Play Service, 1957.
      The Collected Plays. Boston: Little, Brown, 1972.

A11   MONTSERRAT (1949).

      Montserrat (Acting edition). New York: Dramatists Play Service, 1950.
      The Collected Plays. Boston: Little, Brown, 1972.

A12   MY MOTHER, MY FATHER AND ME (1963).

      My Mother, My Father and Me. New York: Random House, 1963.
      The Collected Plays. Boston: Little, Brown, 1972.

II. ARTICLES AND ESSAYS ON DRAMA AND THEATRE

A13   "Author Jabs the Critics." *New York Times* 15 Dec. 1946: II, 3-4.
      Responds to Atkinson's review of *Another Part of the Forest.* Accuses Atkinson of recoiling from action on stage, evil people, and violence. Insists that violence and evil are among the true materials of drama. Approves, however, of the great tradition of writer/critic disagreement.

A14   "Back of Those Foxes." *New York Times* 26 Feb. 1939: X, 1-2.
      Attempts to explain the stages of elation, depression, and hope involved in the writing and mounting *The Little Foxes.* Defends melodrama which has come to have a corrupted modern meaning. Says, "I tried my best."

A15   Introduction. *Four Plays by Lillian Hellman*. New York: Modern Library, 1942; *Six Plays by Lillian Hellman*. New York: Modern Library, 1960.

Admits to shortcomings as a dramatist; defends the well-made play, the melodrama, the pretense and the limitations of theatre; thanks producer/director Herman Shumlin and writer/companion Dashiell Hammett, her biggest critic.

A16   Introduction. *The Selected Letters of Anton Chekhov*. Ed. Lillian Hellman. New York: Farrar, Straus and Cudahy, 1955.

Hellman's introductory essay and prefaces to the letters pay tribute to Chekhov's common sense, workmanship, and social ideals.

A17   "Lillian Hellman Asks a Little Respect for Her Agony, An Eminent Playwright Hallucinates after a Fall Brought on by a Current Dramatic Hit." *Show* 55 (May 1964): 12-13.

Writes a merciless parody of Arthur Miller's *After the Fall*, as a reaction to Miller's dishonoring the profession by exploiting his life with Marilyn Monroe. Hellman titles her autobiographical play, *Buy My Guilt*.

A18   "Scotch on the Rocks." *New York Review of Books* 17 Oct. 1963: 6.

Comments on the Edinburgh Festival and concurrent International Drama Conference which she attended during the summer.

A19   "Theatre." In *Pentimento: A Book of Portraits*. Boston: Little, Brown, 1973. 151-209.

This chapter from the second book of memoirs is particularly relevant to the study of Hellman as a dramatist, as it includes reflections on the writing of the plays, the productions, and related associations.

A20   "The Time of the Foxes." *New York Times* 22 Oct. 1967: D : 1, 5.

Recalls the tensions during out-of-town tryouts and her reactions to success of *The Little Foxes* on Broadway in 1939, while commenting on the 1967 Mike Nichols revival. "Nichols and the cast have taken the play their way, and that is the way they should have taken it" (5).

III. OTHER WORKS

Memoirs:

A21   *An Unfinished Woman*. Boston: Little, Brown, 1969. Reprint London: Macmillian, 1987.

A22   *Pentimento: A Book of Portraits*. Boston: Little, Brown, 1973.

A23   *Scoundrel Time*. Introduction by Garry Wills. Boston: Little, Brown, 1976. Reprint with additional introduction by James Cameron. London: Macmillan, 1976.

A24   *Three*. The collected memoirs with new commentaries by Hellman. Introduction by Richard Poirer. Boston: Little, Brown, 1979.

Nonfiction:

A25   *Maybe: A Story.* Boston: Little, Brown, 1980.

A26   *Eating Together: Recipes and Recollections.* With Peter S. Feibleman. Boston, Little
       Brown, 1984.

Works Edited by Hellman:

A27   *The Selected Letters of Anton Chekhov.* Edited and with an introduction by Hellman.
       Trans. Sidonie K. Lederer. With introduction by Hellman. New York: Farrar,
       Straus and Cudahy, 1955.

A28   *The Big Knockover: Selected Stories and Short Novels,* by Dashiell Hammett. Edited
       and with introduction by Hellman. New York: Random House, 1966; as *The
       Dashiell Hammett Story Omnibus.* London: Cassell and Co., 1966; as *The Big
       Knockover* and *The Continental Op* (2 vols.), 1967.

IV. ARCHIVAL SOURCES:

Columbia University Libraries, Rare Book & Manuscript Library, Butler Library, 6th
Fl, 535 W 114 St., New York 10027. Tel. 212-854-2231, 854-3528. FAX 212-222-0331.
Elec. Mail Lonf@cunixf.cc.columbia. edu. Holdings: Mss. Notes: Forty years of literary
correspondence between the Harold Matson Literary Agency and numerous notable authors.
Restricted use.

New York Public Library Performing Arts Research Center at Lincoln Center,
Billy Rose Collection. Collection contains typescripts of many of Hellman's plays, clipping
files, scrapbooks, photographs, and other archival information on Hellman and the many
actors an directors who worked with her.

University of Texas Libraries, Humanities Research Center, Austin, 78713-7219. Tel.
512-471-9119. FAX 512-471-9646. Collection includes research notes, autographed
manuscripts, and corrected typescripts of Hellman's plays, including *The Little Foxes* and
Toys in the Attic. There is also an extensive correspondence file, with personal
correspondence to and from Dashiell Hammett. Restricted use.

Secondary Bibliography: Reviews

The following secondary bibliography of reviews concentrates on Hellman's career in the theatre.

1934

R1   Anderson, John. "How Child's Lie Brought Ruin to 2 Teachers' Lives Told in Play." *New York Evening Journal* 21 Nov. 1934: 20.
         Review of *The Children's Hour*. A morbid tragedy, literate, adult, and interestingly told, but badly overwritten in the last act, and redeemed only by the sincerity of the writing and the performances of the two teachers.

R2   Atkinson, Brooks. "The Play--*The Children's Hour*, Being a Tragedy of Life in a Girls' Boarding House." *New York Times* 21 Nov. 1934: 23. Reprinted in Bernard Beckerman and Howard Siegman, eds., *On Stage, Selected Theater Reviews from The New York Times*. New York: Arno Press, 1973: 150-51.
         The play should have ended with the suicide, leaving the defeated characters with the dignity of their despair. The work, nonetheless, is "one of the most straightforward, driving dramas of the season, distinguished chiefly for its characterization of little Mary."

R3   Atkinson, Brooks. "*Children's Hour*; Circumstantial Tragedy Set in a Girl's Boarding School--The Disputed Ending to a Swiftly Written Play." *New York Times* 2 Dec. 1934: X, 1.
         Mary is such a brilliantly drawn character that she almost throws the play off balance. Once she makes her entrance "with a petty lie on her lips, she dominates two acts of it with her plots and inverted craft and her mad dissembling. She is a miniature genius of wickedness."

R4   Benchley, Robert. "The Theatre: Good News." *New Yorker* 1 Dec. 1934: 34, 36.
         Review of *The Children's Hour*. The play is finely written until the last quarter. There are "two too many endings, any one of which would have sufficed" (34). Minor objections include the unnecessary departure of the boyfriend and the almost O'Neillian piling up of tragedy at the end. The play,

however, is almost obligatory for any adult with "half a mind." (36). Details the Scottish case whence the play was taken.

R5   Brown, John Mason. "The Play: Katherine Emery and Anne Revere Excellent in an Interesting Play Called *The Children's Hour.*" *New York Post* 21 Nov. 1934: 13.
        The big moments have an undeniable tension, rising above the "slightly threadbare hokum." An absorbing play, the third act needs drastic cutting; and the writing is not always logical or forceful.

R6   Brown, John Mason. "Two on the Aisle: *The Children's Hour* and The Great Drumsheugh Case--Mr. Walbridge Points Out Some Similarities." *New York Post* 26 Nov. 1934: 15.
        Observes an absorbing theatre piece which treats the lesbian issue with sensitivity. Refers to letters from Earle Walbridge who points out that *Bad Companions* is the play's source, challenging Hellman's misleading statement on opening night that she had conceived the Mary's character of out of her own head.

R7   Gabriel, Gilbert W. "*The Children's Hour*--And Excellent Play Most Excellently Acted with Neither Fear Nor Folderol." *New York Journal-American* 21 Nov. 1934: 13.
        The play is brilliantly written "with its own brand of thrills and sympathies, coils and recoils," but it should have ended "five minutes earlier." After the violent death, all else is "sardonic insignificance." All in all, a genuine contribution to the theatre.

R8   Garland, Robert. "*The Children's Hour* a Moving Tragedy; Play at Maxine Elliott's Theatre a Study of Wrecked Lives." *New York World-Telegram* 21 Nov. 1934: 16.
        An ardent and arresting study in abnormality, it presses its point too far-- though written with sincerity. Mary Tilford is an outstanding creation.

R9   Hammond, Percy. "The Theatres: *The Children's Hour*, a Good Play About a Verboten Subject." *New York Herald Tribune* 21 Nov. 1934: 16.
        A sound tragedy about a forbidden subject, the play is told with "honest audacity and honest craftsmanship." Hellman knows the value of suspense. There are "technical lapses in the telling" such as Mrs. Tilford's lack of interest in the details of the suicide.

R10   Hammond, Percy. "The Theatres: Perils of the Advanced Drama." *New York Herald Tribune* 2 Dec. 1934: II, 1, 5.
        Review of *The Children's Hour*. Hammond reads the published edition to confirm that the play is a "first class drama that illustrates, in a thoughtful and disturbing manner, the mysterious and tragic ways in a maiden and another maiden" (1).

R11   Kaufman. "Plays on Broadway." *Variety* 27 Nov. 1934: 52.
        Review of *The Children's Hour*. Praises the splendid dramaturgy that makes for good theatre. The first two acts are a study of the child and its effects,

realistically told and reminiscent of Ibsen. Objects to the third act which turns to sentimentalism in an attempt to tie up loose threads. Suggests the play is a strong candidate for the Pulitzer Prize.

R12   Krutch, Joseph Wood. "Drama: The Heart of a Child." *Nation* 139 (5 Dec. 1934): 656-57.
       Review of *The Children's Hour*. The perverse child is vividly drawn and the center of dramatic interest. When she leaves after two acts, so does the tension.

R13   "Letters and Art: The Thunderbolt of Broadway: *The Children's Hour*," an Adult, Intelligent Study of a Satanic Child, Moves Its New York Audiences to Vast Respect for a Courageous Dramatist." *Literary Digest* 118 (1 Dec. 1934): 20.
       The Children's Hour is written with abiding honesty. It has been thoughtfully treated and skillfully directed. A poignant tragedy, the season's most important play.

R14   Lockridge, Richard. "The New Play--*The Children's Hour*, Interesting Tragedy, Opens at Maxine Elliott's Theatre." *New York Sun* 21 Nov. 21 1934: 17.
       A sensitive tragedy, containing "biting irony," the play is not without weaknesses. The child should not have been taken so seriously; the teachers could have chosen other options; and at the end the investigation of psychological complexities drags on, robbing the play of probability.

R15   Lockridge, Richard. "The Stage in Review; Recapitulation." *New York Sun* 21 Dec. 1934: 8.
       The Children's Hour is an absorbing play, thoughtfully written and admirably acted.

R16   Mantle, Burns. "*Children's Hour* Smashing Tragedy; Adult and Frankly Psychopathic Drama Holds Audience Fascinated." *New York Daily News* 22 Nov. 1934: 59.
       Positive response encapsulated in the title.

R17   Mantle, Burns. "An Exciting Drama Stirs the Town: *The Children's Hour* Pregnant with Debatable Subjects, Wildly Welcomed. *"New York Daily News* 25 Nov. 1934: 74.
       Positive response encapsulated in the title.

R18   Mantle, Burns. "Paging Miss Taylor, Revealing Miss Lillian." *New York Daily News* 2 Dec. 1934: 84.
       Praises Shumlin's direction of *The Children's Hour* and his agreement on the title. Shumlin originally thought the title would be "bad box office," that it did not reflect the "irony" of the piece.

R19   Mok, Michel. "*The Children's Hour*." *New York Post* 23 Nov. 1934.
       In an interview Hellman speaks of the 18th century Scottish law case which served as the "germ" of her play. "What I know about children I only know because I myself have been a child. The imp came out of my own head."

R20   "Other Current Shows." *New Masses* 13 Dec. 1934: 29.
           The Children's Hour is a near tragedy which packs in the audiences
           because its subject is taboo. Faultless dialogue covers too many technical flaws.

R21   Pollock, Arthur. "The Theatre--Bold and Honest Drama is Presented at Maxine
           Elliott's Theatre Under the Disarming Title, *The Children's Hour.*" *Brooklyn
           Daily Eagle.* 21 Nov. 1934: 19.
                    Honest bluntness saves this "arresting tragedy" from sensationalism.
           The play is destined for Mantle's ten best of the season.

R22   Ruhl, Arthur." Second Night: A *Children's Hour* Bearing No Resemblance to
           Longfellow's." *New York Herald Tribune* 25 Nov. 1934: X, 1.
                    Notes two strong acts, a genuine contribution to adult theatre.

R23   "The Theatre: New Plays in Manhattan." *Time* 24 (3 Dec. 1934): 24.
                    Review of *The Children's Hour*. Hellman knows how to write a play.
           She is wise to "the arcane criminality of childhood, to the no less delicate subject
           of female homosexuality." And Shumlin is shrewd enough to know that "plays
           about homosexuals or children seldom fail."

R24   Winchell, Walter. "Tense Drama at Elliott, a New Hit." *New York Daily Mirror*
           21 Nov. 1934: 10.
                    The Children's Hour is three hours of intelligent drama, patterned a little
           after *The Captive* [Edouard Bourdet], the lesbian issue fittingly told.

R25   Young, Stark. Rev. of *The Children's Hour*. *New Republic* 81 (19 Dec. 1934):
           169.
                    Praises the power of Acts I and II, the excellent realistic character
           portrayals; criticizes the adolescent banality of Act III which is "explicit rather
           than creative, sepulchral rather than intense."

                                              1935

R26   Burnshaw, Stanley. "Current Theatre." *New Masses* 14 (8 Jan. 1935): 29.
                    Review of *The Children's Hour*. The play's sensationalism has drawn
           superlatives from the press and crowds who have confused "an unhappy ending
           for a play of real worth."

R27   *The Children's Hour. Stage* 12 (Jan. 1935): 3.
                    Powerfully written, powerfully performed. "One of Broadway's most
           literate and exciting evenings."

R28   *The Children's Hour. Stage* 12 (Jan. 1935): 28.
                    An unidentified student writes, "I enjoyed it tremendously and found it
           an honest and convincing discussion of subjects which are a part of every girl's
           life."

R29   Craven, Thomas. "These American Plays: Are They American?" *Stage* 12 (Jan. 1935): 14-15.

        Review of *The Children's Hour*. Hellman proves the innocence of the accused women--the excuse for the play's existence--, then attempts to convict them "of the charges which, in lying mouths, caused all the trouble" (14).

P30   Gilder, Rosamond. "Theatre Arts Bookshelf." *Theatre Arts Monthly* 19 (May 1935): 392.

        Review of *The Children's Hour*, the published play. *The Children's Hour* is concerned with the psychological rather than the social. The theme concerns "the power of a lie to destroy life and warp human relations."

R31   Gruber, Ide. "The Playbill." *Golden Book* 21 (Feb. 1935): 28A.

        Review of *The Children's Hour* finds the play "powerful and gripping," well-written and well-acted.

R32   Isaacs, Edith J.R. "Without Benefit of Ingenue: Broadway in Review: *The Children's Hour*." *Theatre Arts* 19 (Jan. 1935): 13-15.

        The characters are patently realistic. However, the character of the evil young girl gains such power and impetus that it upsets the balance of the play.

R33   Krutch, Joseph Wood. "Drama: Best Play." *Nation* 140 (22 May 1935): 610.

        Argues that either *The Children's Hour* or Clifford Odets' *Awake and Sing* should have won the Pulitzer. Praises the power and originality of *The Children's Hour*, calling the work "unforgettable," the best of the year, and the best of many years past; yet faults the disappearance of the child in the last act which shifts attention from the Machiavellian child to the two teachers.

R34   Mantle, Burns. "Believe It or--NO!" *Stage* 12 (May 1935): 23.

        Review of *The Children's Hour*. The writing is superbly literate; the performance is an exciting evening in the theatre; the acting is superb.

R35   Nathan, George Jean. "The Theatre: A Play and Some Other Things." *Vanity Fair* 43 (Feb. 1935): 37.

        Review of *The Children's Hour*. The play is "the one material contribution of the season to American playwriting." The last scene is positively essential.

P36   "The New Books: *The Children's Hour*." *Saturday Review of Literature* 11 (2 Mar. 1935): 523.

        Review of published play. Criticizes the disappearance of Mary in the last act. "Miss Hellman feels the need, evidently, of showing the tragic results of the child's unfounded accusations, but has not been able to do this without slowing up and clogging action which, up until the end of the second act, marches straight ahead. The play is not for children but is decidedly a contribution to the adult theatre."

R37   Wyatt, Euphemia van Rensselaer. "The Drama: *The Children's Hour*." *Catholic World* 140 (Jan 1935): 466-467.

The taboo subject matter is treated with relentless loathing, yet saturated with truth. The last act lacks the intensity of the first two. A curtain at the precise moment would have alleviated the prolonged suffering.

1936

R38   Anderson, John. "Labor and Family Crisis Give Theme to New Play by Lillian Hellman." *New York Evening Journal* 16 Dec. 1936: 24.
              Review of *Days to Come*. The plot of *Days to Come* runs in all directions. Its endless talk has neither dramatic power nor literary distinction.

R39   Atkinson, Brooks. "The Play: *Days to Come* on Ethics of Strikebreaking is Lillian Hellman's New Drama." *New York Times* 16 Dec. 1936: 35.
              A laboriously written play, acted with dogged determination, it does not firmly come to grips with the subject matter. The work is plagued with more plot and counterplot than Pinero.

R40   Brown, John Mason. "*Days to Come* Produced at Vanderbilt Theatre." *New York Post* 16 Dec. 1936: 17.
              Starts with a sociological issue, but veers in other directions. This is really several plays in one, none of which merge; an embarrassing failure.

R41   Carr, Philip. "When Spring Comes to Paris." *New York Times* 7 June 1936: IX, 1.
              Review of *The Children's Hour* (retitled *The Innocents*), Paris production. Reports of a "very ordinary melodrama" that was well-received, "largely owing to the impression made by the young actress playing the juvenile evil genius."

R42   "*The Children's Hour* Is Hailed in London, Production at Gate Theatre Studio Is Uncensored--Wins Critical Acclaim." *New York Times* 10 Jan. 1936: 17.
              Report of London production encapsulated in the title. [Private theatre production. Chamberlain still refuses to grant licenses for public performances in England.]

R43   Coleman, Robert. "*The Children's Hour*." *New York Daily Mirror* 16 Dec. 1936: 26.
              Review of the New York Library production. Complains of confused themes and a lack of clarity.

R44   Coleman, Robert. "The Theatre." *New York Daily Mirror* 16 Dec. 1936: 25.
              Review of *Days to Come*. The ideas are jumbled and too many. The dialogue is staccato and stuffy. The characters are third-rate.

R45   ·Darlington, W. A. "A Good Banned Play." *London Daily Telegraph* 13 Nov. 1936.
              Review of *The Children's Hour*, London production. Despite the weakness of the second act, this is "a very good play."

R46   Dexter, Charles E. "Strikes and Strikebreakers." *Daily Worker* 18 Dec. 1936: 7.

Review of *The Days to Come*. Hellman fails to "view the problem through the eyes of the worker, with whom she is so sympathetic." Notes penetrating dialogue and forceful action," especially in the melodramatic moments of the second act," but shallow characters and too much emphasis on "the slowly rotting" capitalism.

R47   Gabriel, Gilbert W. "*Days to Come.*" *New York American* 16 Dec. 1936: 15.
       An awkward mix of a factory strike with a sex scandal, the play amounts to "nice tedium and nothing else."

R48   Gilbert, Douglas. "*Days to Come* Opens at Vanderbilt Theatre." *New York World-Telegram* 16 Dec. 1936: 32.
       This tragedy of strikers ends in a "psychopathic quarrel" within the factory owner's family, only vaguely connected with the issue of the strike. There is plot enough for two plays, neither of which is ever materialized.

R49   Hobson, Harold. "The Week's Theatre." *London Observer* 15 Nov. 1936: 17.
       Review of *The Children's Hour*, London production. Praises Hellman's command of the material, her full-bodied characterizations. "She creates tension by fulfilling anticipation and only stammers when havoc has left its victims to express anguish in words."

R50   Krutch, Joseph W. "Plays, Pleasant and Unpleasant." *Nation* 143 (26 Dec. 1936): 769-70.
       Review of *Days to Come*. Hellman is not a master of Marxist theme. She is a specialist in hate and frustration, and while Ibsen and Chekhov have been connected to her plays, Strindberg seems "nearer, though perhaps still far enough from the mark" (769). There are two themes, but it is not entirely clear which one the play is about.

R51   Lockridge, Richard. "The New Play: Lillian Hellman's *Days to Come* Opens at the Vanderbilt." *New York Sun* 16 Dec. 1936: 42.
       Pans the show as an artless tangle of playwriting, two unequal plots. Observes snatches of "sharp" dialogue in the first act.

R52   Mantle, Burns. "*Days to Come* a Tragic Drama: Story of a Strike That Shook a Town and Shattered a Few Souls." *New York Daily News* 16 Dec. 1936: 61.
       Observes a tragedy of misunderstanding, humans who find themselves in a pitiful impasse, the strike and its theatrical factors no more than incidental contributors.

R53   Morgan, Charles. "American Week in London." *New York Times* 29 Nov. 1936: XII, 2.
       Review of *The Children's Hour*, London production (Gate Studio Theatre). The lesbian theme is not fully developed. The third act is too gloomy. [Private theatre production. Chamberlain still refuses to grant licenses for public performances in England.]

R54   "Plays and Pictures: *The Children's Hour*, at the Gate Theatre." *New Statesman and Nation* 12 (12 Nov. 1936): 810.

Review of *The Children's Hour*, London production. The play lacks poetic imagination, literary and permanent value, yet provides magnificent roles for the actors. The first two acts are hideously convincing.

R55   Pollock, Arthur. "The Theatre: A New Play by Lillian Hellman." *Brooklyn Daily Eagle* 16 Dec. 1936: 20.
          Days to Come is a ponderous drama, written with something of the austerity of Galsworthy's *Strife*. The third act inconsistently runs into the lives of the richman's family, his wife, his friend, his sister, and the cook.

R56   "Strike Breakers: New Theme Utilized in *Days to Come* by Lillian Hellman." *Literary Digest* 122 (26 Dec. 1936): 22-23.
          Review of published play. Hellman seems unable to take sides with either the factory owner or the strikers; instead, she belabors the melodramatic, using "the Rodman family misfortunes as a springboard for some mild interfamily criticism."

R57   Taylor, Alexander. "Lights and Sounds: Miss Hellman's Noble Experiment." *New Masses* 22 (29 Dec. 1936): 27.
          Review of *Days to Come*. Reacts favorably to the insightful and "rather absorbing" work, despite the duality of focus. The piece is "more important as a playwriting effort than as a finished play." It promises "interesting things from her in the future."

R58   Verschoyle, Derek. "Stage and Screen: The Theatre." *Spectator* 157 (20 Nov. 1936): 905.
          Review of *The Children's Hour*, London, Gate Theatre production. The play is "well constructed, sincere, written with taste and skill . . . admirably produced, and extremely well acted by a talented cast." The issue is the malice of gossip and not lesbianism. Audience at this private theatre have a chance to see a play of unusual interest. Regrets that Chamberlain's ban denies a public offering

R59   Watts, Richard, Jr. "The Theatre." *New York Herald Tribune* 16 Dec. 1936: 22.
          Review of *Days to Come*. Hellman has a literary style that is "economical, distinctive and slightly elliptical and some of her scenes, particularly those in which the strikebreakers appear, are shrewdly dramatic. Unfortunately, much of the play seems confused and ineffective, "and the dialogue has an unhappy way of frequently suggesting a novel rather than a play." The play concerns the effects of a class struggle on factory workers, but is more concerned with the employer and his family. Hellman seems interested chiefly in character, but the characters are not clearly defined; the least satisfying is the wife.

R60   Young, Stark. "Social Drama." *New Republic* 89 (30 Dec. 1936): 274.
          Review of *Days to Come*. Applauds the subject matter, but thinks the plays "suffers from an overwhelming stylistic hurdle. It exhibits a combination of stage writing that is elliptical and stage writing that is expressionistic."

1937

R61   Vernon, Grenville. "The Play and the Screen: *Days to Come.*" *Commonweal* 25 (1 Jan. 1937): 276.

      Had Hellman focused on a melodrama with purpose, the play could have worked. Unfortunately, she scattered her focus on too many character studies.

1938

R62   "Lillian Hellman Comes to Brooklyn Schubert." *Brooklyn Daily Eagle* 9 Nov. 1938: 19.

      Review *The Children's Hour*. The play stands up and keeps the audience spellbound.

1939

R63   Anderson, John. "The Season's Theatre." *Saturday Review of Literature* 20 (29 Apr. 1939): 14-15.

      The Little Foxes is slightly over-plotted and occasionally melodramatic, but it has the advantages of keen observation and incisive character drawing. The action "stems directly from the characters as they reveal themselves to make an absorbing drama" (15). Bankhead is brilliant.

R64   Atkinson, Brooks." Miss Bankhead Has a Play: Lillian Hellman's Stinging Drama About Rugged Individualism Provides a Number of Good Acting Parts." *New York Times* 26 Feb. 1939: X, 1. Reprinted in *Broadway Scrapbook*. New York: Theatre Arts, Inc., 1946. 107-110.

      The Little Foxes is an unusually creditable example of the well-made play. Vivid theatre, it is remarkably well-directed. Bankhead gives the finest performance of her career.

R65   Atkinson, Brooks. "Tallulah Bankhead Appearing in Lillian Hellman's Drama of the South, *The Little Foxes.*" *New York Times* 16 Feb. 1939. In New York Theatre Critics' Reviews, 1939. 490. Reprinted in Bernard Beckerman and Howard Siegman, eds., *On Stage, Selected Theater Reviews from The New York Times*. New York: Arno Press, 1973: 210-11.

      Hellman has written a vibrant theatre piece with viable parts that have been perfectly cast. The first act is a masterpiece of exposition. The second and third acts are filled with melodramatic abandon; and the speech of social significance gets lost in the contrivances. Ranks the play second to *The Children's Hour*.

R66   Benchley, Robert. "The Theatre: *The Little Foxes.*" *New Yorker* 15 (25 Feb. 1939): 25.

      A sinister play about sinister people, it panders in no way to its audiences. It is tightly woven and well-conceived, and will probably make a "very significant contribution to the theatre."

R67   Brown, John Mason. "Two on the Aisle: Tallulah Bankhead and *The Little Foxes*; Miss Hellman's Engrossing Play is Compared to Miss Du Maurier's

Rebecca." *New York Post* 11 Mar. 1939: 8. Reprinted in *Broadway in Review*. New York: W.W. Norton, 1940. 116-121.

The play is engrossing, but "too-well-made . . . super-Crime Club stuff." Praises the superb performance by Bankhead, the poignant performance by Collinge, and believes that the play's effectiveness is due to the expert acting.

R68   Cambridge, John. "*The Little Foxes* a Story of Southern Aristocrats." *Daily Worker* 17 Feb. 1939: 7.

Hellman has written a deceptively simple play, "her best and the most consistently tense play of the season. Bankhead gives "perhaps the best performance of her career . . . a fascinating portrait of an evil spirit."

R69   Cambridge, John. "The Stage: Lillian Hellman Shows Ability to Project Social Idea With Dramatic Force in *The Little Foxes*." *New York Sunday Worker* 19 Feb. 1939: 7.

Hellman has written "a penetrating analysis of Southern capitalist mentality on the make . . . what is really a universal parable on this aspect of capitalism."

R70   Fergusson, Otis. "A Play, a Picture." *New Republic* 98 (12 Apr. 1939): 279.

Review of *The Little Foxes*. Criticizes entire company for its acting, especially Bankhead and her baritone register. The play pleases due to our delight in seeing something happen, to the theatre craft and effects. The work is "a thing of some keen edges and no point."

R71   Gassner, John. "The Theatre." *One Act Play Magazine* 2 (Feb. 1939): 746-49.

Review of *The Little Foxes*. The play is admirably produced, but it errs on the side of melodrama and "on the side of ineffective nobility when it indulges in a value declamation in honor of idealism" (748). Regina's character is a triumph of pathos, but calls for a more subtle evocation by Bankhead.

R72   Gilder, Rosamond. "Broadway in Review: *The Little Foxes*." *Theatre Arts Monthly* 23 (Apr. 1939): 244, 246, 247-48.

The first act is gripping; the second act lags, but the third act picks up momentum. Complications of plot are forgotten in the clash of characters, three-dimensionally conceived. Bankhead "radiates ruthlessness" (247).

R73   Kronenberger, Louis. "Greed." *Stage* 16 (1 Apr. 1939): 36-37, 55.

The Little Foxes is an effective protest that reminds us that "our age is not one of personal tragedy but of social confusion and dislocation" (55).

R74   Krutch, Joseph W. "Unpleasant Play." *Nation* 168 (25 Feb. 1939): 244-45.

Review of *The Little Foxes*. The fact that one tolerates this tense and desperate play is a tribute to the writer's skill. Praises superb, vivid characterizations and expert technique, but finds the play occasionally more melodramatic than necessary.

R75   Lockridge, Richard. "Lillian Hellman's *The Little Foxes* Opens at the National Theater." *New York Sun* 15 Feb. 1939.

"The play is steadily interesting and almost, but never quite, more." Bankhead is hard and vicious, as the author's intended, "always authentic in the grain."

R76   Lockridge, Richard. "The Stage in Review: Universality in the Drama, with a Note on Its Absence in *The Little Foxes*." *New York Sun* 19 Feb. 1939: 26. In New York Theatre Critics' Reviews, 1939. 492.

This is an admirable play, yet it lacks universality.

R77   Mantle, Burns. "*The Little Foxes* Taut Drama Of a Ruthless Southern Family." *New York Daily News* 16 Feb. 1939. In New York Theatre Critics' Reviews, 1939. 490.

The play is well-written until the last act which "moves indecisively and haltingly toward its finish."

R78   Mantle, Burns. "Mean Minded Humans Make Good Drama: *The Little Foxes* a Credit to Honesty of Lillian Hellman and Herman Shumlin." *New York Daily News* 26 Feb. 1939: 77.

There are very few moments when the audience is not moved to sympathy or compassion.

R79   McKenney, Ruth. "Sights and Sounds: *The Little Foxes*." *New Masses* 30 (28 Feb. 1939): 29-30.

An unpleasant look at America's future millionaires and America's destiny, the central idea contains "one of the most fascinating stories I have seen in the American theatre" (29. Hellman "comes into her own as one of America's most vigorous and exciting playwrights." This is a theatrical must-see.

R80   Nathan, George J. "Dour Octopus." *Newsweek* 13 (27 Feb. 1939): 26.

Review of *The Little Foxes*. Hellman "has a dramatic mind, and eye for character, a fundamental strength and a complete and unremitting integrity that are rare among her native playwriting sex." She will occupy a distinguished critical place in the theatre when she masters present weaknesses: "a periodic confusion of melodramatic bitterness and suggestive tragedy, intensified and unrelieved acerbity with mounting drama, and a skeletonization of episode with dramatic economy." Notes shades of Ibsen in the handling of theme, touches of Pinero's *The Thunderbolt*, as well as the ghost of Strindberg.

R81   Ross, George. "Decay of the South Play Theme: Tallulah Bankhead Gives Superb Performance in Leading Role of Fine Drama, *The Little Foxes*." *New York World-Telegram* 16 Feb. 1939. In New York Theatre Critics' Reviews, 1939. 491.

Hellman narrates a grim tale in a melodramatic fashion, creating suspense and commanding her audience's attention.

R82   Shipley, Joseph T. "This Week on the Stage: That Spoil the Vine." *New Leader* 22 (4 Mar. 1939): 6.

The Little Foxes is a sharp, bitter conflict which casts our sympathies on one side, making "villains pitch black and the nice characters white as driven snow. Only we hate to be driven."

R83   "The Theatre: New Play in Manhattan." *Time* 33 (27 Feb. 1939): 38.
        Review of *The Little Foxes*. "Playwright Hellman makes her plot crouch,
coil, dart like a snake; lets her big scenes turn boldly on melodrama . . .
capitalizes on it, brilliantly succeeds at it."

R84   Vernon, Grenville. "The Stage & Screen: *The Little Foxes*." *Commonweal* 29 (3
        Mar. 1939): 525.
        The play is admirably written and constructed, a candidate for the Pulitzer.
Hellman is an artist, and whatever her social beliefs, she "does not load the dice
unduly." Praises the character of Regina "who might have stepped out of the
pages of Balzac."

R85   Waldorf, Wilella. "*The Little Foxes* Opens at the National Theatre." *New York
        Post* 16 Feb. 1939: 12. In New York Theatre Critics' Reviews, 1939. 492.
        Bankhead acts with tremendous authority, but this is not "a first-class
vehicle."

R86   Watts, Richard, Jr. "Dixie." *New York Herald Tribune* 16 Feb. 1939: 14. In
        New York Theatre Critics' Reviews, 1939. 491.
        Review of *The Little Foxes*. The work is distinguished and important,
proof of Hellman's standing as a dramatist.

R87   Wyatt, Euphemia van Rensselaer. "The Drama: *The Little Foxes*." *Catholic World*
        149 (Apr. 1939): 87-88.
        The play is "not written for any particular locality, but as a general
exposure to those foxes who run amuck through our social order careless of the
vines they may destroy to reach the grapes they desire" (87). It is technically
better than *The Children's Hour*.

                                              1941

R88   Anderson, John. "*Watch on the Rhine* At the Martin Beck: Lillian Hellman's New
        Play Concerns Conflict in U.S. Over Fascism; Paul Lukas' Acting Brilliant."
        New York Journal and American 2 Apr. 1941. In New York Theatre Critics'
        Reviews, 1941. 342.
        Observes "the sharpness of observation and felicity of characterization that
stamp all of Miss Hellman's most effective work;" yet criticizes the dawdling
beginning, the fumbling conclusion, and concludes that the play misses its mark.

R89   Atkinson, Brooks. "Hellman's *Watch on the Rhine*: Author of *The Children's
        Hour* and *The Little Foxes* Writes of an American Family Drawn into the Nazi
        Orbit." *New York Times* 13 Apr. 1941: IX, 1. *Broadway Scrapbook*. New York:
        Theatre Arts, Inc., 1947. 192-95. 222, 225-257.
        The craftsmanship is inferior to *The Children's Hour* and *The Little
Foxes*, but the characters, most of them, are immediately likable--"humorous,
witty and affectionate in many scenes." This is "incomparably her best work."

R90   Atkinson, Brooks. "Lillian Hellman's *Watch on the Rhine* Acted With Paul Lukas
        in the Leading Part." *New York Times* 2 Apr. 1941. In New York Theatre

Critics' Reviews, 1941. 341. Reprinted in Bernard Beckerman and Howard Siegman, eds., *On Stage, Selected Theater Reviews from The New York Times*. New York: Arno Press, 1973. 235-36.

Carps at technicalities, but finds the play filled with flavor and human characters, the writing enormously skillful.

R91   Bessie, Alvah. "Sights and Sounds." *New Masses* 39 (15 Apr. 1941): 26-28.

Review of *Watch on the Rhine*. While Hellman effectively gets the audience to accept the Müller's anti-Fascism, the movement needs to be redefined in socialist terms.

R92   Brown, John Mason. "Lillian Hellman's *Watch on the Rhine* Presented." *New York Post* 2 Apr. 1941. In New York Theatre Critics' Reviews, 1941. 341.

Lacks tight construction, needs editing, but has rewarding features, such as the witty and eloquent dialogue and several admirably rounded characters. Despite the disappointments, this is one of the fullest and most rewarding plays of the season.

R93   Freedley, George. Rev. of *Watch on the Rhine*. *Morning-Telegraph* 3 Apr. 1941.

This could have been her best play had she not cluttered the play with sub-plots and excessive extraneous action.

R94   Gassner, John. "Stage." *Direction* 4 (July 1941): 42-43.

Review of *Watch on the Rhine*. Praises Hellman's focus on character, particularly on the creation of a "modern hero," brilliantly realized by Lucas.

R95   Gibbs, Wolcott. "The Theatre." *New Yorker* 17 (12 Apr. 1941): 32.

Review of *Watch on the Rhine*. Hellman has treated the fundamental issue of our time "with the dignity, insight, and sound theatrical intelligence that it demands."

R96   Gilder, Rosamond. "Prizes that Bloom in the Spring." *Theatre Arts* 25 (12 Apr. 1941): 409-11.

Review of *Watch on the Rhine*. Criticizes the structure, the slow exposition, the cumbersome sub-plot, yet praises authentic passages that successfully portray "a fundamental human ideal." Müller in Paul Lukas's hands becomes the prototype of all those like Hamlet "who revolt against the 'cursed spite' that calls upon them to set right by violence a world gone out of joint" (411).

R97   Kronenberger, Louis. "*Watch on the Rhine*--The Best Play of the Season: A Melodrama of Anti-Nazism." *New York Newspaper PM*. 2 Apr. 1941: 23. In New York Theatre Critics' Reviews, 1941. 343.

The play ends with a choking scene of farewell between Müller and his family. The dialogue, its wit and fervor, and the characters are admirable.

R98   Krutch, Joseph Wood. "Drama: No Such Animal." *Nation* 152 (12 Apr. 1941): 453.

Review of *Watch on the Rhine*. Hellman has avoided direct confrontation, choosing as her subject a minor incident. She has successfully avoided "flat didacticism and the thinness of characterization." There is, however, a continuous suggestion of contrivance, and the play is "least convincing when it aims to come closest to fact."

R99   Lockridge, Richard. "Lillian Hellman's *Watch on the Rhine* Opens at the Martin Beck." *New York Sun* 2 Apr. 1941. In New York Theatre Critics' Reviews, 1941. 344.

Praises the shrewd and insightful characters.

R100   Mantle, Burns. "*Watch on the Rhine* Stirring Drama of a Family of Refugees." *New York Daily News* 2 Apr. 1941: 59. In New York Theatre Critics' Reviews, 1941. 344.

A tense and exciting play, the father's farewell scene is heart-rending.

R101   "Message Without Hysteria: *Watch on the Rhine* Presents Subtle Indictment of Nazis." *Newsweek* 17 (14 Apr. 1941): 70.

Lacks the craftsmanship and definition of her previous plays. Avoids preaching by approaching the subject from a distance. The first two acts are overly talkative, though witty; the third act is written with warmth, power, and sincerity. The splendid cast makes the melodramatic acceptable.

R102   Nathan, George. "Playwrights in Petticoats." *American Mercury* 54 (June 1941): 750-55. Reprinted as "The Status of Female Playwrights," in *The Entertainment of a Nation*. New York: Alfred A. Knopf, 1942. 34-41.

Review of *Watch on the Rhine*. The play represents "the best of our American women playwrights;" yet it falls short of the mark of our best masculine writers.

R103   "New Play in Manhattan: *Watch on the Rhine*." *Time* 37 (14 Apr. 1941): 64.

An uneven play, yet the best to date on the subject of Nazism, the first two acts are mostly supercharged talk, the last act, "a superbly written and acted picture of a dedicated man."

R104   Vernon, Grenville. "The Stage and the Screen: *Watch on the Rhine*." *Commonweal* 34 (25 Apr. 1941): 15-16.

Faults the structure, much of the dialogue, and many of the characters; criticizes the use of the term "fascist," since the play is really about anti-Nazi propaganda; and finds the occasional communist tinges a contradiction. The melodrama occurs only in the last act, and "the scenes before are probably supposed to be comedy of manners" (16).

R105   Warner, Ralph. "*Watch on the Rhine*: Poignant Drama of Anti-Fascist Struggle." *Daily Worker* 4 Apr. 1941: 7.

Praises skilled craftsmanship, carefully created and believable characters, and the realistic situation that attempts to project the anti-Fascist struggle. Calls it "great theatre," but feels the political issues need explanation.

R106   Watts, Richard, Jr. "Portrait of a German." *New York Herald Tribune* 2 Apr. 1941. In New York Theatre Critics' Reviews, 1941. 342.

Review of *Watch on the Rhine*. A moving and beautiful play, it filled with eloquence and heroic spirit. Defends the melodramatic aspects as truthful reflections of life.

R107   Whipple, Sidney B. "*Watch on the Rhine* Avoids the Soap-Box." *New York World-Telegram* 2 Apr. 1941: 30. In New York Theatre Critics' Reviews, 1941. 343.

"The entire play is a hymn of praise for the courage and nobility of Fascism's opponents rather than an indictment of European political gangsterism."

R108   Wyatt, Euphemia Van Rensselaer. "The Drama: *Watch on the Rhine*." *Catholic World* 153 (May 1941): 215-16.

Criticizes the structure, but praises the brave and human treatment which "gives dramatic impact to the contrast between America's plentiful security and Europe's pitiful and chaotic want" (215).

R109   Young, Stark. "*Watch on the Rhine*." *New Republic* 104 (14 Apr. 1941): 498-99.

Faults the first act for wandering, the last act for devoting entirely too much time to Kurt's farewell to his family, yet praises the expert stagecraft of the melodrama and the remarkably strong characters.

1942

R110   Brown, Ivor. "At the Play." *London Observer* (26 Apr. 1942): 7.

Review of *Watch on the Rhine* (Aldwych Theatre, London). A respectable combination of American writing and background with assorted European acting, the production would have been better if played by Americans, "because the contrast of the two worlds, American and European, is vital to the play." The slow start surges to a tremendous third act, and the direction is praiseworthy.

R111   Brown, Ivor. "At the Play." *Punch* 202 (3 June 1942): 466.

Review of *Watch on the Rhine* (Aldwych Theatre, London). The production suffers somewhat by its "refusal to be suspect of melodrama." It rises slowly to a strong and exciting climax based on "the inner conflict of the hero's struggle between domestic and political ties."

R112   Dent, Alan. "At the Play." *Punch* 202 (28 Oct. 1942): 366.

Review of *The Little Foxes* (Piccadilly Theatre, London). Praises the fine text, the likely plot with its ingenious and surprising turns, the unusual plausible characters. "The one flaw in Miss Fay Compton's masterly presentation of Regina is that she makes too little of the indications of charm, which are most in evidence in the First Act. This steely beauty, with no fascination or even fun to it, brings the whole play perilously near to mere melodrama . . ."

R113   Darlington, W.A. "Americans in London." *New York Times* 1 Nov. 1942: VIII, 2.

Review of *The Little Foxes* (Piccadilly Theatre). Having heard a good deal about the Broadway production and seen the Bette Davis film version, London audiences are disappointed. The play has been received as "a reasonably good melodrama, but nothing more." The play calls for a complete understanding of the subtle nuances which the director and actors have failed to distill.

R114   Martin, Kingsley. " A Fine Play: *Watch on the Rhine* at the Aldwych." *New Statesman and Nation* 23 (2 May 1942): 288.

The scene in which the German family arrives unexpectedly in the drawing room is "as good as anything that has appeared on the London stage in recent years." This is one of the best and most moving plays that London has known in years. The material is truthful, compelling, and harrowing.

R115   Redfern, James. "The Theatre: *The Little Foxes*." *Spectator* 169 (30 Oct. 1942): 407.

Review of the Piccadilly Theatre production (London). A sordid tale of moral downfall, told in vivid, realistic terms, and acted in a convincing manner.

R116   Sobel, Bernard. "Drama: Propaganda and the Play." *Saturday Review* 25 (7 Mar. 1942): 13.

Watch on the Rhine proves that an entertaining well-written propaganda play can succeed. Despite weaknesses, the play is interesting, well-constructed, rich in characters and lifelike dialogue; and the propaganda is intrinsic to the play.

R117   Whitebait, William. "Plays and Pictures: *The Little Foxes* at the Piccadilly." *New Statesman and Nation* 24 (7 Nov. 1942): 304.

Review of Piccadilly Theatre production (London). The production is "slow, uncertain, crude rather than emphatic in its effects. Yet with all these faults, it works up an uneasy excitement and shocks sufficiently."

R118   Wright, Basil. Rev. of *Watch on the Rhine*. *Spectator* (1 May 1942): 419.

Reports of the successful London production at the Aldwych Theatre, starring Dame Peggy Ashcroft as Fanny Farrelly. "Apart from a slightly machine-made opening to the first act, the author manipulates her plot and characters with an assurance, an economy, and a sense of human values to which only an exceptionally talented cast could do justice. Fortunately, such a cast has been assembled."

1944

R119   Barnes, Howard. "Perception and Poetry New York." *New York Herald Tribune* 13 Apr. 1944: 16. In New York Theatre Critics' Reviews, 1944. 218.

The Searching Wind would have gained coherence and feeling had more been made of the wise grandfather and the expatriate son. The final scene in which the son is about to lose his leg for the mistakes of his elders is filled with "undeniable poignancy."

R120   Chapman, John. "*The Searching Wind* A Forceful Drama About World Appeasers." *New York Daily News* 13 April 1944. In New York Theatre Critics' Reviews, 1944. 218.

Absorbing and intelligent theatre, it is not stirring. The individually unhappy trio reach a point of boredom.

R121   Freedley, George. "The Stage Today." *New York Morning Telegraph* 14 Apr. 1944.

Review of *The Searching Wind*. Calls it, "the most and, perhaps, the best serious drama of the new season."

R122   Garland, Robert. "*The Searching Wind* On the Fulton Stage. *New York Journal-American* 13 Apr. 1944. In New York Theatre Critics' Reviews, 1944. 217.

Hellman writes a play of utmost importance with assurance and deep political insight and splendid characterizations.

R123   Gibbs, Wolcott. "Miss Hellman Nods." *New Yorker* 20 (22 Apr. 1944): 42-44.

The Searching Wind alternates, combines, and confuses the issues of love and politics.

R124   Gilder, Rosamond. "*The Searching Wind*." *Theatre Arts* 28 (June 1944): 331-32.

The play wanders from its main political scene, losing itself in an inept love story. Despite its faults, it remains one of the current few that "treats important issues seriously" (332).

R125   "Hellman's Blue Ribbon." *Newsweek* 23 (24 Apr. 1944): 86, 88.

Review of *The Searching Wind*. "The author has something pointedly significant to say and a way of saying it that is given to very few of this country's playwrights."

R126   Ibee [Pulaski, Jack]. "Plays on Broadway; *The Searching Wind*." *Variety* 19 Apr. 1944: 46.

Review of *The Searching Wind*. Ranks the play "the outstanding drama of the season."

R127   Isaacs, Edith. "Lillian Hellman, a Playwright on the March." *Theatre Arts* 28 (Jan. 1944): 19-24.

Review of *The Searching Wind*. Notes the recurring theme of the struggle between good and active evil in Hellman's plays.

R128   Kronenberger, Louis. "A Drama With Teeth to It." *New York Newspaper PM* 13 Apr. 1944. In New York Theatre Critics' Reviews, 1944. 218-19.

Review of *The Searching Wind*. Hellman abandons her mastery of a tight, clenched drama in this rewarding, serious play. There are perhaps two plays here. Notes resemblances to Shaw.

R129   Marshall, Margaret. "Drama." *Nation* 158 (22 Apr. 1944): 494-95.

The Searching Wind lacks clarity of thought and feeling essential to the analysis of both art and politics. Criticizes Hazen's harsh view.

R130   Morehouse, Ward. "Lillian Hellman's Play, *The Searching Wind*, Eloquent and
        Powerful." *New York Sun* 13 April 1944. In New York Theatre Critics'
        Reviews, 1944. 217.
            Hellman "writes with a discernment and considerable bitterness of a
        generation that saw and sensed the rise of Fascism and stood by and let it
        happen." Not her best play, but "a drama of sincerity and stature."

R131   Nathan, George Jean. "Theatre Week." *New York Journal American* 24 Apr.
        1944: 13.
            The Searching Wind is better than most of the plays of the year, but it is
        not Hellman's best.

R132   Nichols, Lewis. "The Play in Review: *The Searching Wind*." *New York Times*
        13 April 1944. In New York Theatre Critics' Reviews, 1944. 218-19.
            Hellman seems more interested in politics than love story, properly so. A
        timely piece.

R133   Nichols, Lewis. "*The Searching Wind*: Lillian Hellman's Latest Play a Study of
        Appeasement and Love." *New York Times* 23 Apr. 1944: X, 1.
            Considers the play a timely credit to the theatre, though not Hellman at her
        best. Needs "more politics and less emotional triangle." Praises Shumlin's
        direction.

R134   New Plays in Manhattan: *The Searching Wind*." *Time* 43 (24 Apr. 1944):
        72.
            The play has bite, but needs focus and/or editing. Theme hinders plot, and
        the love story needs development. This is really two plays.

R135   Phelan, Kappo. "*The Searching Wind*." *Commonweal* 40 (28 Apr. 1944): 40.
            The treatment of the two women is melodramatic Clearly identified as
        heroine and villainess, their motives remain unclear, unproved. Criticizes the
        direction, and the casting of two equally matched females in the leading roles.

R136   Pollock, Arthur. "Playthings." *Brooklyn Daily Eagle* 16 Apr. 1944.
            Review of *The Searching Wind*. "The dramatist most alive in the theatre
        today and the best equipped for living, Miss Hellman stands out as a symbol of
        what the theatre can do and few of its playwrights attempt."

R137   Rascoe, Burton. "*The Searching Wind* Miss Hellman's Finest." *New York
        World-Telegram* 13 April 1944. In New York Theatre Critics' Reviews, 1944.
        218.
            This is a masterpiece of ingenious and thoughtful playwriting, a bitter-sad
        arraignment of the near-sighted and frivolous persons in powerful and influential
        positions who have encouraged the rise of dictatorships.

R138   Shipley, Joseph T. "The Barren Years." *New Leader* 26 (6 May 1944): 26-27.
            Review of *The Searching Wind*. Tricks of the theatre cover a division of
        emphases and a blustery vacuity. Frequent witty or caustic lines, competent
        direction and excellent acting, yet a bad play.

R139   Sillen, Samuel. Rev. of *The Searching Wind*. *New Masses* 51 (2 May 1944): 26-27.

Criticizes the unsuccessful blending of plots, the blurred distinction between appeasement and anti-appeasement Americans.

R140   Waldorf, Wilella. "*The Searching Wind* a Mild Blast at Compromise and Appeasers." *New York Post* 13 April 1944. In New York Theatre Critics' Reviews, 1944. 217-18.

A pretentious, well-meaning drama, *The Searching Wind* always seems on the verge of saying something of tremendous import.

R141   Warner, Ralph. "The New Lillian Hellman Play." *Daily Worker* 17 Apr. 1944: 5.

The Searching Wind captures the picture of Americans aware of Fascism, yet unaware of its monstrous potential. It fails, however, to link the appeasers of yesterday with the defeatists, the nationalists, and isolationists of today.

R142   Winchell, Walter. "*The Searching Wind* Is New Hellman Hit." *New York Daily Mirror* 13 Apr. 1944.

Observes a suspenseful play with real life characters who are civilized but "cruel, selfish and animal-like."

R143   Wyatt, Euphemia Van Rensselaer. "The Drama." *Catholic World*. 159 (May 1944): 170-71.

Review of *The Searching Wind*. "The strength of the play is that the playwright draws no conclusions . . . . it is for us to judge . . . .The characters, all of them down to the waiters, are drawn to perfect scale" (171). The theme of the play--"the world's tragedy is the sum total of all our personal weakness"--places Hellman among our foremost playwrights (170).

R144   Young, Stark. "Behind the Beyond." *New Republic* 110 (1 May 1944): 604.

Review of *The Searching Wind*. The historical scenes hold interest because of their topicality, not their vision. The scenes between the two woman are repetitive, unintense, banal; and the love story unconvincing.

1945

R145   Freedley, George. "The Stage Today; *Children's Hour*." *New York Morning Telegraph* 29 May 1945: 2.

A worthwhile off-Broadway show, the production is enormously effective.

R146   Garland, Robert. "*Children's Hour* at Library." *New York Journal American* 23 May 1945: 8.

The play has not lost its power.

R147   Gassner, John. "The Theatre Arts." *Forum* 106 (Aug. 1945): 175-79.

Review of *The Searching Wind*. Hellman has broken the barriers of the well-made play.

1946

R148   Atkinson, Brooks. "The Play." *New York Times* 21 Nov. 1946: 42. In New
        York Theatre Critics' Reviews, 1946. 248.
            Review of *Another Part of the Forest*. Hellman's hatred for malefactors of
        great wealth in post-war Alabama translates into old-fashioned melodrama. There
        are big scenes in every act, but the play does not measure up to *The Little Foxes*
        or *Watch on the Rhine*.

R149   Atkinson, Brooks. "Lillian Hellman: Eating the Earth." *New York Times* 1 Dec.
        1946: II, 1. Reprinted in *Broadway Scrapbook*. New York: Theatre Arts, Inc.,
        1947. 255-57.
            Another Part of the Forest is less skillfully controlled than *The Little
        Foxes*. One monstrous situation follows another, turning it into a "lurid show."
        Praises the expertly drawn characters of Birdie and Marcus who has "a kind of
        dignity that redeems him from common villainy."

R150   Barnes, Howard. "The Predatory Hubbards of Miss Hellman's Play." *New York
        Herald Tribune* (1 Dec. 1946): V, 1, 3.
            Review of *Another Part of the Forest*. Marcus is much too clever to be
        outwitted by his son. The characters are fascinating, but not always convincing.

R151   Barnes, Howard. "The Theatres: *Another Part of the Forest*." *New York Herald
        Tribune* 21 Nov. 1946: 25. In New York Theatre Critics' Reviews, 1946. 247.
            Most of the tension comes from the building of character. There are
        moments of dramatic impact, but not enough to make the play compelling.

R152   Brown, John M. "Seeing Things: and Cauldron Bubble." *Saturday Review of
        Literature* 29 (14 Dec. 1946): 20-23.
            Review of *Another Part of the Forest*. Equates the "*venomous witches'*
        broth" with Shakespeare. Cites Ibsen and *The Duchess of Malfi* as spiritual
        parents of the work. Finds the "guignol" interesting, yet a detraction from any
        serious intent.

R153   Chapman, John. "*Another Part of Forest* Makes *The Little Foxe*s a Mere
        Warmup." *New York Daily News* 21 Nov. 1946. In New York Theatre Critics'
        Reviews, 1946. 249.
            Praises the successful melodrama, its skillful direction. Suggests that
        Hellman has overplayed her hand in the final scene.

R154   Garland, Robert. "At Fulton--*Another Part of the Forest*." *New York Journal-
        American* 21 Nov. 1946. In New York Theatre Critics' Reviews, 1946. 248.
            Considers the "well-nigh perfect play" the best on Broadway--as a play, a
        performance, and a production.

R155   Gibbs, Wolcott. "The Theatre: Ladies Day." *New Yorker* 22 (30 Nov. 1946): 58-
        60.
            Review of *Another Part of the Forest*. Expresses disappointment in the
        "untidy sequel" (60). Misses the playwright's distinguished style, her almost

impeccable structure and superior thought. Complains of melodramatic ornamentation.

R156   Hawkins, William. "*The Forest* a Modern Theater Classic." *New York World-Telegram.* 21 Nov. 1946. In New York Theatre Critics' Reviews, 1946. 249.

       Review of *Another Part of the Forest.* Hellman directs this classic of the modern theatre as she wrote the play "with the same pains and telling values."

R157   Kronenberger, Louis. "Lillian Hellman Writes Another Compelling Drama." *New York Newspaper PM.* 22 Nov. 1946. In New York Theatre Critics' Reviews, 1946. 247.

       Review of *Another Part of the Forest.* Compared with *The Little Foxes,* the play seems less effective but more interesting, less controlled, but more complex. It is not simply melodrama, for character is more important than plot. Notes a similarity to somber Elizabethan comedies, the cheats, knaves, and evildoers. Praises vigorous characters, Marcus who is perhaps the most interesting, and Hellman's firm and incisive staging.

R158   Krutch, Joseph Wood. "Drama." *Nation* 162 (7 Dec. 1946): 671-672.

       Review of *Another Part of the Forest.* The play is more skillfully written than the earlier works, until the last scene. The relentless depravity lessens enthusiasm and begins to seem. "funny" after awhile. Notes implicit Marxian overtones to the play in "the decline of the Southern feudal aristocracy and the rise of capitalist exploiter" (671).

R159   Morehouse, Ward. "Hellman's *Another Part of the Forest* Is a Fascinating and Powerful Drama." *New York Sun* 21 Nov. 1946. In New York Theatre Critics' Reviews, 1946. 250.

       Portions of the play are overwritten. The strongest material, as in other Hellman pieces, is to be found in the last act.

R160   Nathan, George Jean. "False Alarm Clocks Also Start Ringing." *New York Journal- American* 2 Dec. 1946: 14.

       Review of *Another Part of the Forest.* Notes a resemblance to Strindberg. The play ends "overwrought by melodrama," bordering uncomfortably on travesty.

R161   Phelan, Kappo." The State and the Screen: *Another Part of the Forest.*" *Commonweal* 45 (6 Dec. 1946): 201.

       To make Marcus "a villain, rather than merely villainous, and to cram the work with verging madness, incipient incest, and such fakements as motivating Bibles, pistols, and envelopes of money . . . pulls her whole effort down to the sordid, silly 'shocker' class" (202). The cast is superb.

R162   Schneider, Isidor. "Sights and Sounds: *Another Part of the Forest.*" *New Masses* 61 (24 Dec. 1946): 28-29.

       The play "has great dramatic drive and through the first two acts is convincing; the third act is too trickily balanced on plot pivots for similar conviction" (29). The characters are "flattened out into monotones" (28).

R163   Shipley, John T. "The Meanest Family." *New Leader* 29 (21 Dec. 1946): 12.
            Another Part of the Forest is a study of evil characters--greater and lesser
            --that do not grow. The most pleasant characters are Lavinia and Birdie. "For the
            rest, there is cooked for us a steamy devil's broth. On leaving the theatre, one
            wants to rinse one's mind."

R164   "Theatre: Foxes in the *Forest*." *Newsweek* 28 (2 Dec. 1946): 94.
            Review of *Another Part of the Forest*. "For the first two acts Miss
            Hellman feels out her characters and suspense with delicate jabs. Her final act is
            straight melodrama, but even when she swings from the floor, she knows when
            to pull her punches."

R165   Watts, Richard Jr. "Lillian Hellman's New Play Is Fascinating Drama." *New
            York Post* 21 Nov. 1946. In New York Theatre Critics' Reviews, 1946. 250.
            Another Part of the Forest is a brilliant and distinguished work, of
            enormous power and impact, Hellman's best. Of Marcus, his "sententious but
            earnest striving for culture and his scorn for the romantic pretensions of the
            Confederate South . . . makes one understand a great deal about him." He is a
            scoundrel, but a human being.

R166   Young, Stark. "Theatre." *New Republic* 140 (16 Dec. 1946): 822.
            Review of *Another Part of the Forest*. *The Little Foxes* is twice as
            interesting. "More and more Miss Hellman piles things on from the outside,
            heaps it up into rank melodrama, with an innate lack of essential dignity and
            thrust."

                                              1947

R167   Bentley, Eric. "Broadway and Its Intelligentsia." *Harper's Magazine* 142 (Mar.
            1947): 211-12
            Review of *Another Part of the Forest*. Like *The Little Foxes*, the play is
            grand guignol in the guise of realism. Hideous moments elicit laughter, not
            inappropriately.

R168   Beyer, William. "The State of the Theatre: Midseason Highlights." *School and
            Society* 65 (5 Apr. 1947): 250-52.
            Review of *Another Part of the Forest*. Criticizes the belabored
            contrivances, the "hopped-up" melodrama, the villainies, piled up at a
            preposterous rate, "the papers, robberies, insanity, torture, lechery, more papers,
            even a leer at incest" which add up to an uninspiring evening in the theatre.

R169   Gassner, John. "The Theatre Arts. *"Forum* 107 (Jan. 1947): 81-83.
            Review of *Another Part of the Forest*. Praises well-rounded characters,
            but believes the play misses the highest levels of creativeness, since "it is anti-
            humanistic and befouls the spirit" (82-83). Faults the mechanical aid of
            incriminating papers and testimonies in the last act. Suggests that resolution
            should have come from character, not plot contrivance.

R170   Gassner, John. "The Theatre Arts." *Forum* 107 (Feb. 1947): 172-77.

Review of *Another Part of the Forest* . An over-emphasis of piteous characters takes away from the sultry comic mood, intimating a heavier content.

R171   Gilder, Rosamond. "New Year, New Play: Broadway in Review." *Theatre Arts* 31 (17 Jan. 1947): 14.

Review of *Another Part of the Forest*. The characterizations are "extreme to the point of caricature," yet "so infused with passion that they become horribly alive" (17). The melodramatic aspects are "acceptable symbols of power," cleverly used to heightened tension, yet overused in the last act wherein the maneuvering is much "too prolonged" (17).

R172   Wyatt, Euphemia van Rensselaer. "The Drama." *Catholic World* 164 (Jan 1947): 360.

Calls *Another Part of the Forest* "a melodramatic study of villainy," Marcus "the prime sinner."

1949

R173   Atkinson, Brooks. "*Montserrat* Adapted From the French of Emmanuel Robles by Lillian Hellman." *New York Times* 31 Oct. 1949. In New York Theatre Critics' Reviews, 1949. 246.

This should have been completely devastating theatre, but the writing is barren; the characters are thin; the murders are without motivation; and the direction is monotonous.

R174   Barnes, Howard. "*Montserrat*: Brilliant Adaptation." *New York Herald Tribune* 31 Oct. 1949. In New York Theatre Critics' Reviews, 1949. 244.

The work is conversational and repetitious, a series of melodramatic vignettes which never achieve the eminence of tragedy, yet Hellman has made it "frequently eloquent in her translation and remarkably full of action in her staging."

R175   Beaufort, John. "Three New Plays on Broadway." *Christian Science Monitor* 5 Nov. 1949: 10

Review of *Montserrat*. "Miss Hellman's method is mystifying. The performance moves with such deliberation, such pauses between speeches, that climactic effects are difficult or impossible. . . it is not a very effective play."

R176   Bolton, Whitney. "*Montserrat,* Not Quite Perfect." *New York Morning Telegraph* 1 Nov. 1949: 4..

Criticizes the lack of direction.

R177   Brown, John Mason. "Seeing Things: With and Without Music." *Saturday Review of Literature* 32 (19 Nov. 1949): 53-35.

Review of *Montserrat*. The play is "so repetitious and such a static bore that one can hardly wait to have its victims shot" (53). The good people have no reality. As such they command neither interest nor sympathy. And Hellman's direction is of little help. Izquierdo's ruthless evocation of evil brings the Hubbards to mind.

R178   Chapman, John. "A Brutal Melodrama." *New York Daily News* 31 Oct. 1949. In
        New York Theatre Critics' Reviews, 1949. 244.
                Review of *Montserrat*. Applauds the play's "guts and drive." A formula
        play, it brings the characters to crisis and tests them in Act I, tests them again in
        Act II, but in greater detail and with horror and pity.

R179   Clurman, Harold. "Robles, Hellman, Blitzstein." *New Republic* 121 (5 Dec.
        1949): 21-22.
                Review of *Montserrat*. Hellman wrongly thinks that words intelligibly
        conveyed are all it takes to write a play. She has attempted to make a
        revolutionary document out of a play that is primarily concerned with moral
        issues. Criticizes the direction and the casting.

R180   Coleman, Robert. "*Montserrat* Well Acted But Script Is Bumpy." *New York
        Daily News* 30 Oct. 1949. In New York Theatre Critics' Reviews, 1949. 246.
                This could have been a moving and absorbing play, but it comes across
        too much as melodrama.

R181   Garland, Robert. "Grim." *New York Journal American* 31 Oct. 1949. In New
        York Theatre Critics' Reviews, 1949. 246.
                Review of *Montserrat*. Hellman lets Robles down both in the adaptation
        and in her direction of the play, but the production is still fascinating.

R182   Gassner, John. "The Theatre Arts." *Forum* 112 (Dec. 1949): 337-39.
                Review of *Montserrat*. Identifies flaws in the direction and the writing;
        and finds the effect too repetitive.

R183   Gibbs, Wolcott. "The End of the Means." *New Yorker* 25 (5 Nov. 1949): 56-
        57.
                Review of *Montserrat* . The play interminably repetitive, occasionally
        eloquent.

R184   Hawkins, William. "*Montserrat* Hits Like *Quake*." *New York World-Telegram*
        31 Oct. 1949. In New York Theatre Critics' Reviews, 1949. 245.
                A shattering play, it escapes sensationalism by the suffering tension of
        Hellman's direction.

R185   Marshall, Margaret. "Drama." *Nation* 169 (12 Nov. 1949): 478.
                Review of *Montserrat*. While the source itself is contrived and dated, "the
        adaptation shows the hand of an experienced and skillful worker in the theater."

R186   Morehouse, Ward. "*Montserrat* Disappoints." *New York Sun* 31 Oct. 1949. In
        New York Theatre Critics' Reviews, 1949. 245.
                The violence of the executions takes on a repetitious pattern. For all of its
        excitement, the play is monotonous.

R187   "Moscow Acclaims a Hellman Play." *New York Times* 18 Oct. 1949: I, 34.
                Review of *Another Part of the Forest*, retitled *Ladies and Gentlemen*
        (Moscow Drama Theatre). Reports of a five-hour performance which drew
        twelve curtain calls.

R188   "Moscow Likes Hellman Play." *New York Times* 17 Oct. 1949: I, 19.
        Review of *Another Part of the Forest*, retitled *Ladies and Gentlemen* (Moscow Drama Theatre). Reports of a "packed house."

R189   Nathan, George Jean. "Still Another Stage Battling for Freedom." *New York Journal American* 7 Nov. 1949: 24. Reprinted in *The Theatre Book of the Year 1949-50*. New York: Alfred A. Knopf, 1950. 63-71.
        Review of *Montserrat*. The theme is "altogether too familiar to stimulate the curiosity of audiences."

R190   "New Play in Manhattan: *Montserrat*." *Time* 55 (7 Nov. 1949): 79-80.
        Observes a talkative melodrama, often tense, written with sharpness and bite, especially the characterization of the villain. The play lacks the simple intensity of heroic drama.

R191   "New Plays: *Montserrat*." *Newsweek* 34 (7 Nov. 1949): 80-81.
        Suggests that the faults are inherent in the original play. The first act is given to talk and melodramatic devices; the second act is given to repetitive situations. "*Monsterrat* generates an outward excitement that rarely penetrates to the emotions" (81).

R192   Phelan, Kappo. "The Stage & Screen: *Montserrat*." *Commonweal* 51 (18 Nov. 1949): 179-80.
        Except for "an arpeggio of anguish--gestures, moans, groans, mutterings, and screams," the hero has little to say; yet the play is absorbing, and "gratitude is hereby tendered" (180). "I do not feel capable of tracing the existentialist line which unquestionably motivates the finale" (180).

R193   Shipley, Joseph T. "On Stage." *New Leader* 32 (26 Nov. 1949): 15.
        Review of *Montserrat*. After setting a superb situation in the opening scenes, the play slumps to a close. The rest is anticlimactic.

R194   "Soviet Paper Finds Hellman Play Fails." *New York Times* 13 Nov. 1949: I, 83.
        Review of *Another Part of the Forest*, retitled *Ladies and Gentlemen* (Moscow Drama Theatre). *Soviet Art* faults the play for not adequately espousing the evils of capitalism; further criticizing Hellman and the producers who insinuate the purity of the South in a play that "claims to expose the ruling circles of the United States, in the days when there is unleashed reaction in threatening to lynch one of the most advanced people of America, Paul Robeson."

R195   Watts, Richard Jr. "*Montserrat*, Tragic Play." *New York Post* 31 Oct. 1949. In New York Theatre Critics' Reviews, 1949. 247.
        The horror of the victims is monotonous. The play is provocative and thoughtful, but rarely deeply moving.

R196   Wyatt, Euphemia Van Rensselaer. "Theater." *Catholic World* 170 (Dec. 1949): 227-28.
        Review of *Montserrat*. Robles presents six diverse reactions to sudden death with meticulous enjoyment; but, even with Hellman's help, the play lacks structural strength.

1950

R197   Beyer, William. "Reports: The State of the Theatre: The Strindberg Heritage."
         School and Society 81 (14 Jan. 1950): 25-26.
                 Review of *Montserrat*. The situation is tense with dramatic implications,
         but the unfolding is static and flatly intellectual rather than emotionally
         compelling. Isquierdo is diabolically complex. Montserrat weakly drawn, and not
         enough attention is given to him or the revolutionary cause. Acknowledges that
         the play is difficult to stage; criticizes the direction and the "adequate"
         performances.

R198   "Entertainment: New Bolton's Theatre: *The Children's Hour* by Lillian Hellman."
         London Times 22 Nov. 1950: 10.
                 Comments on the contrivances, the forced probabilities.

R199   "The New Plays: *Montserrat*." *Theatre Arts* 34 (Jan. 1950): 10.
                 Williams plays the ruthless Isquierdo with such chilly skill that his
         adversary, Montserrat, is made "futile milksop." With the situation so unfairly
         weighted, there is little relevance to the moral dilemma.

1951

R200   Atkinson, Brooks. "Lillian Hellman Dramatizes Middle-Aged People in *The
         Autumn Garden*." *New York Times* 8 Mar. 1951. In New York Theatre Critics'
         Reviews, 1951. 326.
                 Hellman usually "controls her plays absolutely. This time she has let the
         characters take charge of their own affairs." The Chekhovian mood puts her at the
         peak of her talents; yet the play is "boneless and torpid," as are "the characters
         whom it admirably describes."

R201   Beaufort, John. "*The Autumn Garden*." *Christian Science Monitor* 17 Mar. 1951:
         6.
                 Notes pungent dialogue and sharp characterizations, yet obscure
         motivations and confusing issues. The play is "an unfairly slanted representation
         of American life. If produced abroad, it may handily serve the Kremlin's
         determined campaign to convince Europe that life in the United States is
         preponderantly decadent."

R202   Brown, John M. "Seeing Things: A New Miss Hellman." *Saturday Review of
         Literature* 34 (31 Mar. 1951): 27-29. Reprinted in *Contemporary Drama: Thirteen
         Plays, American, English, European*. Ed. Stanley A. Clayes and David G.
         Spencer. New York: Charles Scribner's Sons, 1962. 380-82.
                 Review of *The Autumn Garden*. Hellman has shifted from outward
         climaxes to inward crises and to a new form of playwriting that she has not quite
         mastered. While there are too many characters, all are shrewdly observed; and in
         spite of its faults, the play is mature and rewarding, one of the season's best. The
         play has the density of a novel.

R203   Chapman, John. "Hellman's *Autumn Garden* Meaty Comedy Played by Flawless
            Cast." *New York Daily News* 8 Mar. 1951. In New York Theatre Critics'
            Reviews, 1951. 327.
                 This intelligent comedy "makes the point that most people are afraid to take a
            good look at themselves, and the few who are not afraid to take the look seldom
            find anything encouraging."

R204   Clurman, Harold. "Lillian Hellman's *Garden.*" *New Republic* 124 (26 Mar.
            1951): 21-22. Reprinted in *Lies Like Truth.* New York: Macmillan Co., 1958.
            47-49.
                 Review of *The Autumn Garden.* The play is superbly constructed,
            maturely thought, the subtlest and most probing of Hellman's plays; and in its
            failure a far better play than *The Children's Hour.* "Miss Hellman refuses to be
            'metaphysical,' poetic or soft" (49) Criticizes the "astringent, almost cruel"
            approach to character.

R205   Clurman, Harold. "Miss Hellman's New Play: No Message but a Meaning."
            New York Herald Tribune 4 Mar. 1951: IV, 1, 2.
                 The Autumn Garden has no formulaic message. The treatment is
            unsentimental, the structure a garland of twining, merging plots.

R206   Coleman, Robert. "*Autumn Garden* Harps On Depressing Theme." *New York
            Daily Mirror* 8 Mar. 1951. In New York Theatre Critics' Reviews, 1951. 327.
                 Hellman states that the characters "are the sum of their small acts, that
            those who have power and cannot use it should relinquish it." But she does not
            successfully proves this dramatically through her characters. The play is "diffuse
            and not too rewarding."

R207   Darby, Eileen. "*The Autumn Garden.*" *Theatre Arts* 35 (May 1951): 18.
                 Praises the characterizations, but feels the play needs at least one
            redeeming character to leave a glimmer of hope, and more compassion in terms of
            the others.

R208   Dash, Thomas R. Rev. of *The Autumn Garden. Women's Wear Daily* 8 Mar.
            1951.
                 Finds Hellman in a more mellow, Chekhovian mood.

R209   Gassner, John. "Entropy in the Drama." *Theatre Arts* 35 (Sept. 1951): 16-17, 73.
                 Review of *The Autumn Garden* . Hellman's indictment is too general to
            be effective, the resolution too dubious.

R210   Gilder, Rosamond. "Broadway Highlights." *Drama,* New Series 22 (Autumn
            1951): 16-20.
                 The Autumn Garden is less closely knit, less forthright, and less violent
            than Hellman's previous plays.

R211   Guernsey, Otis L. "Some Leaves Are Golden." *New York Herald Tribune* 6 Mar.
            1951: 18. In New York Theatre Critics' Reviews, 1951. 326.
                 Review of *The Autumn Garden.* The separate incidents share a sameness
            in mood and outcome. Fortunately there are the stars and featured actors to
            provide individuality and color beyond the writing.

R212   Hawkins, William. "*Autumn Garden* Is Rich and Mellow." *New York World-Telegram and Sun* 8 Mar. 1951. In New York Theatre Critics' Reviews, 1951. 325.
         Finds the failures exhilarating, the play richly textured.

R213   Kerr, Walter. "The Stage: *The Autumn Garden.* "*Commonweal*   53 (6 Apr. 1951): 645.
         There are too many unrelated characters trapped in the precisely the same situation, a lack of variety or balance in their case histories. Had Hellman focused on one instead of multiples, she may have produced a tragedy. An interesting play, but not engrossing.

R214   Lardner, John. "The First Team Takes Over." *New Yorker* 27 (17 Mar. 1951): 52-54.
         Review of *The Autumn Garden*. Notes a mellowing in Hellman's attitude toward her characters, which does not interfere with the quality of the dialogue. Praises her gift for organization.

R215   Marshall, Margaret. "Drama." *Nation* 172 (17 Mar. 1951): 257.
         Review of *The Autumn Garden* . Finds the plot "unconvincing when it is most like action and boring when it is most convincing. The main interest lies in the characterizations and in the probing of relationships, and here Miss Hellman's shrewdness, competence, and ruthless humor stand in her in good stead."

R216   McClain, John. "Play at Coronet Beautifully Set." *New York Journal American* 8 Mar. 1951. In New York Theatre Critics' Reviews, 1951. 325.
         Review of *The Autumn Garden*. The writing is stimulating and assured, the characters believable. Pardons Hellman's attempt "to juggle too many emotional crises."

R217   "New Plays: *The Autumn Garden.*" *Newsweek* 37 (19 Mar. 1951): 84
         This philosophical play is written with considerably less drive and definition than previous works that have established Hellman as "one of the theater's nosiest dramatists."

R218   "The New Plays: *The Autumn Garden.*" *Theatre Arts* 35 (May 1951): 18.
         The play just misses being "truly extraordinary."

R219   "New Plays in Manhattan." *Time* 57 (19 Mar. 1951): 51.
         Review of *The Autumn Garden*. "What blurs and scatters the general effect is a need, not for more dramatic plot, but for a more incisive pattern." This Southern comedy of manners rubs elbows with Chekhov, although his characters are never allowed to face the truth.

R220   S., F. Rev. of *The Children's Hour. Theatre World* 47 (Jan. 1951): 6.
         Praises the production at the New Bolton's Theatre Club (London).

R221   Shipley, Joseph. "On Stage: Hellman Drags, Herbert Soars." *New Leader* 19 Mar. 1951.

Review of *The Autumn Garden*. The play is earnest, but boring, an "unattractive mishmash."

R222   Watts, Richard Jr. "Lillian Hellman's Latest Drama." *New York Post* 8 Mar. 1951. In New York Theatre Critics' Reviews, 1951. 326.

       The Autumn Garden is a brooding philosophical play, a deviation from the Hellman plays of the past. The characters are believable, but never tremendously interesting.

R223   Wyatt, Euphemia van Rensselaer. "Theater." *Catholic World* 173 (Apr. 1951): 67-68.

       Review of *The Autumn Garden* finds the treatment of middle-aged people resembles Pinero's *The Second Mrs. Tanqueray*.

1952

R224   Atkinson, Brooks. "At the Theatre." *New York Times* 19 Dec. 1952: 35. In New York Theatre Critics' Reviews, 1952. 152.

       Review of *The Children's Hour* revival. Notes ten minutes of excessive, anticlimactic summing up, but acknowledges that Hellman "is entitled to show that the slanderer is doomed as thoroughly as those who have been slandered." Notes broader implications, new political overtones, and a quality of contemporary significance.

R225   Atkinson, Brooks. "*Children's Hour*; Lillian Hellman's First Drama Has Lost None of Its Power or Pertinence." *New York Times* 28 Dec. 1952: II, 1.

       Taut and pertinent, the play fits today's world accurately. Suggests that the audience now has greater understanding of the destructive nature of slander.

R226   Beaufort, John. "Tragic *Children's Hour*." *Christian Science Monitor* 27 Dec. 1952: 4.

       The play remains a powerfully, perceptive study of malevolence, soundly crafted, but suffers from overemphasis. The character that suicides is too troubled from the onset. Thus her confession at the end suffers.

R227   Bolton, Whitney. "*Children's Hour* Still Taut Powerful Drama." *New York Morning Telegraph* 20 Dec. 1952: 4.

       The aging play is still crisp at the seams.

R228   Chapman, John. "Revival of *The Children's Hour*: Strong in Plot, Weak in Acting." *New York Daily News* 20 Dec. 1952: 17. In New York Theatre Critics' Reviews, 1952. 152.

       The play remains taut and vigorous, but needs stronger acting. The three adult roles are not performed to the fullest.

R229   Darlington, W.A. "London Letter." *New York Times* 11 May 1952: II, 3.

       Review of *Montserrat* (London). Finds the action monotonous.

R230   Dash, Thomas R. *"The Children's Hour,* Coronet Theatre." *Women's Wear
        Daily* 18 Dec. 1952: 32.
                Superbly acted, vividly contemporary, well-directed, the play "remains
        one of the best constructed and most meaningful plays of the modern theatre."

R231   Freedley, George. "Off Stage--And On." *New York Morning Telegraph* 26 Dec.
        1952: 2.
                Review of *The Children's Hour.* Stands up well in revival, but "the
        direction robs the play of its subtleties."

R232   Hawkins, William. *"Children' s Hour:* At 18, Still Shocks." *New York World-
        Telegram and Sun* 19 Dec. 1952: 19. In New York Theatre Critics' Reviews,
        1952. 152.
                The characters·are individually and collectively believable. We've learned
        a great deal about slander, since the play was first staged.

R233   Hope-Wallace, Philip. "Last Night at the Theatre." *Manchester Guardian* 10 Apr.
        1952: 5.
                Review of *Montserrat* (London). The captain's dilemma is "perfunctorily
        stated, without variations."

R234   Lambert, J.W. "Plays in Performance." *Drama,* New Series, 26 (Autumn 1952):
        17-20.
                Review of *Monsterrat* . A brief assessment that finds the work cruel and
        unsatisfying.

R235   "The Lyric Theatre, Hammersmith, *Montserrat* by Lillian Hellman, Based on the
        French of Emmanuel Robles." *London Times* (9 Apr. 1952): 6, 10.
                The theatrical shocks are superficially dramatic, tending to lose force in
        their repetitiveness.

R236   Kerr, Walter. *"The Children's Hour."* *New York Herald Tribune* 19 Dec. 1952:
        18. In New York Theatre Critics' Reviews, 1952. 151.
                Applauds Hunter's portrayal of the "teacher who loses both her school
        and her love before justice is done." Neal's mannish interpretation tends to cloud
        the issue from the outset; and the child is too transparent a monster to be believed.
        The play "remains a remarkably shrewd and incisive melodrama, but one which
        has lost a good deal of its vitality through unsubtle, unshaded playing."

R237   McClain, John. *"The Children's Hour--*a Welcome, Though Gruesome,
        Addition." *New York Journal American* 19 Dec. 1952: 18. In New York Theatre
        Critics' Reviews, 1952. 153.
                The play is skillfully written and performed with competence. It is solidly
        professional, and remains a compelling work. The child is a master of the clever
        lie. The scene between the grandmother and the remaining teacher at the end
        "should be recommended to all writers who believe a speech should run two lines
        or not at all."

R238   "Old Play in Manhattan: *The Children's Hour."* *Time* 60 (29 Dec. 1952): 55.

Finds the revival's last act harsher and more humane. "[When] the surviving school-mistress faces an enlightened, remorseful old lady . . . the play takes on, emotionally and morally, a sense of the tragic."

R239   Rev. of *Montserrat. London Times* 9 Apr. 1952: 6d.

The Hammersmith production is criticized. This is "prolonged torture" for the sake of easy theatricality.

R240   "Theater: *The Children's Hour." Newsweek* 40 (29 Dec. 1952): 40.

Praises the production, the effective theatrical writing, and the emphasis placed on the victimized teachers.

R241   Tynan, Kenneth. "Plays." *Spectator* 188 (18 Apr. 1952): 512.

Review of *Montserrat* (London). Harshly attacks the hero's callous reserve, his portrayal as a "sympathetic and honorable idealist."

R242   Watts, Richard, Jr. "Two on the Aisle: *The Children's Hour* Scores Again." *New York Post* 19 Dec. 1952: 45.

Praises Hellman's technical skill and probing intelligence, highly-charged scenes and intense characterizations. Hunter "gives the finest performance I have seen an actress offer all season."

R243   Winchell, Walter. "*Children's Hour* Revival A Spellbinder as in '34." *New York Daily Mirror* 19 Dec. 1952. In New York Theatre Critics' Reviews, 1952. 153.

Just as powerful as it was when first presented, *The Children's Hour* is three hours of intelligent drama. "It should have won the Pulitzer medal (in 1935) but that 'distinction' went to Zoe Akins' *The Old Maid*, a flop."

1953

R244   "The Arts: The Liverpool Playhouse; *Another Part of the Forest* by Lillian Hellman." *London* Times 4 Sept. 1953: 10.

Observes a cleverly contrived melodrama, "now bordering absurdity, now toppling over." "But the Liverpool Repertory company are loyal to their author and do their best to conceal what is transpontine in her drama."

R245   Bentley, Eric. "Hellman's Indignation." *New Republic* 128 (5 Jan. 1953): 30-31. Reprinted in *The Dramatic Event: An American Chronicle.* New York: Horizon, 1953. 74-77.

Review of *The Children's Hour* revival. Finds the mingling of social and psychological themes confusing, the "red-scare" analogy the product of dubious idealism. Criticizes the direction that shares the faults of the script. "Everything on stage seems unreal, inorganic, unrelated to everything else . . . Hence, there is an absence of genuine passion not only in the individual characters but in the whole production" (31).

R246   Beyer, William H. "The State of the Theatre: First Nights." *School and Society* 77 (21 Feb. 1953): 117-18.

Review of *The Children's Hour* revival. The play "irritates by constantly straining at credulity to arrive at 'shock' scenes that sustain purely theatrical suspense rather than create psychological tensions" (118). Hellman's direction propels the melodramatic rather than evoking "the psychologically characterful" (118).

R247   Gassner, John. "Broadway in Review." *Educational Theater Journal* 5 (Mar. 1953): 18-19.
Review of *The Children's Hour* revival. Finds the play more poignantly immediate, given the times. "The highlights of the drama may be Miss Hellman's, but its organization is nearly all Pinero's--entailing some labored exposition and plot contrivance" (19). A powerful play, though not a masterpiece. Regrets Hellman's decision to direct.

R248   Gibbs, Wolcott. "The Theatre: No Pause." *New Yorker* 28 (3 Jan. 1953): 30.
Review of *The Children's Hour* revival. Credits Hellman with "one of the most honest, perceptive, and distinguished plays of our time."

R249   Hayes, Richard. *"The Children's Hour."* *Commonweal* 62 (16 Jan. 1953): 377.
Applauds the exhilarating theatricality of the piece, the "imaginative boldness which has carried Miss Hellman past the failures of realism to a secure and irreproachable ground."

R250   Hewes, Henry. "Broadway Postscripts: Between the Dark & the Dark, Dark Darkness." *Saturday Review* 36 (10 Jan. 1953): 30.
Review of *The Children's Hour*. The current revival might be better titled "The McCarthyites' Hour." The play seems less concerned with the accusers than the credence given them, and is best in the second act where the child spins her web, and worst in the third act "when the most interesting character has dropped out, where the dialogue is unable to rise to any poetic intensity, and where the characters seem to act . . . simply out of the needs of the plot." The improbabilities ring dramatically false and mark the play as old-fashioned melodrama. Harshly criticizes the direction as well.

R251   Marshall, Margaret. "Drama." *Nation* 176 (3 Jan. 1953): 18-19.
Review of *The Children's Hour* revival. The work is fascinatingly written, as a case study of a monstrous child; but it is not genuinely convincing, nor is it moving. The grownups and the child's friend, Rosalie, are all "too perfectly, too predictably, suited to the monster's purposes" (19).

R252   Nathan, George Jean. "Gossip Column." *New York Journal American* 11 Jan. 1953: 20. Reprinted in *The Theatre in the Fifties*. New York: Alfred A. Knopf, 1953: 49-52.
The Children's Hour is an intelligent melodrama. The subject matter has been tastefully handled with restraint. In other hands, it could have been cheap sensationalism. The child's whispered accusations reveal a lack of courage on the playwright's part.

R253   Rev. of *Another Part of the Forest*. *London Times* 4 Sept. 1953: 10a.

The Liverpool Repertory production "runs an ingeniously contrived course . . . brilliantly skirting the edge of absurdity."

R254   "Theater." *Life* 34 (19 Jan. 1953): 51, 54.

The Children's Hour is exceedingly melodramatic, the lesbian issues no longer shocking; yet the character assassination issue remains "timeless and valid."

R255   Wyatt, Euphemia van Rensselaer. "Theatre: *The Children's Hour.*" *Catholic World* 176 (Feb. 1953): 388.

Notes a lack of spiritual development in Karen; faults the dark frustration, the futility of the ending.

1954

R256   Shanley, John. "Theatre: *Montserrat*: Lillian Hellman Drama at Barbizon Plaza." *New York Times* 26 May 1954: 34.

Review of the *Montserrat* revival. The passage of time and the transfer to a more intimate setting have not improved the work.

1955

R257   Atkinson, Brooks. "Theatre: St. Joan With Radiance." *New York Times* 18 Nov. 1955. In New York Theatre Critics' Review, 1955. 206.

Review of *The Lark*. Praises Hellman's skillful adaptation; Harris's finest, most touching performance.

R258   Bentley, Eric. "Theatre." *New Republic* 133 (5 Dec. 1955): 21.

Review of *The Lark*. Discusses the last scene in which Hellman inserts a speech of her own, and the slashing of the inquisitor's speeches, which change Anouilh's intent. Praises the Broadway production and Harris who "is able to say more with her body than one would have believed possible in so very verbal a play."

R259   Chapman, John. Rev. of *The Lark*. *New York Daily News*. 18 Nov. 1955. In New York Theatre Critics' Review, 1955. 208.

The Lark is a "beautiful, beautiful play." Two viewpoints, Joan as a "piece of history" and Joan's own accounting of her life, are deftly portrayed. Harris's performance is electrifying, and "I am still shaken by it."

R260   Coleman, Robert. "*The Lark* Proves Spell-Binding, Witty." *New York Daily Mirror* 18 Nov. 1955. In New York Theatre Critics' Review, 1955. 207.

The play has flashing wit, emotional impact, and the power to make you think and feel.

R261   Cotes, Peter. "A Golden Age. *Plays and Players* 2 (Feb.) 1955: 5.

The Lark is "a masterpiece."

R262   Dash, Thomas. R. Rev. of *The Lark*. *Women's Wear Daily* 18 Nov. 1955.

The play "has verbal sinew, intellectual pitch and integrity."

R263   Gibbs, Wolcott." "The Theatre." *New Yorker* 31 (3 Dec. 1955): 112-13.
            Review of *The Lark*. Discusses the narrative techniques. As in Anouilh,
            "Joan is a much less romantic figure than Shaw's eloquent mystic, but she is
            extremely effective at getting men to give her what she wants" (113).

R264   Hatch, Robert. "Theater and Films." *Nation* 181 (3 Dec. 1955): 485-86.
            The Lark is a clever and deeply-felt work of theatre which presents Joan
            with pride and love, almost playfully as a sprite, yet her presence is intangible.
            "Our hearts go out to youth and innocence, but they do not go out to Peter Pan,
            except when we are young ourselves. There is something complacent about the
            ever-ever child" (486). A splendid evening in the theatre which remains in the
            theatre, as we depart "in a mood of cheerful sentimentality that is not right for
            Joan's victory in martyrdom" (486).

R265   Hawkins, William. "Julie Harris Captures Inner Beauty of Joan. *New York
            World-Telegram and Sun* 18 Nov. 1955. In New York Theatre Critics' Review,
            1955. 207.
            The Lark is a crisp and shining new version of the Joan of Arc story.

R266   Hayes, Richard. "*The Lark*." *Commonweal* 63 (23 Dec. 1955): 304-5.
            Review of *The Lark*. Applauds Harris's performance, but calls the play "a
            genteel muddle."

R267   "A Joan with Gumption." *Newsweek* 46 (28 Nov. 1955): 110.
            Review of *The Lark*. Hellman's heroine is "a crop-haired, sensible little
            warrior . . . less a press-agent symbol than an exalted gamin who understands the
            weakness of the men she inspires." The talented Harris permeates the whole
            show.

R268   Kerr, Walter F. "Theater: *The Lark*." *New York Herald Tribune* 18 Nov. 1955.
            In New York Theatre Critics' Review, 1955. 206.
            A stimulating night at the theatre, despite the extraneous philosophical
            gesture in the second act that attempts to see the Maid as "the natural man."
            Praises Harris's talent.

R269   McClain, John. "Julie Depicts a Vital Joan." *New York Journal American* 18
            Nov. 1955. In New York Theatre Critics' Review, 1955. 208.
            Praises the "tremendously vital and moving" adaptation, Hellman's "lofty
            speeches and towering phrases." The flashback technique supplies suitable action
            without confusing the story line. Calls attention to Harris's "fragile and beguiling
            sincerity."

R270   Shipley, Joseph T. "On Stage: Four Plays That Press Too Hard." *New Leader* 38
            (5 Dec. 1955): 19.
            Review of *The Lark*. "Anouilh is usually fanciful and poetic; this version
            is heavy-handed and flat. Julie Harris works hard with what seems a complete
            misconception of the role." There seems no justification for the confusion of time

levels; and no sound point for the return to the coronation scene after Joan is burnt.

R271   Watts, Richard Jr. "A Stirring Play About Joan of Arc." *New York Post* 18 Nov. 1955. In New York Theatre Critics' Review, 1955. 206.
    The Lark is a beautiful, moving play. It contains a strikingly compact narrative.

1956

R272   "Arts Theatre: *The Children's Hour*, by Lillian Hellman." *London Times* 20 Sept. 1956: 5.
    Review of London production. The acting misses "in the power of its attack," slowing up the already slow play.

R273   Atkinson, Brooks. "The Theatre: *Candide*." *New York Times* (3 Dec. 1956). In New York Theatre Critics' Reviews 1956. 180.
    The eighteenth century philosophical tale is not ideal material for theatre, considering the plotlessness and the repetition.

R274   Atkinson, Brooks. "Musical *Candide*: Lillian Hellman and Leonard Bernstein Turn Voltaire Satire into Fine Play." *New York Times* (9 Dec. 1956): II, 5.
    The story has been compressed, some of Voltaire's documentation of evil omitted. Hellman has ably sketched the character of Candide; and the show itself has put the musical stage on a superior intellectual and artistic level.

R275   Chapman, John. "*Candide* an Artistic Triumph; Bernstein's Score Magnificent." *New York Daily News*. 3 Dec. 1956. In New York Theatre Critics' Reviews 1956. 176-77.
    Considers *Candide* the best light opera since Richard Strauss' *Der Rosenkavalier*; the music a work of genius.

R276   "*The Children's Hour*." *Variety* 3 Oct. 1956: 82.
    Review of London production. The "pallid" production no longer shocks, though the censor's ban remains.

R277   Coleman, Robert. "Musical *Candide* Is Distinguished Work." *New York Daily Mirror* 3 Dec. 1956. In New York Theatre Critics' Reviews 1956. 179.
    The show is not entirely successful, but it has wry humor, manner, grace, and marvelous music.

R278   Clurman, Harold. "Theatre: *Candide*." *Nation* 183 (15 Dec. 1956): 527.
    A sharp, polished, spare, Brechtian treatment might have served better. Furthermore, the artistic talent have forgotten that theatre is a collective art.

R279   Donnelly, Tom. "Best Musical News of Year Is Found in New *Candide*." *New York World-Telegram and Sun* 3 Dec. 1956. In New York Theatre Critics' Reviews 1956. 177.

This has been a tough assignment for Hellman, perhaps "an example of reach exceeding grasp, but what a reach is there!"

R280   Gibbs, Wolcott. "Voltaire Today." *New Yorker* 32 (15 Dec. 1956): 52-54.
        Review of *Candide*. "Miss Hellman's book, though perhaps a little elfin here and there, also has its humor and, of course, the high technical competence for which she has always been noticed" (52).There is something less than satire, however, and few of the characters are really very fascinating.

R281   Hayes, Richard. "The Stage: Mr. Bernstein Cultivates His Garden." *Commonweal* 45 (28 Dec. 1956): 333-34.
        Review of *Candide*. Criticizes Hellman's perversion of tone. She is recriminatory and didactic where Voltaire was passionate and disabused. She insists on will where candor and reason sufficed for him; And folly and chance have been interpreted "in the dry light of the Moral Imperative" (333).

R282   Hewes, Henry. "Broadway Postscript: 'Free Prose' and Free Fall." *Saturday Review* 34 (22 Dec. 1956): 34-35.
        Review of *Candide*. Calls the work "a beautiful bore" (34). The show has its occasional moments of theatrical effectiveness; but Voltaire's satire is missing, as is Candide's absurd gullibility. The libretto wavers. The comedy is labored. And Hellman's attitude is unclear. It seems that she sides with Martin--that we live in the worst of all possible worlds, which, of course, negatives Voltaire's intent.

R283   Hewitt, A. "*The Lark*: Theatrical Bird of Passage." *Theatre Arts* 60 (Mar. 1956): 63-64.
        Comments on the current revival of interest in the Maid. Prefers Anouilh's version to Fry's translation and Hellman's adaptation. Hellman has not hesitated to alter, transpose, shift emphasis, or cut, making her version bolder, less intellectual, and more theatrical. While form and themes are preserved, the tone is changed. There is no humor. "The intent is to tell a serious story, to simplify the crosscurrents of debate, and to appeal to the emotions" (96). Concludes that the French, English and American productions are striking examples of differences in national temperaments/personalities of the interpreters.

R284   Kerr, Walter. "Theater: *Candide*." *New York Herald Tribune* 3 Dec. 1956. In New York Theatre Critics' Reviews 1956. 179.
        Hellman's attempt at satire is academic, blunt, and barefaced. Three talents, Hellman, Bernstein, and Guthrie, have joined hands to create "a really spectacular disaster."

R285   McCarthy, Mary. "The Reform of Dr. Pangloss." *New Republic* 135 (17 Dec. 1956): 30-31.
        Review of *Candide*. Voltaire's social satire has been fizzled into the equivalent of a high school pageant play. The satire is gone. The sex is gone. "The gayety is gone; the dirt is gone; the negativism is gone" (30). One cannot blame the authors for hesitating to attack the Church, but without the daredeviltry, the project is a failure.

R286   McClain, John. "Fine, Bright--But Operetta Lacks Spark." *New York Journal American* 3 Dec. 1956. In New York Theatre Critics' Review, 1956. 178.
        Review of *Candide*. The real "deficiency might have been solved by a more exhaustive examination of the characters involved. We really don't know them." The ambitious score is also lacking.

R287   "New Musical Version of *Candide*." *London Times* 12 Dec. 1956: 5.
        The new musical version of *Candide* at the Martin Beck Theatre in New York City is an artistic success. Its distinction lies in Bernstein's brilliant score; its weakness in Hellman's surprisingly ineffective book which has lost the irony, the pungent satire, and the witty comment of Voltaire.

R288   O'Connor, Frank. "Saint Joans, From Arc to *Lark*." *Holiday* 19 (Mar. 1956): 77.
        Review of *The Lark*. "I nearly jumped out of my seat when the Inquisitor described Joan as an example of 'Natural Man.'" Hellman, it seems, has read herself into the part.

R289   O'Flaherty, Vincent J. "St. Joan Wouldn't Know Herself." *America* 95 (28 Apr. 1956): 109-11.
        Review of *The Lark*. Cites the failure of dramatists to consult history. "Living and dying, she [Joan] makes sense only as a daughter of the church and in a Catholic context."

R290   Watts, Richard, Jr. "Voltaire's *Candide* as an Operetta." *New York Post* 3 Dec. 1956. In New York Theatre Critics' Reviews 1956. 178.
        While the libretto is true to the Voltaire outline, it lacks powerful satire and dramatic effectiveness.

R291   Wyatt, Euphemia van Rensselaer. "Theater: *The Lark*." *Catholic World* 182 (Jan. 1956): 308-309.
        Observes "a far less voluble version in clean, crisp English without a trace of Gallicism" (308). As in the Anouilh version, Joan is portrayed as a child, denounced for her love of Man, identified with the "Natural Man." Her vacillation, weighing old age with heroic death, is completely out of character.

1957

R292   "*Candide*." *Theatre Arts* 41 (Feb. 1957): 17-18.
        This has been a tough assignment for Hellman. She has "lost a good deal of the bite--if not the essential spirit of the original" (18). Despite the travelogue, the libretto grows fairly static by Act II.

R293   Driver, Tom F. "On the Run: Drama." *Christian Century* 124 (6 Feb. 1957): 171-72.
        Candide fails as a piece of theatre, because the book requires the hero to travel in too many episodes to find his final truth.

R294   Gassner, John. "Broadway in Review." *Educational Theatre Journal* 9 (Mar. 1957): 42-43.
        Review of *Candide*. Contributes nothing to the mixed reactions, merely commenting that "we are somehow moving toward some *modus vivendi* in America between the art of theatre and the art of opera" (43).

R295   Kolodin, Irving. "Candied *Candide*." *Saturday Review* 40 (23 Feb. 1957): 49.
        A review of the Columbia OL 5180 recording excludes comment on the dramatic values. Finds the score, aside from the clever, busy overture, "deficient in melodic content, padded out by formula instead of creative impulse, constantly trying to live beyond its musical means."

R296   Mannes, Marya. "Views and Reviews." *Reporter* 16 (24 Jan. 1957): 35.
        Review of *Candide*. The show has definite faults, "but it has the best new music and the wittiest lyrics and the handsomest production in town." Criticizes the lagging pace and solemn periods, especially in the first act. Finds it surprising that Hellman has blunted the satire.

R297   Wyatt, Euphemia van Rensselaer. "Theater: *Candide*." *Catholic World* 184 (Feb. 1957): 384-85.
        The decor and the musical score are the most important contributions. Despite Hellman's skill and enthusiasm, the adaptation has lost its sting.

1960

R298   Ashton, Frank. "*Toys in Attic* Takes Apart Lives of Five." *New York World-Telegram and Sun* 26. Feb. 1960. In New York Theatre Critics' Reviews 1960. 345.
        With heartless accuracy and subtle pity, *Toys in the Attic* seems to be Hellman's most hellishly hypnotic play.

R299   Atkinson, Brooks. "Theatre: Hellman's Play." *New York Times* 26 Feb. 1960. In New York Theatre Critics' Reviews 1960. 347.
        Not the greatest play in the world, *Toys in the Attic* is still "head and shoulders above the level of the season."

R300   Bohle, Bruce. "The Openings: *Toys in the Attic*." *Theatre Arts* 44 (May 1960): 57-58.
        The characters need definition, and the storyline needs to be tightened. Still, Hellman "bring[s] a dramatic situation to a boil, and there is no questioning her unrelenting integrity" (57). The strong cast carries the play.

R301   Brustein, Robert. "The Play and the Unplay." *New Republic* 142 (14 Mar. 1960): 22-23.
        Review of *Toys in the Attic*. Despite the perfect form, and despite the intelligence and the quiet dignity of the piece that is rare on Broadway, the play is only moderately interesting. The action is too contrived, and the characters, other than the Southern mother, "do not have much life beyond their dramatic function"

(22-23). Calls Hellman a "playwright in the true Ibsenite tradition" (23), yet finds the play "too corseted a work to let its author breathe the free inspired air" (23).

R302   Chapman, John. "Miss Hellman's *Toys in the Attic* Vigorous and Absorbing Drama." *New York Daily News* 26 Feb. 1960. In New York Theatre Critics' Reviews 1960. 348.
        The brilliant portrayal of characters offers much to remember.

R303   Clurman, Harold. "Theatre." *Nation* 140 (19 Mar. 1960): 261-62.
        Review of *Toys in the Attic*. The theme of self-deception is "related to the one more fully (and convincingly) stated in *The Autumn Garden*" (261). Faults confused narrative structure, jumbled themes, and irrelevant melodramatic "turns of plot, implausibilities and jabs of lurid violence" (261). Praises the dialogue, the "combination of selective realism and subtly rhetorical phrasing" (261).

R304   Coleman, Robert. "*Toys in the Attic* Sure-Fire Hit." *New York Mirror* 26 Feb. 1960. In New York Theatre Critics' Reviews 1960. 346.
        The characters are attention grippers, complete and absorbing in their portrayals. The dialogue "crackles and probes." Ends his rare review with a rush to the box office notice to his readers.

R305   Driver, Tom F. "Puppet Show." *Christian Century* 77 (27 Apr. 1960): 511-12.
        Review of *Toys in the Attic*. The social themes (greed for money, racial equality) are not developed; and the characters are not believable. Except for the chauffeur and the mother-in-law, all of the characters are "very mixed up or very mean or both" (511). Stapleton and Revere are miscast; but the direction is "very skillful" (512).

R306   "English Finesse in an American Play." *London Times* 11 Nov. 1960: 16.
        Review of *Toys in the Attic* (London). Finds Hellman's approach to character too clinical: "we ought perhaps to be more deeply moved by their frustrations than we are in fact." Praises the intensely American play that perhaps requires American actors, yet compliments the British players who leave no doubt as to the author's intentions.

R307   "First Nights: Broadway Comes Alive." *Newsweek* 55 (7 Mar. 1960): 89.
        Review of *Toys in the Attic*. Praises taut writing and acute characterizations. "Not at all pretty, but pretty wonderful."

R308   Gassner, John. "Broadway in Review, *Toys in the Attic*." *Educational Theatre Journal* 12 (May 1960): 113-15. Also in Dramatic Sounding: Evaluations and Retractions Culled from 30 Years of Dramatic Criticism. New York: Crown Publishers, 1968. 481-84.
        "Among her earlier works only *The Little Foxes*, her masterpiece of the strenuous Thirties, possesses as much penetration and dramatic vitality; and rarely before has Miss Hellman written dialogue with such vigor and virtuosity" (113). Even the faults, as the slow, meandering first act, contribute to the powerful effect. A mordant rather than a morbid drama.

R309   Hayes, Richard. "The Stage: Forecast." *Commonweal* 71 (18 Mar. 1960): 677.

Review of *Toys in the Attic*. The play "extends the rectitude and intransigence of Miss Lillian Hellman's later method into something very like spiritual fantasy, overdeveloped undeniably, but suggesting, if not the flush of life, an intimation of its pressure and the insistent toll of its past."

R310   Hewes, Henry. "Broadway Postscript: Love in the Icebox." *Saturday Review* 43 (2 Mar. 1960): 71-72.
Review of *Toys in the Attic*. The play gives us another glimpse of Hellman's "tough, naked attitudes and literate dialogue" (72). There is a touch of Brecht in Julian's discovery of the true nature of Carrie's love for him. A difficult play to direct, Penn has avoided the Chekhovian stillness and kept the action moving.

R311   Kerr, Walter. "First Night Report: *Toys in the Attic*." *New York Herald Tribune* 26 Feb. 1960: 12. In New York Theatre Critics' Reviews 1960. 348.
For all the aridity, "there is the splendor of straight-forward, uncompromised writing."

R312   Kerr, Walter. "Theater: *Toys in the Attic*: Lillian Hellman Whets the Knife of Language." *New York Herald Tribune* 6 Mar. 1960: IV, 1, 3.
Praises the lucidity and control and language that has been painstakingly whetted to a cutting-edge; and finds the play as powerful as *The Little Foxes*.

R313   Mannes, Marya. "Miss Hellman's *Electra*." *Reporter* 22 (31 Mar. 1960): 43.
Review of *Toys in the Attic*. Praises the well-rounded characters, composed of remembered realities, as those of Tennessee Williams. Hellman's characters, however, are devoid of gratuitous shock or sensation. She has done nothing for effect alone, "although she well knows how."

R314   McClain, John. "Top Writing--Top Acting." *New York Journal American* 26 Feb. 1960. In New York Theatre Critics' Reviews 1960. 346.
Review of *Toys in the Attic*. Complains of being tired of plays about decadent Southern families, yet thinks the play is not to be dismissed. The work is solidly constructed, brilliantly cast, and acted. But wonders why all of the characters have to be so perverse.

R315   Shipley, Joseph T. "On Stage: James Thurber's Empty Carnival and Hellman's Crowded Attic." *New Leader* 43 (21 Mar. 1960): 21.
Review of *Toys in the Attic*. There is little emotional depth in the "play's piled situations which individually might be exciting but which cumulatively remind one of an acrobat trying to balance six chairs on top of one another." This is really three plays in one.

R316   "The Theatre: New Plays on Broadway." *Time* 75 (7 Mar. 1960): 50
Review of *Toys in the Attic*. "Playwright Hellman's old mordant power is in evidence again and again, but *Toys* combines it with a broadened sense of humanity. She is more probing and wideranging about character." Praises the taut structure, the power and insight of the piece; faults manipulated action and talky beginning.

R317   Trewin, J.C. "The World of the Theatre: Deep Down." *Illustrated London News* 237 (26 Nov. 1960): 964.

Review of *Toys in the Attic* at the Piccadilly (London). Hellman's discussion of various types of love and possessiveness turns disturbingly to "a parody of the sultrier Deep South drama. At the extreme end of the third act the play appears for a moment to right itself; by then it is time to go home." The play is overcharged with theatrics. May have worked better in a smaller house.

R318   Tynan, Kenneth. "The Theatre: Deaths and Entrances." *New Yorker* 36 (5 Mar. 1960): 124-25.

Review of *Toys in the Attic*. Criticizes the shift in focus from an inquiry into the moral consequences of wealth to a "treatise on abnormal psychology"(124). Compares the play favorably to Tennessee Williams.

R319   Watts, Richard, Jr. "Lillian Hellman's Striking Drama." *New York Post* 26 Feb. 1960. In New York Theatre Critics' Reviews 1960. 347.

Review of *Toys in the Attic*. Compares Hellman to Tennessee Williams in her portrayal of Southern decadence. Hellman is more devious, complex, and subtle in her methods, "sneaking up on the playgoer to twist his emotions into troubled shreds."

R320   Watts, Richard, Jr. "That 'Shabby Season' in Perspective." *Theatre Arts* 44 (July 1960): 13, 16, 63.

Review of *Toys in the Attic*. Bears a superficial resemblance to Tennessee Williams, yet the play is in no way imitative. Hellman's straightforward plotting and writing is "realistic, dramatic and distinguished" (16).

1961

R321   Balliett, Whitney. "Off Broadway: Martyrs and Misery." *New Yorker* 36 (21 Jan. 1961): 68-70.

Review of *Montserrat* revival at the Gate Theatre (New York City). This "Gallic seminar on morality" has too much talk, too little action.

R322   Lambert, J. W. "Plays in Performance." *Drama*, New Series, no. 60 (Spring 1961): 20-26.

Review of *Toys in the Attic* at the Piccadilly Theatre (London). This is simply a bad play. Very powerful acting might have given the play theatrical validity.

R323   Lewis, Theophilus. "Theatre." *America* 104 (28 Jan. 1961): 577.

Review of *Montserrat* revival at the Gate Theatre (New York City). Hellman's adaptation is "an intellectual horror play." The acting is better than in the original Broadway production.

R324   Taubman, Howard. "Theatre: *Montserrat*." *New York Times* (9 Jan. 1961): I, 30.

Review of *Montserrat* revival at the Gate Theatre (New York City). "In its tight plotting and sharp thrust of characterization *Montserrat* bears the stamp of Miss Hellman's craftsmanship. It also carries the fervor of her hatred for injustice and her belief in man's right to shape his own destiny." The play "deserves a rehearing."

1963

R325   Chapman, John. Review of *My Mother, My Father and Me*. *New York Daily News* 22 Mar. 1963. In New York Theatre Critics' Reviews, 1963. 304.
         The script is too free-wheeling; it lacks focus.

R326   Clurman, Harold. "Theatre." *Nation* 196 (20 Apr. 1963): 334.
         Review of *My Mother, My Father and Me*. Criticizes the direction which fails to capture "the needed abandon or ferocity of imagination." Regrets his lack of praise, "for despite everything I was 'on its side.'"

R327   Coleman, Robert. "Lillian Hellman Play Is Depressing Farce." *New York Mirror* 1 Apr. 1963. In New York Theatre Critics' Reviews, 1963. 303.
         Review of *My Mother, My Father and Me*. The fun deteriorates rapidly into a "tasteless, far-fetched and often depressing farce."

R328   "Family of Gargoyles." *Newsweek* 61 (8 Apr. 1963): 85.
         Review of *My Mother, My Father and Me*. Starts out as farce and ends up Theatre of the Absurd. Lacks contour and climax, but has "vivacity, daring, and a three-ply thread of irony."

R329   Gottfried, Martin. Review of *My Mother, My Father and Me*. *Women's Wear Daily* 25 Mar. 1963.
         A foolhardy attempt at comedy by a playwright who has "no sense of humor."

R330   Hewes, Henry. "Last Laughs and Last Tapes." *Saturday Review of Literature* 46 (27 Apr. 1963): 27.
         My Mother, My Father and Me moves desperately from one situation to another in its attempts to target the middle class. There are outrageously funny moments which accurately capture the monstrous insanity that we substitute for purposeful action, but the cumulative effects are "an unpleasantness and unconcern grimly suffered by the audience to no apparent dramatic purpose."

R331   Kerr, Walter. Rev. of *My Mother, My Father and Me*. *New York Herald Tribune* 22 Mar. 1963. In New York Theatre Critics' Reviews, 1963. 303.
         Faults the tone, which is "indeterminate, vacillating, uncommitted."

R332   Mannes, Marya. "The Half-World of American Drama." *Reporter* 27 (25 Apr. 1963): 48-50.
         My Mother, My Father and Me lacks the sparseness and structural clarity of Hellman's earlier plays. Often comic, it contains too many targets--"Jews, Negroes, white liberals, psychiatrists, beatniks, nursing homes, folk singers, and of course, mother-loves-son and wife-loathes-husband, and amply reciprocal conditions" (49).

R333   McCarten, John. "The Theatre: Domestic and Foreign." *New Yorker* 29 (30 Mar. 1963): 108.

   Review of *My Mother, My Father and Me*. Domestic comedy is not Hellman's forte. "While some of the observations are amusing, the work as a whole is disjointed and at times both incoherent and vulgar."

R334   McClain, John. Rev. of *My Mother, My Father and Me*. *New York Journal American* 2 Mar. 1963. In New York Theatre Critics' Reviews, 1963. 303.

   Predicts success with the "wild and utterly outlandish romp which kids the britches off the U.S. Establishment."

R335   Nadel, Norman. "*My Mother, My Father and Me*." *New York World-Telegram and Sun* 22 Mar, 1963. In New York Theatre Critics' Reviews, 1963. 302.

   Regards this as one of the sorriest plays of the season, and wonders how "someone of her established merit" went wrong.

R336   Oppenheimer, George. "I Dismember Mama." *Newsday* 27 Mar. 1963.

   My Mother, My Father and Me is a strange "mixture of the abstract and representational."

R337   Pryce-Jones, Alan. "*My Mother, My Father and Me*." *Theatre Arts* 47 (May 1963): 69-70.

   Some of the sketches are funny, but Hellman cannot write comedy. "The play is cut into a number of short scenes, some of them hardly more that revue sketches. Their weakness is that they do not represent any credible family of period (70). The original book from which the play is adapted is savagely amusing; most of the venom is lost in "this newest attack on Momism" (70).

R338   Taubman, Howard. "*My Mother, My Father and Me*." *New York Times* 22 Mar. 1963. In New York Theatre Critics' Reviews, 1963. 302.

   The play is a "sardonic hymn to hate," neither conventionally engaging nor charming." It is too preoccupied with speaking "furious truths."

R339   "The Theatre: Gathering Toadstools." *Time* (5 Apr. 1963): 63.

   Review of *My Mother, My Father and Me*. "As a satirist, Lillian Hellman can be cuttingly observant despite the familiarity of her targets, but she lacks the moral suasion of satire that comes from being half in love with what one loathes, cherishing the sinner while hating the sin." In this catalogue of latter-day evils she manages only "to turn bile into bilgewater."

R340   Watts, Richard, Jr. "Two on the Aisle: Angry Comedy by Lillian Hellman." *New York Post*. 25 Mar. 1963. In New York Theatre Critics' Reviews, 1963. 304.

   Review of *My Mother, My Father and Me*. Finds it interesting to see Hellman using methods of the avant-garde, yet misses the hard-driving efficiency of her earlier works.

1967

R341   Barnes, Clive. "Theatre: Return of *The Little Foxes*." *New York Times* 27 Oct. 1967: 53. In New York Theatre Critics' Reviews, 1967. 238.

The play is a well-turned, machine-made drama, that thrives on evil, "a superlative vehicle for the actors." Nichols has directed the work as if it were a film.

R342   Bolton, Whitney. "Revival: Lillian Hellman's *The Little Foxes*." *New York Morning Telegraph* 28 1967: 3.
        The show retains its original power.

R343   Chapman, John. "Lincoln Center Rep Revival of *The Little Foxes* a Humdinger." *New York Daily News* 27 Oct. 1967: 70. In New York Theatre Critics' Reviews, 1967. 239.
        The melodrama has been directed with flair by Nichols, and seems more "intensely interesting now." Praises the acting, especially the performance by Leighton.

R344   Cooke, Richard P. "The Theatre: A Well-Acted Revival." *Wall Street Journal* 30 Oct. 1967: 18.
        Review of *The Little Foxes*. Hellman's knowledge of character is sure. The play benefits from the casting.

R345   Gottfried, Martin. "Theatre: *The Little Foxes*." *Women's Wear Daily* 27 Oct. 1967: 84. In New York Theatre Critics' Reviews, 1967. 239.
        Finds little merit in the "absurdly naturalistic" play which relies heavily on "opportunistic materialism in the Old South." The play fails the test of a classic. Leighton was splendid as Birdie, "a startling precursor of William's' Blanche DuBois."

R346   "Greedy Lot." *Time* 90 (3 Nov. 1967) 64, 69.
        The Little Foxes remains stage-sturdy and retains its power to please. "A 1939 audience would have understood the play as an attack on predatory capitalist morality. A 1967 audience is more likely to relish it as an indictment of greed, hate, and the lust for power at any time, in any place" (69).

R347   Hardwick, Elizabeth. "*The Little Foxes* Revived" *New York Review of Books* 9 (21 Dec. 1967): 4-5.
        The production suffers from "piety and money" (5). The spring of the action is Regina's determination to share in the new industrial prosperity by getting her dying husband to release his money for the cotton mill; yet Hellman fails to do justice to complications, revealing "much about our theatre and our left-wing popular writers of the Thirties" (4). Regina and her brothers are not typically Southern. Horace is simply a puppet in service of an idea. The servants are another deviation from probability; and the daughter is ill-equipped to repudiate the villainy of her mother.

R348   Hewes, Henry. "The Crass Menagerie." *Saturday Review* 50 (11 Nov. 1967): 26.
        Review of *The Little Foxes* revival. Shows us the "graceless behavior of a society in which the more ambitious become scoundrels and the more decent stand by and let them get away with exploiting the poor."

R349   Kerr, Walter. "We Could Have Five *Little Foxes.*" *New York Times* 5 Nov. 1967: II, 1. In New York Theatre Critics' Reviews, 1967. 237-38. Reprinted in *Thirty Plays Hath November.* New York: Simon and Schuster, 1969. 129-32.

A well-crafted melodrama, filled with cunning characters, the "level of the performance literally makes you hold your breath." Praises the play as a classic piece of Americana.

R350   Kroll, Jack. "Theater: Chasing the Fox." *Newsweek* 70 (6 Nov. 1967): 86.

The Little Foxes captures the liberalism and social concerns of the American stage of the 1930s. "Mike Nichols has directed an 'all-star cast' in a version that tries for effects rather than depth or balance, and makes an intelligently calculated play seem like an obvious-melodrama."

R351   Lewis, Theophilus. "Theatre: *The Little Foxes.*" *America* 117 (9 Dec. 1967): 723.

Ranks the play beside the works of Ibsen and Strindberg, "as distinctively American as the hotdog and as universal in impact as *Tartuffe.*"

R352   McCarten, John. "The Theatre: Low Jinks." *New Yorker* 43 (4 Nov. 1967): 162.

Review of *The Little Foxes* revival. Calls the play a mechanical melodrama, "socially on par with Faulkner's *Snopeses.*" Suggests that the director has not "supplied enough lubrication" to the clanking plot. Criticizes the thrust stage which takes away from familial intensity.

R353   Morrison, Hobe. "Show on Broadway: *The Little Foxes.*" *Variety* 1 Nov. 1967: 58.

The plays holds up after 28 years and gets the Lincoln Center season off to a fine start.

R354   Simon, John. "The Stage: Tally Ho!" *Commonweal* 87 (1 Dec. 1967): 304-05. Rprt *Uneasy Stages: A Chronicle of New York Theater 1963-73.* New York: Random House, 1975. 117-18.

Review of *The Little Foxes* revival. The Hellman play is "inferior to Chekhov, whom in its best moments it tries to resemble . . . Only when villainy snarls or smiles as it stabs does the work come to life--and then only to the second-rate life of melodrama" (304). Criticizes the playwright, the director, the acting, and the lack of ensemble playing.

R355   Watts, Richard, Jr. "Two on the Aisle--Ruthlessness of the Hubbards." *New York Post* 25 Dec. 1967: 45.

Review of *The Little Foxes* revival. The play is still powerfully absorbing.

1968

R356   Barnes, Clive. "Theatre: *The Little Foxes* Revisited, Leighton and Marshall Appear in New Roles, Geraldine Chaplin Acts with Spirit and Force." *New York Times* 6 Jan. 1968: 24.

In its transfer to Broadway's Barrymore Theatre, the play has lost some of the gusto.

R357   Weales, Gerald. "What Kind of Fool Am I?" *Reporter* 38 (11 Jan. 1968): 36.
        Considers the revival of *The Little Foxes* flagrantly overpraised, "sloppily performed and ineptly directed."

R358   Wilson, Edmund. "An Open Letter to Mike Nichols." *New York Review of Books* 9 (4 Jan. 1968): 32.
        Review of *The Little Foxes* revival. Praises Hellman's work and suggests the production might lead to an American National Theatre in which *The Little Foxes* would be a classic. The letter is written in response to Hardwick's attack (See R349).

1970

R359   Johnson, Wayne. "*Little Foxes* Superb at Rep." *Seattle Times* 23 Feb. 1970: A, 15.
        Review of *The Little Foxes* (Seattle Repertory production). The play is a "consistently engrossing, entertaining piece of theater."

R360   Stromberg, Rolf. "Acting Saves Hokey Foxes." *Seattle Post Intelligencer* 23 Feb. 1970: 5.
        Review of *The Little Foxes* (Seattle Repertory production). Finds the play dated.

1972

R361   Coe, Richard L. "Dated *Little Foxes* at ACTF." *Washington Post* 22 Apr. 1972: B, 2.
        The Little Foxes is presented at the American College Theatre Festival, and is considered a museum piece.

1975

R362   Aaron, Jules. "*The Little Foxes*." *Educational Theatre Journal* 27 (Dec. 1975): 553-54.
        Review of the University of California, San Diego, production. "The plot centers on the growing awareness of a young woman, Alexandra, of the evil surrounding her, but the script's problem remains that she is just not a very interesting character." Despite structural flaws, this is a compelling show, and the audience loved it.

1976

R363   Gussow, Mel. "Dour *Autumn Garden* at Long Wharf." *New York Times* 16 Nov. 1976: 52.

Review of New Haven production. "Hellman's incisiveness and urbanity as a playwright . . . makes one wish that she were still active in the theater."

R364   Kerr, Walter. "This *Garden* is Nearly Perfect." *New York Times* 28 Nov. 1976: D, 3, 42.

Review of Long Wharf production (New Haven). Notes changes from the original production. Sophie's blackmail no longer seems melodramatic. She is a girl of independence, wants no favors. The play emerges, at last, as Hellman's best.

1978

R365   Clurman, Harold. Rev. of *Days to Come. Nation* 25 Nov. 1978: 588.

Revived at the WPA theatre, Off-Off Broadway. The play is intelligent enough to command attention. It is about the strike for the first two acts, though Hellman insists that this is not her main concern. The plot "does not wholly convey its intended meaning or creative impulse" (588).

R366   Fox, Terry Curtis. "Early Work." *Village Voice* 6 Nov. 1978: 127, 129.

Review of *Days to Come,* Off Off Broadway revival. The family structure resembles the one later perfected in *The Little Foxes.*

1979

R367   Gussow, Mel. "*Watch on the Rhine* Revived." *New York Times* 16 Oct. 1979: C, 20.

The play has more staying power than most antiwar plays. Sara resembles "the fictional representative of the author's friend, Julia."

1981

R368   Barnes, Clive. "Liz' Glamour Brings Glitter to *Little Foxes*." *New York Post* 8 May 1981. In New York Theatre Critics' Reviews, 1981. 232.

Review of Broadway revival. Hellman's "boulevard melodrama" has never been a great play. "Something has been made of nothing--but the something is presence, and the nothing is brightly colored tinsel." Taylor is more of a trouper than an actress. Pendleton has staged the play with considerable finesse.

R369   Beaufort, John. "Elizabeth Taylor Effective in Lillian Hellman's *Little Foxes*." *Christian Science Monitor* 8 May 1981. In New York Theatre Critics' Reviews, 1981. 233.

Review of Broadway revival. With Elizabeth Taylor starring, the production "luxuriates in a kind of timeless grandeur well suited to Lillian Hellman's 1939 play." This old-fashioned melodrama is treated in obvious terms. A financial success (sold out for its 10-week run), the production's artistic merits are questionable.

R370   Cunningham, Dennis. "*The Little Foxes.*" WCBS-TV2 (7 May 1981). In New
            York Theatre Critics' Reviews, 1981. 234.
                     Review of 1981 Broadway revival. Taylor performs in a first class
            production of a classic of the American realistic theatre. Stapleton is mentioned
            for her "astonishing" supporting role.

R371   Kalem, T.E. "The Theater: Plunders in Magnolia Land." *Time* 19 May, 1981. In
            New York Theatre Critics' Reviews, 1981. 231.
                     Review of *The Little Foxes* 1981 Broadway revival. Taylor displays more
            confidence than craft. The audience is more interested in her than in the play.
            Without diminishing her performance, Stapleton takes top honors.

R372   Kissel, Howard. "*The Little Foxes.*" *Women's Wear Daily* 8 May 1981. In New
            York Theatre Critics' Reviews, 1981. 229-30.
                     Review of the 1981 Broadway revival. The production plods along,
            veering between melodrama and soap opera, partly because of the ineffectual
            direction. This is a shallow play. There is no character revelation, and the cast is
            disappointing.

R373   Kroll, Jack. "Elizabeth Taylor in the Fox's Den." *Newsweek* 18 May 1981. In
            New York Theatre Critics' Reviews, 1981. 231-32.
                     Review of the 1981 Broadway revival of *The Little Foxes*. Taylor's
            performance relies on personality rather than style. She lacks Bankhead's gothic
            force, Davis's magnolia quality. Criticizes the direction, designed "possibly to
            help Taylor's oddly Victorian rhythms."

R374   Rich, Frank. "Stage: The Misses Taylor and Stapleton in *Foxes.*" *New York
            Times* 8 May 1981: C, 3. In New York Theatre Critics' Reviews, 1981. 228.
                     Review of *The Little Foxes 1981* Broadway revival. Praises the
            entertaining melodrama, which is "as good as the genre gets," the bristling
            language. Is impressed by Taylor's acting, except in the second act, and with
            Stapleton "who digs beneath the surface to add a Chekhovian dimension."

R375   Siegel, Joel. "*The Little Foxes.*" *WABC-TV* Channel 7 (7 May 1981). In New
            York Theatre Critics' Reviews, 1981. 233.
                     Review of 1981 Broadway revival. Praises Taylor, the excellent cast, and
            the well-written play.

R376   Watt, Douglas. "Liz Seems a Reticent Regina in *Foxes.*" *New York Daily News*
            8 May 1981. In New York Theatre Critics' Reviews, 1981. 229.
                     Review of the 1981 Broadway revival. Criticizes Taylor's performance;
            and calls the direction "spotty."

R377   Wilson, Edwin. "Elizabeth Taylor Arrives on the Broadway Stage." *Wall Street
            Journal* 12 May 1981. In New York Theatre Critics' Reviews, 1981. 230.
                     Review of the 1981 Broadway revival. The melodrama "condemns
            avariciousness and greed . . . in blatantly overstated terms." Is impressed with
            Taylor's debut, which "is as much an event as the play itself."

1994

R378   Mackay, Shena. "They Were Divide." *Times Literary Supplement* 4775 (7 Oct. 1994): 26.

Review of *The Children's Hour* (Lyttleton Theatre, London). The play is not about lesbianism. It is about mendacity and malice; the persecution and corruption pointing to the anti-Communist witchhunts of the 1950s in which Hellman was blacklisted. The production touches but needs Audrey Hepburn of the film version (*The Loudest Whisper*) to "break the heart."

1997

R379   Auchincloss, Louis. "A Morality Play That Retains Its Punch." *New York Times* 23 Mar. 1997. Clippings, Theatre Collection, New York Public Library.

Preopening press, regarding *The Little Foxes* revival (Vivian Beaumont Theatre at Lincoln Center, NYC). Suggests that play is still popular because the villains that Hellman "hated live on. In fact, today they're worse. In her day, at least, they might have felt shame."

R380   Barnes, Clives. "*Foxes* still Lifeless." New York Post 28 Apr. 1997. Clippings, Theatre Collection, New York Public Library.

Review of *The Little Foxes* 1997 revival (Vivian Beaumont Theatre at Lincoln Center, NYC). The present production is more notable for its set than its cast. Stockard Channing's portrayal is "baldly calculated"; and the play "screams" for knockdown, knockout performances, which the director has not managed to extract from his cast. Suggests that *The Children's Hour* is a more worthy candidate for revival.

R381   Brantley, Bent. "Freud Strays Into a Well-Furnished Foxes' Den Down South." *New York Times* 28 Apr. 1997. Clippings, Theatre Collection, New York Public Library.

Review of *The Little Foxes* 1997 revival (Vivian Beaumont Theatre at Lincoln Center, NYC). Criticizes the Freudian shadings that the director has given the production; and finds the play "wildly miscast" and "haplessly misconceived." Coldblooded Regina "emerges as a jittery, fluttery neurotic" incapable of the higher stakes intended by the author.

R382   Feingold, Michael. "Antique Shows." *Village Voice* 13 May 1997. Clippings, Theatre Collection, New York Public Library.

Review of *The Little Foxes* 1997 revival (Vivian Beaumont Theatre at Lincoln Center, NYC). The director has gone for internal subversion. Regina has become "a frail and desperate creature, a little afraid of her big brother and longing for tenderness from her estranged husband."

R383   Kissel, Howard. "*Foxes* Need Vixen Up." *New York Daily News* 28 Apr. 1997. Clippings, Theatre Collection, New York Public Library.

Review of *The Little Foxes* 1997 revival (Vivian Beaumont Theatre at Lincoln Center, NYC). Criticizes the weak central performances, Regina's lack of credibility, the lack of theatricality and ideological underpinnings.

R384   Simon, John. "Second Helpings." *New York Magazine* 19 May 1997. Clippings,
         Theatre Collection, New York Public Library.
             Review of *The Little Foxes* 1997 revival (Vivian Beaumont Theatre at
         Lincoln Center, NYC). Praises the director for trying a new and risky
         interpretation of Regina which is psychologically and socially believable. The
         director sheds new light on the play which is "convention-bound and somewhat
         suspect classic, lifting it to a higher, subtler level of unforgettability."

Secondary Bibliography: Books, Articles, Sections

The following secondary bibliography of books, articles, and sections concentrates on Hellman's career in the theatre. Biographic material is also included.

1934

S1   Mok, Michel. "*The Children's Hour* Had to Be Written; 18th Century Gave Idea for Modern Play; Hellman Inspired by Scotch Law Case." *New York Post* 23 Nov. 1934: 5.
          Background information on the play, including a brief biographical sketch.

1935

S2   "Asides: Hellman." *Stage* 12 (Jan. 1935): 34.
          Describes opening night reception given *The Children's Hour*. George Jean Nathan stayed until the final curtain to give his cheerful benediction. Others shouted "Second Ibsen! New O'Neill! American Strindberg! 1934 Chekhov." Comments on the difficulties in casting the show, summarizes *The Great Drumsheugh Case*, and provides a biographical sketch.

S3   "American Play Banned: English Censor Forbids Presentation of *The Children's Hour*." *New York Times* (12 Mar. 1935): 24.
          Lord Chamberlain has banned public performances of *The Children's Hour* in London. Finds the theme offensive.

S4   "*Children's Hour* Banned in Boston: Mayor Acts After Report by City Censor Who Saw Play Here: Private Showing Banned: Mansfield Rejects Manager's Offer--Drama Was Backed by Guild Affiliate." *New York Times* 15 Dec. 1935: 42.
          Major Mansfield never read the script or attended a performance, but based his decision to ban the play on a report made by the censor who labeled it "indecent."

S5   *"Children's Hour* Ban Extended." *New York Times* 18 Dec. 1935: 33.
            Report of the ban in Beverly, MA. Concerns the touring company.

S6   "London Success Seen for *Children's Hour*: Producer Regrets Action of Lord
            Chamberlain Banning Play and Considers Appealing. *New York Times* 15 Mar.
            1935: 24.
            Chamberlain's action has bitterly disappointed producer Alec L. Rea, who
            comments, "It is a great play . . . If people here would only stand for the theme, it
            would be a success."

S7   Maney, Richard. "Even the Keyhole Was Absent in the Real *CH*." *New York
            Herald Tribune* 4 Aug. 1935: V, 1.
            Summarizes and compares William Roughead's "Closed Doors" to the
            Hellman play.

S8   Mantle, Burns, ed. *The Best Plays of 1934-35.* New York: Dodd, Mead and
            Company, 1935. 33-65.
            The Children's Hour is included among the season's ten best plays.
            Summarized version. Brief comments.

S9   Reed, Edward. "New Faces, 1935, Lillian Hellman." *Theatre Arts* 19 (Apr.
            1935): 268-77.
            Biographical sketch with comments on *The Children's Hour* and the
            controversy over its theme.

S10   Shumlin, Herman. "Seeks to Remove Taboo on *The Children's Hour*." *New
            York World-Telegram* 13 Apr. 1935: 20.
            The Broadway producer opposes the London ban. Insists the play is
            "highly moral."

S11   Vernon, Grenville. "The Pulitzer Award." *Commonweal* 12 (31 May 1935): 134.
            Recounts Clayton Hamilton's article in the *American Mercury* about the
            Pulitzer Committee's decision to award the prize to Zoë Akins' *The Old Maid.*
            Vernon states his belief that *The Children's Hour* should have won the award.
            Despite the unpleasant subject, it is "a powerful and an honest piece of work, and
            certainly does not make any plea or apology for vice."

S12   Walbridge, Earl. "Closed Doors." *Saturday Review of Literature* 11 (16 Mar.
            1935): 548.
            A letter to the editor calls attention to Roughead's *Bad Companions* as the
            source of Hellman's *The Children's Hour*, arguing that Roughead should have
            received credit in the program or in the printed text of the play. (See R6).

S13   "Winter's Harvest: A Paean of Praise for Some of the Novas in Our
            Entertainment World This Season." *Stage* 12 (Mar. 1935): 8-9.
            Regarding *The Children's Hour*, Florence McGee, who plays the spiteful
            child of fourteen, is actually twenty-four and a newcomer to Broadway.
            Katherine Emery, one of the teachers, was also unknown before the season.
            Anne Revere, the other teacher, made a name for herself last season in *Double*

Door. Hellman never wrote a play before this, yet her dialogue is "strong, clear, expert, and right" (9).

1936

S14   Beebe, Lucius. "An Adult's Hour Is Miss Hellman's Next Effort." *New York Herald Tribune* 13 Dec. 1936: VII, 2. Reprinted in *Conversations with Lillian Hellman.* Ed. Jackson S. Bryer. Jackson: University Press of Mississippi, 1986. 3-6.
           In this preopening interview regarding *Days to Come*, Hellman says that her primary interest has been the family, that the strike and social manifestations served merely as background material. "It's the story of innocent people on both sides who are drawn into conflict and events far beyond their comprehension. It's the saga of a man who started something he cannot stop, a parallel among adults to what I did with children in *The Children's Hour*" (*Conversations*, 5).

S15   *"The Children's Hour"* is Weighed in Chicago." *New York Times* 10 Jan. 1936: 17.
           The Corporation Counsel of Chicago has banned the production in its city.

S16   "The Fruits of a New Symposium." *New York Times* 8 Mar. 1936: IX, 2.
           Discloses the results of a survey, taken by producer/director Shumlin, of why audiences have seen *The Children's Hour*. Some said "for folly." Others said critical reviews and recommendations of friends. Only one person cited the Boston ban.

S17   Lawson, John Howard. *Theory and Technique of Playwriting.* New York: G.P. Putnam's Sons, 1936. 223, 263-67. Rprt. New York: Hill and Wang, 1960.
           Examines the structure of *The Children's Hour* which is disorganized because of the author's inability to integrate the two lines of action. The climax splits the play in two. The situation itself seems implausible, because it is not put into a solid social framework. There is no way to "gauge the effect of the child's gossip within the community" (264); and "the psychological effect on the two women is also vague, and is taken for granted instead of being dramatized" (265).

S18   Nathan, George. *Theatre of the Moment.* New York: Alfred A. Knopf, 1936. 248-50.
           Praises *The Children's Hour*, as a material contribution to American theatre, despite the ending. Confirms his opinion that the grandmother's apologies and the explanation of the child's malfeasance are necessary to the ending of *The Children's Hour* (See P35). Disputes colleagues who find the play's title misleading, the actions of the adults lacking in common sense. Hellman has written that which "is essential to the integrity of her theme, even if in stage practice it becomes discommodious to an audience's patience. Her show may be over and done with the aforesaid re-introduction and explanation, but her play--that is her manuscript in all its honesty--is not" (250).

S19   "Whisper Opposed in Play, Ruling on Injunction Against *Children's Hour* Ban
          Delayed." *New York Times* 30 Jan. 1936: 14.
                    Reports of the Boston's mayor objections to the theme of lesbianism. In
          the play the accusation is whispered by the child to her grandmother. Concerns
          the touring company.

1937

S20   Lawson, John H. "A Comparative Study of *The Children's Hour* and *Days to
          Come*." *New Theatre & Film* Mar. 1937: 15-16, 60-61.
                    An analysis of the two plays shows that the problems inherent in *The
          Children's Hour* are developed in a more complex form in *Days to Come*. The
          faults of the latter play "are due to the intensity of the author's growth. Her search
          for dramatic truth leads her beyond her present ability to organize and unify her
          material" (15).

1939

S21   Beebe, Lucius. "Stage Asides: Miss Hellman Talks of Her Latest Play, *The Little
          Foxes*." *New York Herald Tribune* 12 Mar. 1939: VI, 1, 2. Reprinted in
          Conversations with Lillian Hellman. Ed. Jackson S. Bryer. Jackson: University
          Press of Mississippi, 1986. 7-10.
                    In this interview Hellman speaks of her current sellout success, *The Little
          Foxes*. Choosing the South as a setting was purely incidental. She wanted to set
          the time of the play about the turn of the century, and it happened that the cotton
          states in these years had witnessed the sort of exploitation she wanted to write
          about. The play, in essence, represents "the sort of person who ruins the world
          for us" (8).

S22   Block, Anita Cahn. *The Changing World in Plays and Theatre*. Boston: Little,
          Brown and Company, 1939. 122-26. Reprinted New York: DeCapo Press,
          1971.
                    A chapter entitled "Contemporary Drama: The Individual in Conflict with
          Changing Sexual Standards" praises Hellman for making the focal point of *The
          Children's Hour* "not the question of homosexuality itself, but society's savage
          treatment of the homosexual.

S23   Krutch, Joseph Wood. *The American Drama Since 1918*. New York: Random
          House, 1939: 130-33.
                    Surveys *The Children's Hour*, *Days to Come*, and *The Little Foxes*.
          Finds the stories "too highly colored and too extraordinary to justify an attitude so
          inclusive as that which she [Hellman] has adopted . . . When their author has
          discovered a theme more truly central to her own concerns she may not
          unreasonably be expected to produce a genuinely important play" (133).

S24   Mantle, Burns. *The Best Plays of 1938-39*. New York: Dodd, Mead and
          Company, 1939. 75-109.

The Little Foxes is included among the season's ten best plays. Summarized version. Brief comments.

S25   O'Hara, Frank Hurburt. "Comedies Without a Laugh." *Today in American Drama.* Chicago: University of Chicago Press, 1939. 83-101.

Examines the social factors that loom behind the main action of *The Little Foxes.* Hellman looks at her family with relentless realism, commenting upon the present by means of scenes from another day; her characters are fully drawn; the form is somewhat novelistic.

S26   "Writing a Play Isn't Half of It for This Author: Six Months of Research and Much Thought Take Place Before She Begins." *New York Herald Tribune* 19 Feb. 1939: VI, 2.

With *The Little Foxes* in previews, Hellman comments on the two years it took to complete the play.

1941

S27   Atkinson, Brooks. "Critics' Prize Plays." *New York Times* 17 Apr. 1941: IX, 1.

Announces that *Watch on the Rhine* has been awarded the Drama Critics' Circle Award for the best American play. Identifies members who voted for the play and those who did not.

S28   Freedley, George, and John A. Reeves. *A History of the Theatre.* New York: Crown Publishers, 1941. 598.

A one-paragraph survey praises Hellman who "has demonstrated greater dramatic power than any woman now writing for our stage." Calls *The Little Foxes,* "one of the most satisfactory dramas seen on the New York stage in recent years." Praises the flawless acting that heightened the effect of the play.

S29   "Founts on Headliners: Producer." *New York Times* (27 Apr. 1941): IV, 2.

Announces *Watch on the Rhine* as the recipient of the New York Drama Critics' Circle Award. Reviews Shumlin's career as producer and director of *The Children's Hour* and *The Little Foxes.*

S30   Gould, Jack. "Paul Lukas, Late of Hollywood: Random Notes on the Central Figure in Lillian Hellman's New Drama, *Watch on the Rhine.*" *New York Times* 6 Apr. 1941: IX, 1, 2.

A strong believer in repertory theatre and ensemble playing, Lukas encouraged actors to "a little higher degree of excellence even if here and there it meant overshadowing of his own role" (1).

S31   Harriman, Margaret Case. "Profiles: Miss Lily of New Orleans. *New Yorker* 17 (8 Nov. 1941): 22-26, 28-29, 32, 34-35. Reprinted in *Take Them Up Tenderly.* New York: Alfred A. Knopf, 1944, 94-109. Also reprinted in *Critical Essays on Lillian Hellman.* Ed. Mark W. Estrin. Boston, MA: G.K. Hall & Co., 1989. 219-29.

A biographical portrayal which includes a survey of the plays. Describes the notebooks for *Watch on the Rhine,* which Hellman made available to her.

Quotes at length from the notes which provide data on contemporary history, local customs, and political events.

S32   Hughes, Charlotte. "Women Playmakers." *New York Times Magazine Section* (4 May 1941): 10-11, 27.
           A biographical sketch which includes Hellman comments on *Watch on the Rhine*, her research on the underground movement, her "decent" German protagonist, the general difficulties she has in writing parts for male characters. Hellman says, "I did eleven rough versions of *Watch on the Rhine*, and four complete versions, before I was satisfied" (11).

S33   Landman, Isaac, ed. *The Universal Jewish Encyclopedia*. New York: Universal Jewish Encyclopedia, Inc., 1941. V, 311-12.
           Brief biographical sketch and discussion of plays through *Watch on the Rhine*.

S34   Mantle, Burns. *The Best Plays of 1940-41*. New York: Dodd, Mead and Company, 1941.64-93.
           Watch on the Rhine is included among the season's ten best plays. Summarized version. Brief comments.

S35   Van Gelder, Robert. "Of Lillian Hellman: Being a Conversation with the Author of *Watch on the Rhine*." *New York Times* 20 Apr. 1941: IX, 1, 3. Uncut interview reprinted in *Conversations with Lillian Hellman*. Ed. Jackson S. Bryer. Jackson: University Press of Mississippi, 1986. 11-15.
           Hellman speaks of her research methods and other work habits. She made digests of twenty-five books on political argument, memoirs, and German history before writing *Watch on the Rhine*.

1942

S36   Gilder, Rosamond. "Theatre Arts Bookshelf." *Theatre Arts* 26 (May 1942): 346.
           Comments on Hellman's remarks in the preface to the Modern Library edition of four of her plays, *The Children's Hour*, *Days to Come*, *The Little Foxes*, *Watch on the Rhine*.

S37   *Twentieth-Century Authors*. Eds. Stanley Kunitz and Howard Haycraft. New York: Wilson, 1942: 634. Updated 1955.
           Brief biographical sketch with discussion of plays through *Watch on the Rhine*.

S38   Parker, Dorothy. Foreword to Limited Edition of *Watch on the Rhine*. New York: Privately Published by the Joint Anti-Fascist Committee in cooperation with Random House, 1942.
           Comments on the playwright and the eleven well-known artists who illustrated the book (Rockwell Kent, Hans Mueller, Philip Reisman, Benjamin Kopman, Donald Gelb, William Gropper, Lawrence Beall Smith, Don Freeman, William Sharp, Luis Quintanilla, Fritz Eichenberg), commending them for their early fight against Fascism and their courageous efforts which will live within the

349 numbered copies, privately published for the benefit of the Joint Anti-Fascist Refugee Committee.

S39   *"Watch on the Rhine* Seen by President." *New York Times* (26 Jan. 1942): IV, 18.
       President Franklin Delano Roosevelt attended a command performance in Washington, DC; his first public appearance away from the White House since the war began, other than to address Congress and attend church."

1944

S40   Clark, Barrett. "Lillian Hellman." *College English* 6 Dec. 1944: 127-33.
       Examines the first five plays, all propagandist except *The Searching Wind*. Hellman "never wrote a line without trying to say something that would help man to escape or offset the effects of ignorance and wrong thinking" (127).

S41   Drutman, Irving. "Herman Shumlin's Favorite Dramatist." *New York Herald Tribune* 7 May 1944.
       Profiles the director/playwright relationship through *The Searching Wind*.

S42   "How Lillian Hellman Writes a Play." *PM* Magazine 12 Mar. 1944: 11-12.
       Discusses the writing of *The Searching Wind*, the rewrites and revisions common to her work.

S43   Maney, Richard S. "From Hellman to Shumlin to Broadway." *New York Times* 9 Apr. 1944: X, 1.
       Hellman's longtime press agent profiles the Hellman/Shumlin collaboration on the eve of the opening of *The Searching Wind*. To date, all of Hellman's shows have been produced and directed by Shumlin who considers her a perfectionist and the ablest of playwrights.

S44   Nathan, George Jean. *The Theatre Book of the Year, 1943-44*. New York: Alfred A. Knopf, 1944: 259-99.
       The Searching Wind resembles Strindberg's *The Stronger*. There is a lack of clarity in both political and love plots, the promise of an important statement that never is expressed.

S45   "New York Drama Critics's Circle Award." *New York Times* 26 Apr. 1944: 25.
       The Searching Wind received seven votes from the Drama Critic's Circle as the best play of the year, one short of a majority. Circle's members voted against any award this season, having argued that no American play was good enough.

S46   Ormsbee, Helen. "Miss Hellman All But Dares Her Next Play to Succeed." *New York Herald Tribune* 9 Apr. 1944: IV, 1.
       The Searching Wind preopening interview. Hellman says that the title came from a "colored" maid who worked for her. "It's a searching wind today," the maid would say to describe a wind that chilled to the bones. "I suppose in my title I was thinking of the wind that's blowing through the world."

1945

S47   Fleishman, Earl. E. *"The Searching Wind* in the Making." *Quarterly Journal of Speech* 3 (Feb. 1945): 22-28.
          Fleishman's stage name is Eugene Earl. He is the actor who played Sears (Hazen's secretary in Paris). His analysis of the Broadway production--the acting, setting, direction, and writing, blames the play's difficulties on Shumlin's direction and the acting. The emotional scenes were mechanical, the pauses too deliberate, the emphasis too rational.

1946

S48   Von Wein, Florence. "Playwrights Who Are Women." *Independent Woman* 25 (Jan. 1946): 12-14.
          Ranks Hellman among the best American playwrights, a painstaking and keenly perceptive playwright who "has an awareness of the sick anxieties of humanity, intellectual indignation and the technical skill to express what she wants to say" (13).

S49   Wilson, John S. "No First Night Jitters for Playwright Lillian Hellman." *PM* 17 Nov. 1946: 16-17.
          The Searching Wind, pre-opening press interview. Hellman says that she still intends to write another play about the later period in the lives of *The Little Foxes* family. Includes a biographical sketch.

1947

S50   Atkinson, Brooks. *Broadway Scrapbook*. New York: Theatre Arts, Inc., 1947. 107-110, 192-95, 222, 225-257.
          Reprints of Sunday *New York Times* reviews. *The Little Foxes*, *Watch on the Rhine*, *Another Part of the Forest*.

S51   Gagey, Edmond. *Revolution in American Drama*. New York: Columbia University Press, 1947: 126, 137-38, 142, 268.
          Surveys of *The Children's Hour*, *The Little Foxes*, and *Watch on the Rhine*.

S52   Gassner, ed. *Best Plays of the Modern American Theatre*. New York: Crown, 1947: 641-82.
          Watch on the Rhine is anthologized. Includes introductory comments to the play.

S53   Mantle, Burns, ed. *The Best Plays of 1946-47*. New York: Dodd, Mead and Company, 1947. 163-203.
          Another Part of the Forest is included among the season's ten best plays. Summarized version. Brief comments.

S54 Nathan, George Jean. *The Theatre Book of the Year*, 1946-1947. New York: Alfred A. Knopf, 1947. x-xx, 201-204.
Surveys the plays through *Another Part of the Forest*.

1948

S55 Hartley, Lodvick C. and Arthur Ladu. *Patterns in Modern Drama*. Englewood Cliffs, NJ: Prentice-Hall, Inc., 1948. 417-494.
Includes *The Little Foxes* (under the rubric of melodrama) in a collection of seven plays that are well-established in the repertory of the contemporary theatre. Includes a chronology of the playwright, an introduction to the play, and a brief critical bibliography.

S56 Nagelberg, Munjon Moses, ed. *Drama of Our Time*. New York: Harcourt, Brace & World, Inc., 1948. 31-96.
The text of *Watch on the Rhine* is introduced with an explanatory note and a brief biographical sketch of the author. Includes preparatory material materials entitled "Before Reading, study aids and questions in "While Reading, and finally the section entitled, "After Reading," designed to stimulate student interest and creativity.

S57 Spiller, Robert E., et al, eds. *Literary History of the United States*. Vol. 2. New York: Macmillan Press, 1948. 1330.
Considers Hellman's plays propagandistic, making it "difficult to take her artistic pretensions with full seriousness." The war plays exhibit considerable theatrical dexterity but are "limited by immediate political considerations." *Another Part of the Forest* is theatrically her "most dexterous" play.

1949

S58 Mersaud, Joseph. *The American Drama Since 1930: Essays on Playwrights and Plays*. New York: Modern Chapbooks Press, 1949.
A chapter entitled "Some New Playwrights" includes a discussion of Hellman contribution, her "capacity for sharp characterization and powerful situations" (248). Comments on *The Children's Hour*, *Days to Come*, *The Little Foxes*, and the Hellman-Bankhead relationship. Includes biographical information. Another section comments on *Another Part of the Forest*, a thoroughly creditable job of playwriting, though "a lesser play than *The Little Foxes*" (290).

S59 Morehouse, Ward. *Matinee Tomorrow, Fifty Years of Our Theater*. New York: Whittlesley House, McGraw-Hill Book Company, Inc., 1949.
References to *The Children's Hour*, and *The Little Foxes*.

S60 Schumach, Murray. "Miss Hellman Discusses Directors." *New York Times* 23 Oct. 1949: II, 1, 3. Reprinted in *Conversations with Lillian Hellman*. Ed. Jackson S. Bryer. Jackson: University Press of Mississippi, 1986. 19-21.

Pre-opening press interview, *Montserrat*. Hellman expresses her decision to stage her plays, her quarrel with directors whose interpretation is not always in keeping with the playwright's intent. Since the stage business of her plays is so carefully detailed, she believes that the director's input need not be that of a genius.

1951

S61   Clurman, Harold. "Letters Found in the Drama Mailbag: Director's Explanation." *New York Times* 22 Apr. 1951: II, 3.
         Responds to a letter to the editor from a playgoer who wrote that he did not understand the Sophie character of *The Autumn Garden*. Clurman explains that Sophie is pivotal to the play. She represents the typical contemporary European point of view: an impatience with generalizations and ideals not founded on concrete fact.

S62   Davis, Owen. *My First Fifty Years in the Theatre*. Boston: Walter H. Baker, 1950. 125-26.
         Davis's recollections include a brief comment on *The Children's Hour*. He considers the confrontation scene between Mrs. Tilford and the two school mistresses the best in modern drama. "These three women were beautifully drawn and every word they spoke, in a long harrowing scene, was exactly what these three women under the circumstances would have said" (125-26).

S63   Downer, Alan S. *Fifty Years of American Drama, 1900-1950*. Chicago: Henry Regnery, 1951. 60-61, 137, 139-41.
         A critical survey with comments on *The Little Foxes*, *The Watch on the Rhine*, *The Searching Wind*, *The Autumn Garden*. One section discusses Hellman and Odets, labeling them propaganda playwrights whose "conviction can sometimes overcome craftsmanship to the serious detriment of even theatrical effectiveness" (60). Finds Hellman more technically skilled than Odets.

S64   Drutman, Irving. "Author's Problem--What to Do After Play Opens?" *New York Herald Tribune* 18 Oct. 1951: IV, 2.
         Hellman discusses the writing of *The Autumn Garden* and talks about the emotional letdown that she experiences after opening night.

S65   Gilroy, Harry "Lillian Hellman Drama Foregoes a Villain." *New York Times* 25 Feb. 1951: II, 1, 3.
         Preopening interview comments on the absence of evil characters in *The Autumn Garden*. The theme centers on empty lives and the importance of not wasting life; and of changing courses. Hellman says, "It is meant to say the opposite--they can do a great deal with their lives . . . I don't like cheerless plays . . . I don't feel cheerless about the world" (1).

S66   Halline, Allan G.   Introduction to *Six Modern American Plays*. New York: Random House, 1951. xx-xxii.
         Finds Hellman's representative plays moralistic and serious, somber without being classically tragic. "She chronicles and exposes vicious aspects of

our national scene and character; but she does not cheer her age" (xxii). Anthologizes *The Little Foxes* (200-296).

S67   Morehouse, Ward. "*Garden* Pleases Miss Hellman." *New York World-Telegram and Sun* 3 Mar. 1951: 7. Reprinted in *Conversations with Lillian Hellman*. Ed. Jackson S. Bryer. Jackson: University Press of Mississippi, 1986. 22-23.

In a pre-opening interview Hellman discusses *The Autumn Garden*, which she calls her most satisfying play in the writing. "Perhaps in the play, I've wanted to say that if you've had something to stand on inwardly when you reach the middle years you have a chance of being all right; if you haven't you just live out your life" (23). Expresses great respect for Tennessee Williams and Arthur Miller, Sean O'Casey and Bernard Shaw.

S68   Nathan, George Jean. *Theater Book of the Year 1950-1951*. New York: Alfred A. Knopf, 1951. 241-44.

The Autumn Garden is "diffused and somnambulistic." The characters are "essentially comic figures pulled into tragic postures at the end of wires manipulated by a puppet master dressed in the blouse of Turgenev and the hat of Chekhov" (243).

S69   Rice, Vernon. "Curtain Cues: Lillian Hellman: Frankfurter Expert." *New York Post* 6 Mar. 1951: 38.

Over hot dogs during rehearsals, Hellman comments on the title of *The Autumn Garden*. "An autumn garden is one which by winter will fade and not be a garden any more. It's a chrysanthemum garden. The people of the play are coming into the winter of life."

1952

S70   Bankhead, Tallulah. *Tallulah*. New York: Harper & Brothers, 1952.

Recalls her experiences in *The Little Foxes*, including her running feud with Hellman.

S71   Gilroy, Harry. "The Bigger the Lie." *New York Times* 14 Dec. 1952: II, 3, 4. Reprinted in *Conversations with Lillian Hellman*. Ed. Jackson S. Bryer. Jackson: University Press of Mississippi, 1986. 24-26.

In an interview on the eve of *The Children's Hour* revival opening, Hellman says the play is not about lesbianism, but about a lie. She's changed some of the original lines that seemed too literary, resisted the urge to rewrite, and believes "that people who have seen the play before will find that this is in many ways a different interpretation" (26).

S72   Morgenstern, Joseph. "New *Children's Hour*--Grim Power of Gossip." *New York Herald Tribune* 4 Mar. 1952: IV, 1, 4.

Hellman says *The Children's Hour* was never meant to be a lesbian play. "I meant no more than this: that if the child's lie hadn't driven her to suicide, Martha would have ended up at fifty, with headaches, a lonely, irritable, neurotic spinster who had no idea of what brought her to where she was" (1).

S73   "Testimony of Miss Lillian Hellman, Accompanied by her Counsel Joseph L. Rauh, Jr." in Communist Infiltration of the Hollywood Motion Picture Industry-- Part 8, Wednesday, May 21, 1952." *Hearings Before the Committee on Un- American Activities, House of Representatives, Eighty-Second Congress, Second Session*. Washington, DC: U.S. Government Printing Office, 1952. 3541-49.

1953

S74   Bloomgarden, Kermit. "The Pause in the Day's Occupation." *Theatre Arts* 37 (May 1953): 33.
        Post-opening comments on *The Children's Hour* revival. The producer provides background material on the original production. He was called in as general manager shortly after the play opened.

S75   "Chicago Sees *Children's Hour*." *New York Times* 10 Nov. 1953: 39.
        Banned in 1936, the play has opened at the Harris Theatre without interference.

S76   Nathan, George Jean. *The Theatre in the Fifties*. New York: Alfred A. Knopf, 1953.
        In a section entitled "Lillian Hellman," comments on the revival of *The Children's Hour* revival. The play is a tight, intelligent melodrama, its theme of scandalmongery tastefully turned. Restraint has been Hellman's best critical weapon. Cites weaknesses in the casting and the direction. Confesses that he is still troubled that the child whispered, but did not speak out her accusations against the two schoolteachers. "It is not the child that is hesitant about articulating them; it is the playwright who evidently has qualms about putting them into words and who shrinks from possible censorship (*vide The Captive*). Miss Hellman has cheated" (52).

1954

S77   Gassner, John. *Masters of the Drama*. New York: Dover Publications, Inc., 1954. 737.
        Comments on *The Autumn Garden*. Notes incisive dialogue and a measure of human sympathy, and an "affecting indirection and stasis unusual for a writer who had usually favored overt conflicts on the stage" (737).

1955

S78   "Julie Harris as Joan of Arc: A Fiery Particle." *Time* 66 (28 Nov. 1955): 76 to 78+.
        Cover story on Harris, who is featured in *The Lark*. The article includes comments on the play. Hellman's adaptation lacks the emotional substance of important drama, but it has the cerebral excitement and the visual flair of superior theater" (76). Hellman has cut 43 pages of Anouilh and the *ennui*, and "the result is intellectual theatre at close to its best" (76).

S79   Schumach, Murray. "Shaping a New Joan. " *New York Times* 13 Nov. 1955: II,
        1.
             The Lark reopening press interview. Hellman insists that she will do no
        more adaptations.

S80   *Twentieth Century Authors, First Supplement 1955*. Ed. Stanley J. Kunitz. New
        York: H.W. Wilson, 1955. 432-33. Supersedes entry *Twentieth Century
        Authors*, 1942.
             A brief biographical sketch and survey of plays.

1956

S81   Gaver, Jack, ed. *Critics' Choice: New York Drama Critics' Circle Prize Plays*.
        London: Arco Publications, 1956.
             An anthology of New York Drama Critics' Circle Award plays, which
        includes *Watch on the Rhine* (1940-41). An introduction to the book recounts the
        history of the organization which was founded as a reaction to the awarding of the
        Pulitzer to Akins's *The Old Maid*.

S82   Griffin, Alice. "Books--of a Different Feather." *Theatre Arts* 40 (May 1956): 8-10.
             A book review that compares the Hellman adaptation of Anouilh's *The
        Lark* to Christopher Fry's translation. Hellman's is shorter by about a third,
        romantic in tone, the ending different, more appealing to American audiences.
        Joan is the main character; the theme is that man's courage will prevail. The
        burning takes place off stage; and in the coronation scene, Joan is depicted as the
        savior of her country.

S83   Kronenberger, Louis, ed. *The Best Plays of 1955-56*. New York: Dodd, Mead
        and Company: 189-213.
             The Lark is included among the season's ten best plays. Summarized
        version. Brief comments. Production information.

1958

S84   Gunther, John. *Inside Russia Today*. New York: Harper and Brothers, 1958.
             Discusses the success of *The Autumn Garden* in Moscow. Several
        amateur critics thought the play reminded them of Chekhov, but didn't think it
        was "representative of conditions in the United States. Americans simply could
        not behave like that!" (313).

S85   Knepler, Henry W. "*The Lark*, Translation vs. Adaptation: A Case History."
        Modern Drama 1 (May 1958): 15-28. Excerpted version reprinted in *Critical
        Essays on Lillian Hellman*. Ed. Mark W. Estrin. Boston, MA: G.K. Hall & Co.,
        1989. 64-71.
             Posits the superiority of the Hellman adaptation over the Fry translation.
        Hellman took into consideration the theatrical traditions and expectations of her
        New York audience. Fry "did not do the same for his London public" (65).

1959

S86   Bowers, Faubion. *Broadway, U.S.S.R.* Edinburg: Thomas Nelson and Sons, 1959. 75, 76, 89, 90-92.
            Describes the Moscow Art Theatre (MHAT) repertory production of *The Autumn Garden*, the 1957-58 season. The play "represents an exquisitely drawn portrait of a number of people drawn in the autumnal clarity and helplessness of age" (90).

S87   Guthrie, Tyrone. *A Life in the Theatre.* New York: McGraw-Hill, Inc., 1959. 240-41.
            Recalls the artistic skirmish regarding the *Candide* collaboration. The eminent group lost whatever share of lightness, gaiety, and dash that they might have been able to contribute as "an unconscious reaction to the diamond quality of Bernstein's brilliance" (241). Singers were chosen to do justice to the score, but not the text; and Hellman's qualities were lost.

S88   Stern, Richard. "Lillian Hellman on Her Plays." *Contact* 3 (1959): 113-119. Transcript of interview printed in *Conversations with Lillian Hellman.* Ed. Jackson S. Bryer. Jackson: University Press of Mississippi, 1986. 27-43.
            Interviewed while teaching an English course at the University of Chicago, Hellman comments on the theatre and on her own plays, particularly *Toys in the Attic* which she has been in the process of writing for some time.

1960

S89   Dusenbury, Winifred L. *The Theme of Loneliness in Modern American Drama.* Gainesville: University of Florida Press, 1960. 134-49.
            A chapter entitled "Socioeconomic Forces" includes Hellman's plays in a discussion of the valuable contributions to the modern theatre of plays portraying the isolating effects of the particular conditions of the south. Briefly discusses *Another Part of the Forest* before analyzing *The Little Foxes*. These are not thesis plays, and the fact that Hellman was "interested enough in her characters to study their past and seek out the sociological and moral causes of their rapaciousness proves that she did not consider them mere figures in melodrama" (146). In addition, the two plays "contrast the loneliness of the rising and falling family, highlighting the two women, Birdie and Regina" (147-48).

S90   Felheim, Marvin. "*The Autumn Garden*: Mechanics and Dialectics." *Modern Drama* 3 (Sept. 1960): 191-95. Reprinted in *Critical Essays on Lillian Hellman.* Boston: G.K. Hall & Co., 1989. 49-53.
            Examines Hellman's move from the "well-made" play to the direction of Chekhov, the logical development of her lifelong study of Chekhov. Concludes that *The Autumn Garden* "makes for modern tragedy" (53).

S91   Gassner, John. *Theatre at the Crossroads.* New York: Holt, Rinehart, Winston, 1960. 132-39, 247-49.
            An overview of significant plays, especially *The Autumn Garden* and *The Searching Wind*; and *The Lark*.

S92   Nannes, Caspar H. *Politics in American Drama*. Washington, DC: Catholic
        University, 1960.
            A chapter entitled "Naziism and Fascism" includes a discussion of *The
        Searching Wind*, depicting the politicians and the political society of the day. The
        Hazen son is shown as one of the American servicemen whose lives had been
        uprooted because of the war; one of many who "were particularly bitter about the
        businessmen who had played ball with Hitler" (143-44). A chapter entitled
        "Evolution of a Liberal" comments on Kurt Müller (*Watch on the Rhine*), "the
        liberal driven to the extremity of committing an act inherently repulsive to him so
        freedom can live" (171).

S93   Thorp, Willard. *American Writing in the Twentieth Century*. Cambridge, MA:
        Harvard University Press, 1960. 96-97.
            Surveys the plays. Observes that Hellman's "plots are carefully
        constructed but they are not 'well-made' in the manner of Scribe and Sardou....
        She is a specialist in the evil in men's lives, and as the titles of her plays suggest,
        she is also an ironist" (96).

1961

S94   Adler, Jacob H. "The Rose and the Fox: Notes on the Southern Drama." *South:
        Modern Southern Literature in its Cultural Setting*. Eds. Louis D. Rubin, Jr. and
        Robert Jacobs. Garden City, NY: Dolphin Books, 1961. 349-375.
            Examines the important plays of Tennessee Williams, then compares them
        to Hellman's plays, citing useful contrasts and parallels. Concludes that Williams
        is more profound due to a wider variety of technique and his "far greater ability to
        make characters function both as characters and as multiple symbols" (375). *Little
        Foxes, Another Part of the Garden, The Autumn Garden, Toys in the Attic,
        Watch on the Rhine*, and *The Searching Wind*.

S95   "The Complete Text of *Toys in the Attic* by Lillian Hellman." *Theatre Arts* 45
        (Oct. 1961): 25+.
            Comments on Hellman's career. She "is a superb craftsman, a writer of
        great integrity and intense vitality."

S96   *Current Biography* 1960. Ed. Charles Moritz. New York: H.W. Wilson, 1961.
        186-87.
            A biographical sketch with comments on the plays through *Candide*.
        Supersedes the article which appeared in *Current Biography* in 1941.

S97   Gassner, John, ed. Introduction to *The Little Foxes. A Treasury of the Theatre*
        [From Henrik Ibsen to Eugene Ionesco]. New York: Simon Schuster, 1961. 983-
        84.
            Considers *The Little Foxes* an effective stage piece, the strongest and
        most closely knit of Hellman's plays. The play exists on many levels, "as
        character drama, melodrama, and comedy" (984), and brings to mind the
        intermediate genres of Ibsen, Strindberg, and Becque, as well as the "dark
        comedies" of Shakespeare.

S98   Knepler, Henry. "Translation and Adaptation in the Contemporary Drama."
         Modern Drama 4 (May 1961): 31-41.
                  Proposes a concept of transfer which adapts rather than translates. Argues
         that Christopher Fry, as translator, adheres closed to the instructions of the
         Anouilh's *L'Alouette*, while the Hellman play (*The Lark*) has been adapted to the
         American experience.

S99   Miller, Jordan Y. *American Dramatic Literature: Ten Modern Plays in Historical*
         Perspective. New York: McGraw-Hill, 1961. 87-130.
                  Critiques *The Little Foxes* as an introduction (87-90). Considers the play
         "one of the finest examples of the craft of playmaking combined with the qualities
         of excellent realistic drama" (87). Defends the use of melodrama which arises
         from established character and situation, furthering the plot without distraction.
         Includes a brief biographical sketch (90).

1962

S100   Biascoechea, Rosario. *Three Plays by Lillian Hellman, A Study in Modern*
         American Melodrama. Unpublished Dissertation (Catholic University), 1962.
                  An unverified reference.

S101   Brockington, John. *A Critical Analysis of the Plays of Lillian Hellman*.
         Unpublished Dissertation (Yale University),1962.
                  Not available from UMI.

S102   Meehan, Thomas. "Miss Hellman, What's Wrong with Broadway." *Esquire* 58
         (Dec. 1962): 140-42, 235-56. Reprinted in *Conversations with Lillian Hellman*.
         Ed. Jackson S. Bryer. Jackson: University Press of Mississippi, 1986. 44-52.
                  In this interview, Hellman complains that the theatre of the sixties is a
         bleak state of affairs, that advances in technique and avant-garde ideas do not
         necessarily make a good play. She praises Beckett, "the only writer of importance
         to come along in the theatre in the last ten or twelve years" (*Conversations*, 47).
         Calls Brecht's *The Three Penny Opera* and *Mother Courage* "big league"
         (Conversations, 49).

S103   Strasberg, Lee, ed. *Famous American Plays of the 1950s*. New York: Dell,
         1962. 18-19.
                  Blames the production style for the failure of *The Autumn Garden*. The
         set needed to be open to create a Chekhovian environment--to bring out the
         inherent humanness of character in the acting.

1963

S104   Adler, Jacob. "Miss Hellman's Two Sisters." *Educational Theatre Journal* 15
         (May 1963): 112-17. Reprinted in *Critical Essays on Lillian Hellman*. Ed. Mark
         W. Estrin. Boston, MA: G.K. Hall & Co., 1989. 43-49.
                  Compares *Toys in the Attic* to Chekhov's *The Three Sisters*. Although the
         play is tightly constructed, the basic outline comes from Chekhov. Like the

Russian master, Hellman "displays compassion and detachment in the process of revealing character and demonstrating universal uncontroversial truth" (117).

S105   Bradbury, John M. *Renaissance in the South: A Critical History of the Literature, 1920-1960*. Chapel Hill: University of North Carolina Press, 1963.
        A chapter entitled "Later Poetry and Drama" includes a critical survey of the Hellman plays. Compared to Williams, Hellman's picture of the South has softened over the years, as his has grown harsher. Over the years, "The fiery social liberalism which gave power, sometimes an all but melodramatic power, to Miss Hellman's plays has been lost, but it has been replaced by a more balanced, more delicate sense of human motivations and involvements [*The Autumn Garden* and *Toys in the Attic*]" (192).

S106   Breault, Sister Mary Armata, O.P. *A Comparative Analysis of the Structure of Selected Plays by Lillian Hellman and William Inge*. Unpublished Dissertation (Catholic University), 1963.
        An unverified reference.

S107   Himelstein, Morgan Y. *Drama Was a Weapon, the Left-Wing Theatre in New York*, 1929-1941. New Brunswick, NJ: Rutgers University Press, 1963. Rprt. Westport, CT: Greenwood Press, 1976. 200-201, 205, 208-209, 213-15, 222-23.
        Examines indirect Marxist sympathies in *Days to Come* and *The Little Foxes*, and the "curiously limited" anti-Nazi sentiments of *Watch on the Rhine*.

S108   Kerr, Walter. "Miss Hellman," in *The Theatre in Spite of Itself*. New York: Simon and Schuster, 1963. 235-38.
        Revised *Toys in the Attic* 1960 review. Praises the cool, resolute reaffirmation of primary virtues, the lucidity and control, the painstakingly sharp language, Hellman's perceptions grown deeper.

1964

S109   Bentley, Eric. *The Life of Drama*. New York: Atheneum, 1964.
        The chapter entitled "Melodrama" merely mentions Hellman. "It was the melodramatic touch that O'Neill brought to the American theatre already in the twenties, that Lillian Hellman and Clifford Odets brought to it in the thirties . . ." (214).

S110   Johnson, Joann H. *A Production Study and Text of Jean Anouilh's The Lark adapted by Lillian Hellman as Presented at Catholic University*. Ph.D. Dissertation. Catholic University, 1964.
        An unverified reference.

S111   Quinn, Arthur Hobson. *A History of The American Drama From the Civil War to the Present Day*. New York: Appleton-Century-Crofts, 1964. 300-01.
        Comments on the "irritating" critical and popular reaction to *The Children's Hour*. Finds Hellman "much more talented playwright than Clifford Odets, and when she finds a theme worthy of her, she may make important

contributions" (300). Having established the situation in *The Children's Hour*, she didn't know what to do with it in the last act.

S112   Rabkin, Gerald. *Drama and Commitment: Politics in the American Theatre of the Thirties*. Bloomington: Indiana University Press, 1964.

In a chapter entitled "The Committed Decade and Its Drama" mentions Hellman's three plays of that decade which reflect social concerns: *Days to Come*, the theme of a strike, and *The Children's Hour* and *The Little Foxes*, the vindictiveness and rapacity of bourgeois society. Excludes Hellman's work from the discussion of important dramatists of 1930s, since the corpus of her work is too small and there is limited space in his study.

1965

S113   Goldstein, Malcolm. "Body and Soul on Broadway." *Modern Drama* 7 (1965): 411-21.

Includes Hellman in a discussion of playwrights who have contributed to American psychological drama.

S114   Lewis, Allan. *American Plays and Playwrights of the Contemporary Theatre*. New York: Crown Publishers, Inc., 1965. 99, 105-199.

Surveys the Hellman plays in a chapter devoted to the three most prominent playwrights to come out of the economic depression of the thirties: Hellman, Odets, and Shaw. "All were committed writers, deeply concerned with the fight for social justice, and critical of long-held myths that induced complacency in times of success and panic in the face of disaster" (99).

S115   Phillips, John and Anne Hollander, "The Art of the Theater I: Lillian Hellman, An Interview." *Paris Review* 33 (Winter-Spring 1965): 64-95. Reprinted in *Writers at Work: The Paris Review Interviews, Third Series*. Ed. George Plimpton. New York: Viking Press, 1967. 115-140. Reprinted in *Conversations with Lillian Hellman*. Ed. Jackson S. Bryer. Jackson: University Press of Mississippi, 1986. 53-72. Reprinted in *Critical Essays on Lillian Hellman*. Ed. Mark W. Estrin. Boston, MA: G.K. Hall & Co., 1989. 230-47.

In an interview that took place on three afternoons during a busy Labor Day weekend on Martha's vineyard, Hellman comments on her plays, her playwriting theories, her contemporaries, Arthur Miller and Tennessee Williams, Hammett's influence, the House Un-American Activities Committee affair, and Mary McCarthy. Includes a copy of the letter sent to Congressman John S. Wood, Chairman of HUAC, dated 19 May 1952.

1966

S116   Clurman, Harold. *The Naked Image: Observations on the Modern Theatre*. New York: Macmillan Co., 1966.

Comments on the Edinburgh Festival and concurrent International Drama Conference sessions (1963), which Hellman attended. Reports on the current

Parisian theatre (1963), noting that *The Little Foxes* is on the boards. The Hellman play is "a success despite poor notices because of the presence in the cast of Simone Signoret and Suzanne Flon" (209).

S117   Drutman, Irving. "Hellman: A Stranger in the Theatre?" *New York Times* 27 Feb. 1966: II, 1, 5.

Hellman discusses a Yale University seminar for selected freshman and other projects that have kept her busy, expressing her increasing disenchantment for the theatre. One of her last happy memories is *Pal Joey*, which she saw five times; but she considers most of Broadway a bore. She has felt happy and excited when she has seen or read Beckett. She has completed the first act to *My Mother, My Father and Me*, but has not looked at it in three years.

S118   Gassner, John. *Directions in Modern Theatre and Drama*. New York: Holt, Rinehart and Winston, Inc., 1966.

Lists the 1939 Broadway production of *The Little Foxes* in a chronology of important developments in the theatre. Hellman's play is "a social drama with naturalistic, *comedie rosse*, qualities that invite comparison of the play with Becque's *Les Corbeaux*" (418).

S119   Gould, Jean. "Lillian Hellman." In *Modern American Playwrights*. New York: Dodd, Mead and Co., 1966. 168-86.

A comprehensive essay that covers biographical material, the Hammett relationship woven throughout, and an analysis of the plays.

S120   Keller, Alvin Joseph. *Form and Content in the Plays of Lillian Hellman: A Structural Analysis*. Unpublished Dissertation (Stanford University). DAI 26 (1966), 6715.

Examines the original plays according to the mode of literal scientific criticism, analyzing the six qualitative parts of each play to determine their relationship, pertinence to the whole, and artistic power. Concludes that Hellman is a social thinker and a moralist, a theatrical playwright and superb ironist, concerned with human hypocrisy and evil; and that she is best when dealing with the complexities of dynamic characters and the powerful assertion of their wills.

S121   Kerr, Walter. *Thirty Days Hath November*. New York: Simon and Schuster, 1966. 129.

Praises Mike Nichols' brilliant revival of *The Little Foxes*, the tightly crafted melodrama, and the cunning characters.

S122   Laufe, Abe. *Anatomy of a Hit: Long-Run Plays on Broadway from 1900 to the Present Day*. New York: Hawthorn Books, Inc., 1966.

Comments on *The Children's Hour* and *Toys in the Attic*. Regarding *The Children's Hour*: "Even if the third act lacks the vigor of the first two the entire play holds audience interest because Miss Hellman has handled the subject of abnormality frankly in a forceful drama which illustrates the tragedy wrought by malicious gossip and lies" (140). Notes controversial issues in *Toys in the Attic*, the interracial marriage and the affair between the white woman and her Negro chauffeur deftly developed so that "audiences are quizzical rather than incredulous about these relationships" (293).

S123   Murray, Robert and Gary Waldhorn. "A Playwright Looks at the Theater Today." *Yale Reports* 402 (5 June 1966): 1-8. Reprinted in *Conversations with Lillian Hellman*. Ed. Jackson S. Bryer. Jackson: University Press of Mississippi, 1986. 73-83.
            Hellman discusses problems confronting the young American playwrights and conditions necessary for the revival of meaningful original work. She is disenchanted with the theatre of the day, expressing also her concern that "expense account" audiences no longer want serious plays.

S124   Triesch, Manfred. *The Lillian Hellman Collection at the University of Texas.* Austin, TX: Humanities Research Center, University of Texas at Austin, 1966.
            A descriptive catalogue of manuscripts, notebooks, and letters in a collection open solely to Hellman's official biographer, William Abrahams.

1967

S125   Bentley, Eric. *The Theatre of Commitment.* New York: Atheneum Publishers, 1967. 39-40.
            A chapter entitled "The American Drama [1944-54]" charges that *The Children's Hour* (1952-53 season) gives expression to a particular ambiguity which is strikingly characteristic of a quasi-liberal movement that has been overawed by Communism.

S126   Calta, Louis. "Lead Is Dropped by Miss Leighton: Actress Takes a Smaller Part in *Little Foxes* Here." *New York Times* 16 May 1967, 49.
            British actress Margaret Leighton will play the part of Birdie in the Lincoln Center Repertory Theatre's production of *The Little Foxes*, relinquishing the leading role of Regina as originally scheduled. (An Actors Equity faction, opposed to foreign performers, had recently picketed the *Galileo* production at the Vivian Beaumont because of Anthony Quayle.)

S127   Findlater, Richard. *Banned! A Review of Theatrical Censorship in Britain.* London: MacGibbon & Kee Ltd., 1967. 135, 136, 165.
            Lists *The Children's Hour* among the plays that Lord Chamberlain prohibited, since its performance "would have been a real scandal" (135). "When Henry Sherek applied to the Chamberlain to stage *The Children's Hour*, Lord Scarbrough called him a *corrupter of youth*--and said no" (165).

S128   Freedman, Morris. *The Moral Impulse: Modern Drama from Ibsen to the Present.* With a Preface by Harry T. Moore. Carbondale, IL: Southern Illinois University Press, 1967.
            A chapter entitled "Bertold Brecht and American Social Drama" compares *The Little Foxes* and *Watch on the Rhine* to Brecht. Finds characters caricatured in *The Little Foxes*, stereotyped in *Watch on the Rhine*. Describes the treatment that Brecht would have employed.

S129   French, Warren. "The Thirties--Drama." In *The Thirties: Fiction, Poetry, Drama.*
        Ed. Warren French. Deland, FL: Everett Edwards, Inc., 1967. 177-78.
            Briefly mentions Hellman in a survey of the achievements of the 30s.
        Believes her plays will outlast those of Odets. *The Children's Hour* and *The Little
        Foxes* still have impact, though they will never become period pieces.

S130   Goldstein, Malcolm. "The Playwrights of the 1930s." *The American Theatre
        Today.* Ed. Alan S. Downer. New York: Basic Books, 1967. 34-36.
            Comments on *The Children's Hour* and *The Little Foxes.* Compares
        Hellman to Clifford Odets. Finds Hellman "the more impressive dramatist, by
        virtue of her avoidance of the easy answer; her plays have a life outside the
        context of the Depression years. Moreover, her art continues to develop in
        admirable though infrequent contributions to the stage" (36).

S131   Hartnoll, Phyllis, ed. *The Oxford Companion to the Theatre.* 3r ed. London:
        Oxford University Press, 1967. 438.
            Brief biographical sketch and critical overview of Hellman's plays by
        John Gassner.

                                    1968

S132   Funke, Lewis. "Interview with Lillian Hellman." 1968. From *Playwrights Talk
        About Writing: 12 Interviews With Lewis Funke.* Chicago: Dramatic Publishing
        Co., 1975. 90-110. Reprinted in *Conversations with Lillian Hellman.* Ed.
        Jackson S. Bryer. Jackson: University Press of Mississippi, 1986. 84-106.
            Having just published *An Unfinished Woman,* Hellman expresses
        opinions on the lack of female playwrights, the art of playwriting, and her
        English classes wherein she never gives rules, because she doesn't believe in
        them.

S133   Gardner, Fred. "An Interview with Lillian Hellman." 1968. Audio cassette:
        Jeffrey Norton Publishers, Guilford, CT. Printed in *Conversations with Lillian
        Hellman.* Ed. Jackson S. Bryer. Jackson: University Press of Mississippi, 1986.
        107-123.
            Interviewed by a former student, who took a English course that she
        taught at Harvard in 1961, Hellman comments on her plays and the current state
        of theatre from which she has become increasingly alienated. She believes that
        Broadway audiences have changed, as has Broadway theatre which "has declined
        in the quality of writing" (108).

S134   Haller, Charles David. *The Concept of Moral Failure in the Eight Original Plays
        of Lillian Hellman.* Unpublished Dissertation (Tulane University). DAI 28
        (1968), 4303.
            An examination of the concept of moral failure in the plays concludes that
        Hellman views the absence of good (moral failure) in terms of destructive action
        or nonaction, of active and passive killers, harshly judging her characters by
        holding them responsible as individuals and not society.

1969

S135   Adler, Jacob H. *Lillian Hellman--Southern Writers Series* 4. Austin, TX: Steck,
         Vaughan Company, 1969.
                 Includes biographical information, analyzes the plays, explores their
         relationship to Ibsen, and to the influence of Chekhov in *The Autumn Garden*.
         Considers Hellman's methods viable, her mastery minor. The first extended study
         (44 pages).

S136   Goldman, William. *The Season: A Candid Look at Broadway*. New York:
         Harcourt, Brace and World, Inc., 1969.
                 A chapter entitled "Culture Hero" discusses the Mike Nichols' production
         of *The Little Foxes* . Nichols took an excellent melodrama, gave it "an execrable
         production, and triumphed nonetheless" (263). The work was "ecstatically
         received," and Nichols became a "culture hero."

S137   Miller, Jordan Y. "Drama: The War Play Comes of Age." *The Forties: Fiction,
         Poetry, Drama*. Ed. Warren French. Deland, FL: Everett Edwards, 1969. 63-81.
                 The chapter includes *Watch on the Rhine* in an examination of the
         development of the war play from naiveté to the "sophisticated exploration of the
         war's effects on the men who fight it" (64). Praises the construction of the play,
         the characters, and the understatement that makes its point.

S138   Whitesides, Glenn B. *Lillian Hellman: A Biographical and Critical Study*.
         Unpublished Dissertation (Florida State University). DAI 29 (1969), 2287.
                 Discusses, interprets, and evaluates Hellman's contributions to America
         literary activity and the relationship of her private life to her literary work.

1970

S139   Ackley, Meredith Erling. *The Plays of Lillian Hellman*. Unpublished Dissertation
         (University of Pennsylvania). DAI 30 (1970), 4441.
                 An examination of dramatic patterns in the plays concludes that while the
         works are intended to be more than entertaining theatre, no attention has been
         given to definition of the black and white forces of their action. Participants are
         named but not explored. Only the "inactive" main character is fully delineated; and
         the action exists solely to bring this character to awareness.

S140   Atkinson, Brooks. *Broadway*. New York: Macmillan Co., 1970. 258, 262, 298-
         300, 357, 446.
                 Comments on the Pulitzer and Drama Critics' Circle Awards in
         relationship to Hellman's plays. Surveys *The Children's Hour*, *The Little Foxes*,
         Watch on the Rhine, and *Another Part of the Forest*.

S141   "Lillian Hellman Reflects upon the Changing Theatre." *Dramatists Guild
         Quarterly* 7 (Winter 1970): 17-22. Reprinted in *Playwrights, Lyricist, Composers
         on Theater*. Ed. Otis L. Guernsey, Jr. New York: Dodd, Mead and Company,
         1974. 250-257. Edited version reprinted in *Conversations with Lillian Hellman*.
         Ed. Jackson S. Bryer. Jackson: University Press of Mississippi, 1986. 124-131.

During a question-and-answer session at the Drama Guild headquarters, Hellman states her dissatisfaction with the theatre. She has always been interested in the writing of the play, yet the commercial aspects of production have always been to her disliking. She believes that theatre "has gone steadily down hill. Even musical theater isn't as good as it used to be . . . [and] films now are more exciting than plays" (Conversations, 127).

S142   Heilman, Robert B. "Dramas of Money." *Shenandoah* 21 (Summ. 1970): 20-33.

Includes *The Little Foxes* in a discussion of money plays. Melodrama dominates the Hellman play, yet the money-theme is treated with generic diversity. In the end evil is triumphant, but "the play seems less to evoke the divided response of the best melodrama than to give us some comforting reassurance that sooner or later the bad guys will have their troubles, if only at the hands of each other" (28).

S143   Keats, John. *You Might as Well Live, The Life and Times of Dorothy Parker.* New York: Simon and Schuster, 1970.

Contains references to the Parker/Hellman friendship and to the production of *Candide* and Parker's "very minor role" (269). According to Parker, "It didn't work out very well. There were too many geniuses in it, you know" (269).

S144   Sievers, W. David. "Lillian Hellman." *Freud on Broadway: A History of Psychoanalysis and the American Drama.* New York: Cooper Square Publishers, Inc., 1970. 279-289.

Devotes a section to Hellman in the chapter entitled, "Freudian Fraternity of the Thirties." Her plays reflect the turbulent thirties and the war-torn forties, and the psychoanalytic insight, derived from her own psychoanalysis.

1971

S145   Bentley, Eric, ed. *Thirty Years of Treason, Excerpts from Hearings before the House Committee on Un-American Activities, 1938-1968.* New York: Viking Press, 1971. 533-43.

Includes a copy of Hellman's testimony before the Committee as well as the text of her letter. Comments on her tactics.

S146   Block, Anita. *The Changing World in Plays and Theatre.* New York: Da Capo Press, 1971. 120, 122-126.

A chapter entitled "Conflict with Changing Sexual Standards" praises *The Children's Hour*, despite its structural flaws, for treating a subject of grave import with meaning and significance. The real victim is Martha who, whether shocked into illuminating knowledge or so devastated as to believe herself abnormal, "steps quietly into the next room and shoots herself" (125).

S147   Johnson, Annette Bergman. *A Study of Recurrent Character Types in the Plays of Lillian Hellman.* Unpublished Dissertation (University of Massachusetts). DAI 31 (1971), 6614.

Analyzes four categories of character types within the Hellman plays: the masters, the lost ladies, the ineffectual males, and the enlightened and their counselor, usually the spokesmen for the playwright. The "types" undergo transformations through the plays and adaptations in accordance with Hellman's growth and development. Concludes that there is nothing positive in Hellman's vision of society, no solutions to the problems posed. She rails against evil, but withdrawing through the counselor types denies that there is an ideal which can be achieved.

S148   Larimer, Cynthia D.M. *A Study of Female Characters in the Eight Plays of Lillian Hellman*. Unpublished Dissertation (Purdue University). DAI 31 (1971), 5410.

Examines the female characters in the eight original plays according to autobiographical significance, dramatic portrayal, and significance of character, concluding that through continuous experimentation and reuse of basic types, the female characters become more dramatically effective.

1972

S149   Adler, Renata."The Guest Word." *New York Times Book Review* 9 July 1972: 39.

Novelist and reviewer Adler dismisses the Samuel review of *The Collected Plays* as sign of pure ineptitude. (See S157)

S150   Angermeier, Brother Carrol. *Moral and Social Protest in the Plays of Lillian Hellman*. Unpublished Dissertation (University of Texas at Austin). DAI 32 (1972), 3986.

Examines the original plays as examples of topical drama that protest moral and social delinquency, as a study of social irresponsibility, and in terms of the relationship between Hellman's social and moral value system and its milieu. Includes a chapter on Hellman's biography.

S151   Bentley, Eric. *Are You Now or Have You Ever Been? The Investigation of Show Business by the Un-American Activities Committee, 1947-1958*. New York: Harper-Colophon Books, 1972. 109-113.

The dialogue of this play *Are You Now or Have You Ever Been?* is taken from the hearings before the Un-American Activities Committee and from a record published by the United States Government. In one part of the play Hellman is named by screenwriter by Martin Berkeley. The scene is followed by a reading of Hellman's letter to Congressman Woods.

S152   Blitgen, Sister Carol B.V.M. *The Overlooked Hellman*. Unpublished Dissertation (University of California, Santa Barbara), 1972.

An unverified source.

S153   Clurman, Harold. *On Directing*. New York: The Macmillan Company, 1972. 47-50, 83, 197-205.

The director comments on his production of *The Autumn Garden*. Includes director's notes (197-205).

S154 Israel, Lee. *Miss Tallulah Bankhead*. New York: G.P. Putnam's Sons, 1972. 186-200.

Chapter 17, entitled *The Little Foxes*, contains information on the Shumlin/Hellman relationship, including the dispute over a special benefit performance for the Finnish cause. The show gave Bankhead the greatest property of her career. After a year on Broadway, she took the show on the road.

S155 Moody, Richard. *Lillian Hellman: Playwright*. New York: Pegasus, 1972.

Introduction by Harold Clurman. The first of the critical biographies that consider the development of Hellman's plays. Includes detailed plot summaries, play analyses, manuscript revisions, and critical overviews. Relies excessively on material in *An Unfinished Woman* and the *Paris Review* interview.

S156 Phillips, Elizabeth C. "Command of Human Destiny as Exemplified in Two Plays: Lillian Hellman's *The Little Foxes* and Lorraine Hansberry's *A Raisin in the Sun*." *Interpretations* 4 (1972): 29-39.

Examines parallels within the two plays, literary derivation of titles, families as *dramatis personae*, theme, techniques, and values, which affirm the belief that man may command his own destiny.

S157 Samuels, Charles Thomas. *New York Times Book Review* 18 June 1972, 2-3, 16, 18.

A combined appraisal of Moody's book and The Collected Plays. Finds the Moody book "deplorable and inept." Criticizes skimpy biographical information, which is based largely on Hellman's memoirs. Attacks Hellman's reputation as a serious playwright. (See Adler rebuttal, S149)

S158 Smiley, Sam. *The Drama of Attack: Didactic Plays of the American Depression*. Columbia: University of Missouri Press, 1972.

While not purely Marxist, Hellman's plays represent "the highest achievements of the leftist writers "in their organization, communication of social awareness and intensive employment of thought" (59).

S159 Szogyi, Alex. "The Collected Plays by Lillian Hellman." *Saturday Review* 12 Aug. 1972: 51-52.

An affectionate review that celebrates Hellman's accomplishments and acknowledges her as one of the most important American playwrights of our time.

1973

S160 Armato, Philip M. "*Good and Evil* in Lillian Hellman's *The Children's Hour*." *Educational Theatre Journal* 25 (1973): 443-47.

Explores the interpersonal relationships which are "patterned after the structure of human association in the Venice of Shakespeare's *Merchant . . .* [and] best described as a victim-victimizer syndrome" (444). Argues that school mistresses are first the victimizers then the victims.

S161 Bonin, Jane. *Prize-winning American Drama, a Bibliographical and Descriptive Guide*. Metuchen, NJ: Scarecrow Press, 1973.

Includes comments on the Pulitzer decision disqualifying *The Children's Hour* as recipient of its award. The Prize went instead to Zoë Akins's *The Old Maid*.

S162   Eatman, James. "The Image of American Destiny: *The Little Foxes*." *Players* 48 (Dec.-Jan. 1973). 70-73.
       Examines the potential of the historical play to construct "meaning by illuminating simultaneously the past, the present, and the future" (70). Considers the play as a resilient construction of history, a distinctive representative of social realism--although the setting is not contemporary--, and concludes that, "By a synthesis of rational formulation and moral commitment, *The Little Foxes* gains particular authority in casting an image of American destiny--the continuing dialectic of the privileges versus the responsibilities of liberal democracy" (730).

S163   Ephron, Nora. "Lillian Hellman Walking, Cooking, Writing, Talking." *New York Times Book Review* Section 23 Sept. 1973: 2, 51. Reprinted in *Conversations with Lillian Hellman*. Ed. Jackson S. Bryer. Jackson: University Press of Mississippi, 1986: 132-37.
       Having just published her second memoir, *Pentimento*, Hellman talks about Hammett, Parker, the McCarthy period, getting old (she's now 67), the women's movement, and more.

S164   Falb, Lewis W. *American Drama in Paris 1945-1970: A Study of Its Critical Reception*. Chapel Hill: University of North Carolina Press, 1973.
       A section entitled "Lillian Hellman" (54-55) describes the critical reception of *The Little Foxes* in Paris in 1962 which was "universally and vehemently negative" (54). The play was a moderate success, however, due to leading ladies, Simone Signoret and Suzanne Flon.

S165   Heilman, Robert. *The Iceman, The Arsonist and the Troubled Agent: Tragedy and Melodrama on the Modern Stage*. Seattle: University of Washington Press, 1973.
       A chapter entitled "Dramas of Money: Some Variations Since 1875" includes a section on *The Little Foxes*. Notes the straightforward melodramatic pattern, yet the attempt at a general validity that lies beyond stereotypes; the pervasive irony of dishonor among thieves as in Jonson's *The Fox*; the touch of black comedy as in Becque's *The Vultures*.

S166   Hasbany, Richard. *Rituals of Reassurance: Studies in World War II American Drama*. Unpublished Dissertation (Michigan State). DAI-A 34 (1973), 3398.
       Chapter two includes a discussion of Hellman's works, arguing that she moves from a vision in which the individual and his moral experience is of primary concern to a vision in which individual destiny is linked to communal destiny, that this identification is imaged in the figure of Christ who also sacrificed his life to save the community.

S167   Holmin, Lorena Ross. *The Dramatic Works of Lillian Hellman*. Uppsala, Sweden: Almquist and Wiksell (distr.), 1973. Ph.D. dissertation, Uppsala University, published in Uppsala University's English Studies series. Austin, TX: Humanities Press.

Examines the original plays, excluding *Days to Come*, emphasizing plot summary rather than analysis.

S168   Vinson, James, ed. *Contemporary Dramatists*. Preface by Ruby Cohn. London, St. James Press; New York, St. Martin Press, 1973. 363-66.

Entry, entitled "Hellman, Lillian (Florence)," reprints Clurman's Introduction to Moody's *Lillian Hellman: Playwright*, 1972 (S155). Includes biographical information, publications lists.

1974

S169   Chusmir, Janet. "Lillian Hellman on Lillian Hellman. *Miami Herald* 17 Mar. 1974: F, 1, 10. Reprinted in *Conversations with Lillian Hellman*. Ed. Jackson S. Bryer. Jackson: University Press of Mississippi, 1986. 159-164.

Hellman comments on getting older, her relationship with Hammett, and her lack of interest in the theatre which was really not her world, although it had been her life.

S170   Goldstein, Malcolm. *The Political Stage: American Drama and Theatre of the Great Depression*. New York: Oxford University Press, 1974. 149.

The Children's Hour demonstrates "the playwright's ability to weave tough-minded expressions of liberal social attitudes into a suspenseful plot."

S171   Moyers, Bill. "Lillian Hellman" *The Great Playwright Candidly Reflects on a Long, Rich Life*. Telecast on National Educational Television, Apr. 1974. Available on audio cassette from the Center for Cassette Studies. Reprinted in *Conversations with Lillian Hellman*. Ed. Jackson S. Bryer. Jackson: University Press of Mississippi, 1986. 138-158.

Hellman comments on her life experiences, the celebrities that she's known, her relationships, the women's movement, her books, her plays; and reads selected passages from the Julia chapter of *Pentimento*.

1975

S172   Carlson, Eugene T. *Lillian Hellman's Plays as a Reflection of the Southern Mind*. Unpublished Dissertation (University of Southern California), 1975.

An unverified reference.

S173   De Pue, Stephanie. "Lillian Hellman: She Never Turns down an Adventure." *Cleveland Plain Dealer* 28 Dec. 1975: V, 2. Reprinted in *Conversations with Lillian Hellman*. Ed. Jackson S. Bryer. Jackson: University Press of Mississippi, 1986. 184-191.

Recently named Ladies Home Journal Woman of the Year in Creative Arts, cited for embodying woman's potential as an artist since the production of her first play, Hellman comments on the women's movement, her plays, and her fascination with villains.

S174   Going, William T. *Essays on Alabama Literature: Studies in Humanities* No. 4.
         Tuscaloosa: University of Alabama Press, 1975. 142-55.
             Chapter 8, entitled "The Prestons of Talladega and the Hubbards of
         Bowen: a Dramatic Note," considers *The Little Foxes* and *Another Part of the
         Forest* which demonstrate Hellman's interest in the historical, social, and political
         aspects of the Alabama she knew partially at firsthand. She "used her mother's
         Alabama family, particularly her Uncle Jake, as models for the rapacious
         Hubbards" (144). Sophronia Mason, Hellman's Negro nurse, was "the probable
         model for Addie in *The Little Foxes*" (143).

S175   Reed, Rex. "Lillian Hellman Remembers." *New York Sunday News* 9 Nov.
         1975; and *The [Baltimore] Sun* 9 Nov. 1975: D, 3. Reprinted in *Valentines &
         Vitriol.* New York: Delacorte Press, 1977. 103-08. Reprinted in *Conversations
         with Lillian Hellman.* Ed. Jackson S. Bryer. Jackson: University Press of
         Mississippi, 1986. 179-183.
             Interview having to do with the tribute to Hellman that evening at the
         Circle in the Square, NYC, "for her contribution to the theatre, to literature and to
         the protection of civil liberties" (103). Celebrities read and performed excerpts
         from her plays. The proceeds went to the Committee for Public Justice, an
         organization Hellman founded five years prior to support the Bill of Rights and to
         protect private citizens.

                                          1976

S176   Edmiston, Susan and Linda D. Cirino. *Literary New York: A History and Guide.*
         Boston: Houghton Mifflin Co., 1976.
             Includes addresses where Hellman lived.

S177   Hershey, John. "Lillian Hellman." *New Republic* 18 Sept. 1976: 25-27.
         Reprinted in *Life Sketches*: New York: Knopf, 1989. 367-74. Reprinted in
         Critical Essays on Lillian Hellman. Ed. Mark W. Estrin. Boston: G.K. Hall &
         Co., 1989. 248-252.
             An homage to Hellman, written on the occasion of her receiving the
         Edward MacDowell Medal for her contribution to literature, affectionately
         portrays her as a spunky, rebellious life force. "She cuts through all ideologies to
         their taproot: To the decency their adherents universally profess but almost never
         deliver" (27).

                                          1977

S178   Buckley, William F., Jr. "*Scoundrel Time* & Who Is the Ugliest of Them All?"
         National Review 24 (21 Jan. 1977): 101-06.
             Buckley scathingly denounces *Scoundrel Time.* A direct personal attack is
         keynoted by the magazine's cover, depicting a reproduction of the Hellman
         Backglama fur advertisement on which is superimposed in large type "& Who Is
         the Ugliest of Them All?" Hellman had posed in a mink coat advertisement titled
         "What Becomes a Legend Most?"

S179   Doudna, Christine. "A Still Unfinished Woman: A Conversation with Lillian
         Hellman." *Rolling Stone* 233 (24 Feb. 1977): 52-57. Reprinted in *Conversations
         with Lillian Hellman*. Ed. Jackson S. Bryer. Jackson: University Press of
         Mississippi, 1986. 192-209.
                 During a July 4th weekend on Martha's Vineyard, Hellman elaborates
         upon her writings, her views of the feminist movement, the movie *Julia*, her
         relationship with Hammett, and growing old. Speaking of the psychiatric therapy
         that she had undergone, she says: "The man who analyzed me once said I was the
         only patient he'd ever had in his life who talked about herself as if I were another
         person. He meant no compliment. He meant that I had too cold a view of myself"
         (*Conversations*, 201).

S180   McPherson, Michael Lewis. *Lillian Hellman and Her Critics*. Unpublished
         Dissertation (University of Denver). DAI 37 (1977), 3989.
                 Analyzes the critical reaction to Hellman's original plays, concerning
         style, form, language, subject matter, and theme. Finds the plots predominantly
         melodramatic, the characters brilliantly drawn, a reflection of skillful dialogue;
         Hellman's high standards of emotional impact matched by few of her
         contemporaries.

S181   Patraka, Vivian Mary. *Lillian Hellman, Dramatist of the Second Sex*.
         Unpublished Dissertation (University of Michigan). DAI 37 (1977), 3989.
                 Investigates Hellman's female characters in terms of fulfilling the
         requirements for characterization as dictated by dramatic realism and also in terms
         of being rounded portrayals of women, revealing circumstances unique to women
         and common to humanity. Concludes that, in the artistically successful plays,
         female characters are depicted as autonomous and complex.

S182   Rather, Dan. "A Profile of Lillian Hellman." Interview broadcast on CBS-TV, 8
         Mar. 1977. Available on audio cassette from Encyclopedia Americana/CBS News
         Audio Resource Library. Transcript printed in *Conversations with Lillian
         Hellman*. Ed. Jackson S. Bryer. Jackson: University Press of Mississippi, 1986.
         210-217.
                 Now the subject of *Julia*, the film in which Jane Fonda plays her
         character, and her recent bestselling memoir, *Scoundrel Time*, that has stirred
         controversy among critics and friends, Hellman grants an interview. She denies
         revisionist writing of the McCarthy era. Her position on the women's movement
         is restated: its concerns are and should be more on economic demands. Includes
         Fonda's comments on Hellman's complexities and contradictions, having met
         with Hellman to confer on the upcoming film.

1978

S183   Dillon, Ann and Cynthia Bix. *Contributions of Women: Theater*. Minneapolis:
         Dillon Press, Inc. 1978. 76-99. An unverified source

S184   Falk, Doris V. *Lillian Hellman*. New York: Frederick Ungar Publishing Co., 1978.
                 The first book-length analysis of both plays and memoirs, the critical
         biography examines the relationship between the two. Insists that Hellman is a

well-made, realistic playwright. Divides the eight original dramas into despoiler and bystander categories. Omits discussion of adaptations.

S185   Friedman, Sharon P. *Feminist Concerns in the Works of Four Twentieth-Century American Women Dramatists: Susan Glaspell, Rachel Crothers, Lillian Hellman, and Lorraine Hansberry.* Unpublished Dissertation (New York University). DAI 39 (1978), 858.
        Applies feminist theory to the works of the four dramatists. In the Hellman plays, social and economic powerlessness of the women can at times give rise to the most demonic behavior. Women characters are varied. Far from being stereotypes, "they are firmly rooted in their circumstances as women.

S186   Jelinek, Estelle C. *The Tradition of Women's Autobiographies.* Dissertation (State University of New York, Buffalo). DAI-A 38 (1978), 5479. Published Twayne, 1986.
        One chapter analyzes *An Unfinished Woman, Pentimento,* and *Scoundrel Time,* wherein she converts the personal into the psychological, viewing political and social events from her own eccentric perspective, and relying on anecdotes to narrate her shaped but discontinuous portraits.

S187   Laufe, Abe. *The Wicked Stage, A History of Theater Censorship and Harassment in the United States.* New York: Frederick Ungar Publishing Company, 1978. 70, 71, 72.
        The Children's Hour was rumored to be the leading contender for the Pulitzer Prize, but censored by the Committee who bypassed the play and selected *The Old* Maid by Zoë Akins. Incensed critics reactivated the New York Drama *Critics Circle* the following year in order to award their own prizes.

S188   Long, Norma Rae. *Creative Autonomy of the Literary Woman: Case of Hellman.* Unpublished Dissertation   (University of Maryland College Park). DAI 39 (1978), 781.
        Investigates Hellman's creative autonomy, as manifested in her life and personality, using a framework of six value orientations: theoretical, aesthetic, religious, social, political, and economic. Demonstrates that Hellman's lifestyle was emotionally fulfilling and artistically rewarding, concluding that other creative women would benefit similarly from an assessment of their relations to their art, their loved ones, and their culture.

S189   Scanlan, Tom. *Family, Drama, and American Dreams.* Westport, CT: Greenwood Press, 1978.
        A chapter entitled "The Family World of American Drama" discusses the Hellman plays and concludes that in most of Hellman's works "the corrosive effect of the enclosed family is the central situation of her dramatic world. She is at her best when presenting a well-made family war" (185). Compares Hellman's family themes to those of Odets.

1979

S190   Adam, Peter. "Unfinished Woman." *The Listener* 191 (8 Feb. 1979): 213-16. Originally broadcast as a BBC programme on "Omnibus," 8 Feb. 1979, and excerpted from an interview conducted in late autumn 1978. Printed in

Conversations with Lillian Hellman. Ed. Jackson S. Bryer. Jackson: University Press of Mississippi, 1986. 218-231.

Hellman elaborates upon her struggles with the theatre as a woman whose need for privacy could not be reconciled with a profession that demanded collaboration. In retrospect, she believes that she took her moral stands too sharply. Comments on her plays and Hammett's influence.

S191   Berger, Marilyn. "Profile: Lillian Hellman." Interview, 1979. Transcript of a five-part interview broadcast on KERA-TV Dallas/Fort Worth, 5, 7, 8, 9, 10 Apr. 1981. Printed in *Conversations with Lillian Hellman*. Ed. Jackson S. Bryer. Jackson: University Press of Mississippi, 1986. 232-273.

In Part I, Hellman explains her preference for writing novels. She is not a collaborator by nature; and she intensely dislikes the commercial aspects of putting on a play. In Part II, she touches on her plays and her relationship with Hammett. In Part III, she speaks of the McCarthy episode of her life; Part IV to the aftermath. In Part V, she regrets having wasted time, not having committed herself more to her writing, not having gone on for an M.A. and a Ph.D.; and wants to be remembered for her writing.

S192   Bills, Steven H. *Lillian Hellman: An Annotated Bibliography*. New York: Garland Publishing, Inc., 1979.

An introductory study of Hellman's life and work which attempts to cover comprehensively the critical reception of her work. Entries include biographical material; interviews and news concerning Hellman's plays and books; reviews, scholarly works and critical surveys of the eight original plays and the four adaptations; reviews of screenplays; reviews of autobiographies; and graduate studies. Descriptive and evaluative comments. Errors in listing number of performances of each play, in volume and page numbers in all sections, and in the contents of annotations (see Adler, Three Books 470-71).

S193   Lederer, Katherine. *Lillian Hellman*. Boston: Twayne Publishers, 1979. In DiscLit. American Authors. Twayne United States Authors Series and OCLC American Authors Catalog, 1991.

Introductory study of Hellman's life and work which debunks "automatic genre labeling." Analyzes the eight original plays and includes plot summaries. Uses the categories in Robert Boies Sharpe's *Irony in the Drama* to illustrate the constant use of dramatic irony in the Hellman plays, concluding that Hellman's best plays are ironic (and novelistic).

S194   Morrison, Frances Rowena. *Seeing, and Seeing Again: Self-Discovery in the Plays of Lillian Hellman*. Unpublished Dissertation (University of North Carolina at Chapel Hill). DAI 40 (1979), 251.

Isolates a single theme, the moral necessity of self-awareness and purposive action in life, that is worked out in Hellman's dramas against the field of social, political, and psychological problems. Shows how the theme of self-discovery is expressed in various patterns from play to play, relying on Hellman's memoirs, where relevant, for interpretive detail.

1980

S195   Estrin, Mark W. "Lillian Hellman." *Contemporary Dramatists*, 3d ed. Ed. James
        Vinson. London: St. James Press, 1980: 374-78.
          A critical essay with biographical and bibliographic information.

S196   Estrin, Mark W. *Lillian Hellman: Plays, Films, Memoirs: A Reference Guide.*
        Boston: C.K. Hall & Co., 1980.
          This well-annotated bibliography includes a detailed critical assessment of
        the plays, adaptations, films, memoirs, and other studies. Works by Hellman
        make up the first major section of the book and are listed by genre. The writings
        about Hellman, 1934-79, form the second section and are assembled
        chronologically and then alphabetically with the year of publication.

S197   Lederer, Katherine. "The Foxes Were Waiting for Horace, Not Lefty: The Use of
        Irony in Lillian Hellman's *The Little Foxes.*" *West Virginia University
        Philological Papers* 26, 1980. 97-104.
          Examines the use of ironic technique in *The Little Foxes*. Points out that
        "tone" is all-important in Hellman's works, that Hellman has trenchantly
        expressed a frequently funny, uncomfortably accurate ironic vision of her foxes.

S198   Riordan, Mary Marguerite. *Lillian Hellman: A Bibliography, 1926-1978.*
        Methuchen, NJ, & London: Scarecrow Press, 1980.
          A lengthy chronology introduces other sections: plays and adaptations,
        screenplays, books, contributions to newspapers and periodicals, unpublished
        works, recordings, and an index to letters and manuscripts. Not all entries are
        annotated.

S199   Tischler, Nancy M. "The South Stage Center: Hellman and Williams." *The
        American South: Portrait of a Culture.* Ed. Louis D. Rubin, Jr. Baton Rouge:
        Louisiana State University Press. 323-33.
          Compares Hellman to Williams, who began his theatrical career shortly
        after the publication of *The Little Foxes*. While Hellman does not cotton to defeat,
        Williams dotes on the defeated. He sees the enemy as time or fate, she is "more
        inclined to see it as human malevolence" (331). Her portrayals are effective
        vignettes of *home and frightening land* (333); his are more poetic, more moving.

S200   Warga, Wayne. "Hellman at 75: Fragile but Furious." *Los Angeles Times* 10
        Aug. 1980, calendar, 1, 6-7. Reprinted in *Conversations with Lillian Hellman.*
        Ed. Jackson S. Bryer. Jackson: University Press of Mississippi, 1986. 274-281.
          Hellman talks about her recent controversy with Mary McCarthy, who has
        called her a bad and dishonest writer on the Dick Cavett Show; and her fourth
        memoir, *Maybe,* which has just been published, the theme of which is memory.

1981

S201   Adler, Jacob H. "Three Books on Hellman." *Mississippi Quarterly: Journal of
        Southern Culture* 34 (Fall 1981): 463-71.

Book reviews of Katherine Lederer's *Lillian Hellman*, Mary Marguerite Riordan's *Lillian Hellman: A Bibliography*, and Steven H. Bills *Lillian Hellman: An Annotated Bibliography*. A discerning appraisal by the scholar who wrote the first extended study on Hellman's plays.

S202   Broe, Mary Lynn. "Bohemia Bumps into Calvin: The Deception of Passivity in Lillian Hellman's Drama." *Southern Quarterly* 19 (Winter 1981): 26-41.

Examines the negligible women in five plays, *The Children's Hour*, *The Little Foxes*, *Another Part of the Forest*, *The Autumn Garden*, and *Toys in the Attic*, to show how cleverly Hellman tailors passivity, a socially assigned role, to "variegated moral and dramatic authority" (40). Catalysts for truth telling and deception, these socially negligible women serve to clarify recurring themes.

S203   Drake, Sylvie. "Lillian Hellman as Herself." *Los Angeles Times* 18 Oct. 1981, calendar, 1, 6. Reprinted in *Conversations with Lillian Hellman*. Ed. Jackson S. Bryer. Jackson: University Press of Mississippi, 1986: 287-292.

In Los Angeles for the opening of *The Little Foxes* at the Ahmanson, Hellman grants an interview, even though she doesn't like being interviewed. "Its silly to say because it sounds fake-modest, but I'm not crazy about talking about myself" (Conversations, 287. She comments on decency, courage, her disillusionment with the theatre, her work, being Jewish and a woman.

S204   Hungerford, Robert Walker. *Minutes in Lillian Hellman's The Children's Hour: Composition of the Play from Inception to Publication*. Unpublished Dissertation (University of South Carolina). DAI 42 (1981), 215.

Provides historical and critical information on the sources and composition of *The Children's Hour*, based on materials held in the Lillian Hellman Collection of the Humanities Research Center at the University of Texas at Austin. Notes problems with the third act and Martha's suicide which were present in pre-composition stages and continued through six stages of composition.

S205   Meras, Phyllis. "Lillian Hellman Hasn't Gone Fishin'." *Providence Journal* 5 July 1981: H, 9. Reprinted in *Conversations with Lillian Hellman*. Ed. Jackson S. Bryer. Jackson: University Press of Mississippi. 1986: 282-286.

An interview granted while *The Little Foxes* was in revival on Broadway with Elizabeth Taylor playing Regina. Hellman talks of politics, the current state of literature, and of her failing eyesight that hinders work on a new book about children.

S206   Mooney, Theresa Rose. *"Southern Influences in Four Plays by Lillian Hellman*. Dissertation (Tulane University). DAI 42 (1981), 2677. Available Ann Arbor: UMI, 1984.

Analyzes the elements of Southern influence in *The Little Foxes* (1939), *Another Part of the Forest* (1946), *The Autumn Garden* (1951), and *Toys in the Attic* (1959), tracing autobiographical details and discussing the growth of Hellman's political commitment.

S207   Olauson, Judith. *The American Woman Playwright: A View of Criticism and Characterization*. Troy, NY: The Whitston Publishing Company, 1981.

Includes Hellman in her discussion of women who have made extensive contributions to the body of American dramatic literature, but were presumed to be second rate and undeserving of thorough critical attention.

1982

S208   Bigsby, C.W.E. *A Critical Introduction to Twentieth-Century American Drama 1900-1940*. Cambridge, UK: Cambridge University Press, 1982.
        A careful and unpatronizing critical analysis of the plays in a chapter devoted entirely to Lillian Hellman (274-297).

S209   Dick, Bernard F. *Hellman in Hollywood*. Rutherford: Fairleigh Dickinson University Press, 1982.
        Critiques the film adaptations of the plays, the films Hellman adapted for the screen from others sources, the film adaptation of the "Julia" section of *Pentimento*, and includes a filmography. Chapter 2 (32-49) analyzes *The Children's Hour*, the stage play, in terms of classical tragedy before discussing the film adaptations. Chapter 4 (58-80) integrates information about the stage plays, *The Little Foxes* and *Another Part of the Forest*, in a discussion of the screen versions. Chapter 5 (81-96) examines *Watch on the Rhine*, stage to screen versions. Chapter 7 (108-118) *The Searching Wind*, Chapter 8 (119-135) *Toys in the Attic*. Chapter 10 (152-165) traces the Julia figure throughout the plays.

S210   Williams, Philip. "Homage to Lillian Hellman: Notes on *The Children's Hour*." *Doshisha Studies in English* 28 (1982): 91-113.
        Although Hellman resisted the "woman playwright" label, an examination of *The Children's Hour* shows that the play makes "striking points which are important for better understanding of 'Woman and Literature,' and there is no question that they mirror personal attitudes and experiences of the playwright"(95).

1983

S211   Lyons, Bonnie. "Lillian Hellman: The First Jewish Nun on Prytania Street." In *From Hester Street to Hollywood: The Jewish-American Stage and Screen*. Ed. Cohen, Sarah Blacher. Bloomington: Indiana University Press, 1983. 106-122.
        An examination of Hellman's works reveals a distinctly unJewish and ultimately anti-Jewish worldview. Rigid, excessively judgmental, unloving, and unforgiving, characteristic of a stereotypical nun, she insists on "extreme, undivided, absolute commitment and projects a world in which moral complexity is flattened into a simplified relief of good and evil" (121).

S212   O'Brien, Susan. "The Image of Woman in Tony-Award-Winning Plays 1960-1979."
        Includes *Toys in the Attic* in a discussion of dramas that contain "insights as pertinent as Ibsen's plays of the late nineteenth century into woman's need to accept responsibility for her own liberation and establishing of self-identity, separate from being a function of a relationship." Anna, at the end of the play,

opts out of relationships, cloying and false, in favor of a new sense of personhood.

S213   Sargeant, Alvin. *Two Lives: Dashiell Hammett/Lillian Hellman*. Burbank, CA: Richard Roth Productions, in association with Warner Bros., 1983.
        A screenplay, held solely by Amherst University. Not available for loan.

1984

S214   Binder, Wolfgang. "Manners, Morals and Success in Modern American Drama." In *Rags to Riches: Le Mythe du Self-Made Man*. Ed. Serge Ricard. (Aix en Provence: Univ. de Provence, 1984). 121-35.
        Dramas by Clifford Odets, Lillian Hellman [*The Little Foxes*], and Arthur Miller are examined as examples of partial ideological critiques of individualism and family values in the context of an acquisitive, competitive society. Concludes that all three authors see, "The sterile venality of a materialistically conceived American Dream . . . as a menace to the integrity of human beings" (133).

S215   Dukore, Bernard F. *American Dramatists 1918-45*. New York: Grove Press, 1984. 142-155.
        Chapter 8, entitled "Lillian Hellman," examines the dramatist, providing an overview of dramatic and theatrical characteristics. Surveys *The Children's Hour*, *Days to Come*, *Watch on the Rhine*, and *The Searching Wind*. Concentrates on *The Little Foxes* for a more intensive analysis. "Better crafted than her other works, it is varied in characterization and language. Of particular importance to the theatre, it is an effective acting vehicle not only for a female star but also for supporting characters" (155).

S216   Friedman, Sharon. "Feminism as Theme in Twentieth Century American Women's Drama." *Journal of American Studies* 25 (Spring 1984): 69-89.
        Includes Hellman's *The Little Foxes* and *Another Part of the Forest* in an examination of the works of four women dramatists whose plays make a statement about women's role and status in contemporary society. (See S185)

S217   Krammer, Hilton. The Life and Death of Lillian Hellman. *New Criterion* 3 (Oct. 1984): 1-6.
        Finds profound misrepresentations and distortions in the Hellman autobiographical trilogy, such as the "Julia" story which is actually based on the anti-fascist experiences of Muriel Gardiner who was married to Ernest Hemingway at the time. Suggests, as does Marsha Norman, that it is the theatre that Hellman made of her life that we are asked to admire. Reminds us that Hellman died an unrepentant Stalinist, leaving half of a substantial estate to the establishment the Dashiell Hammett Fund to be guided by the political, social and economic beliefs of the late "Hammett, who was a believer in the doctrines of Karl Marx" (6).

S218   *"The Little Foxes."* In *The American Experience: Drama*. Ed. Marjorie Wescott Barrows et al. New York: Macmillan, 1984. 3-85.

Includes text of play with an introduction, study questions, and composition suggestions.

S219   McCracken, Samuel. "*Julia* and Other Fictions by Lillian Hellman." *Commentary* 77 (June 1984): 35-43.
Argues that Julia was modeled on Muriel Gardiner and suggests that the eventual portrayal of Hellman's reputation "will tell us a good deal about the health, intellectual no less than moral, of our literary establishment" (43).

S220   Norman, Marsha. "Articles of Faith: A Conversation with Lillian Hellman." *American Theatre* 1 (May 1984): 10-15.
Robert Brustein made the arrangements for this interview and joined Hellman and Norman as they talked at Martha's Vineyard during the summer of 1993. Hellman says that she never felt comfortable in the theatre, that she found most theatre people silly and vain. As for advice for success in the theatre, "Just earn the money and forget it" (14).

S221   Norman, Marsha. "Lillian Hellman's Gift to a Young Playwright." *New York Times* 26 Aug. 1984: C, 1, 7.
Writes of Hellman's advice to playwrights, of her legacy. Writers like Lillian Hellman "make it possible for those who come after them to survive" (7).

S222   Shaver, Sara Hurdis. *Feminist Criticism As Role Analysis for the Interpreter: Women in Lillian Hellman's Major Plays*. Dissertation (University of Arizona). DAI-A 15 (1984), 344. Published. Tokyo, Ann Arbor: Yushodo, UMI, 1986.
An original method of analysis, based on the tenets of feminist criticism, is applied to the women in the major plays, focusing on character analysis and featuring inquiry into the character's role, values, self image, finances, attitudes toward sex, and measure of power.

1985

S223   Adler, Jacob H. "Modern Southern Drama." *The History of Southern Drama*. Eds. Louis D. Rubin, Jr., Blyden Jackson, S. Moore Rayburn, Lewis P. Simpson, Thomas Daniel Young. Baton Rouge: Louisiana State University Press, 1985. 436-42.
Surveys Hellman's plays and provides a brief biographical sketch. Determines that *The Little Foxes, Watch on the Rhine, The Searching Wind*, and *Another Part of the Forest* "show strong affinities to Ibsen: in their well-made qualities, taut dialogue, unresolved endings, use of the end-play technique, interest in social issues, symbolic titles, use of blackmail, and depiction of clear cut characters, including in two of the plays, children" (439). Considers Hellman second to Arthur Miller as an American Ibsenian, second in importance to Tennessee Williams as a Southern playwright.

S224   Grossman, Anita Susan. "Art versus Truth in Autobiography: The Case of Lillian Hellman." *Clio* 14 (Spring 1985): 289-308.

Examines the controversies associated with the memoirs, concluding that the issue of truth in autobiography raised by her work will continue to be debated for years to come.

S225   Higdon, David Leon. "Henry James and Lillian Hellman: An Unnoted Source." *Henry James Review* 6 (Winter 1985): 134-35.

Regina Giddens' refusal to get her husband's medicine when he suffers his fatal attack has become one of the most famous scenes in American theatre. A very similar scene occurs in Chapter 22 of Henry James's *The American*.

S226   Parrish, Richard Dale. *Style in Lillian Hellman's Pentimento: The Rhetoric of Elusiveness*. Ann Arbor: UMI, 1985.

Doctoral thesis (East Texas State University) which examines the memoir.

1986

S227   Albert, Jan. "Sweetest Smelling Baby in New Orleans." *Conversations with Lillian Hellman*. Ed. Jackson R. Bryer. Jackson: University Press of Mississippi, 1986. 165-178.

A radio interview conducted on WBAI-NY, 1975. The audio cassette (available from Pacifica Tape Library, Los Angeles, CA) was transcribed and edited for print. Hellman talks about her childhood, her plays, her relationship with Hammett, her first trip to Russia, her appearance before the House Un-American Activities Committee, and being blacklisted in Hollywood.

S228   Barker-Nunn, Jeanne Beverly. *A More Adequate Conception: American Women Writers' Quest for a Female Ethic*. Unpublished Dissertation (University of Minnesota). DAI-A 46 (1986), 3069.

Chapter 3 looks at the plays and memoirs of Lillian Hellman as an example of a moral intelligence burdened by the myth of female moral inferiority.

S229   Bryer, Jackson R., ed. *Conversations with Lillian Hellman*. Jackson: University of Mississippi, 1986.

Contains uncut interviews, for the most part, which Hellman gave, usually before or just after one of her plays opened on Broadway, or about the time a film she had written was released. The twenty-seven selected interviews also include some which focus on Hellman's views on the state of the American theatre and film industries and discussions of aspects of her life, principally her relationship with Hammett and her 1952 appearance before the House Un-American Activities Committee, and lastly those which occurred as her memoirs appeared.

S230   Denham, Cynthia Bailey. *Lillian Hellman's Revisions in the Collected Plays*. Unpublished Dissertation (Auburn University). DAI-A 47 (1986): 897.

Collates the revisions in the first editions and in *The Collected Plays* which is considered the definitive 1972 edition, noting subtle changes in dialogue, the elimination of overly explicit stage directions, and the correction of structural faults. Assesses the effect of the revisions on structure, thematic purpose, and characterization, concluding that the major effect has been to strengthen characterization and theme with no significant effect on structure. The most extensive revisions appeared in *Days to Come*; almost 25 percent of the text cut.

S231   Doudna, Christine. "A Still Unfinished Woman: A Conversation with Lillian Hellman." *Conversations with Lillian Hellman.* Ed. Jackson R. Bryer. Jackson: University Press of Mississippi, 1986. (See S179)

S232   Jelinek, Estelle C. *The Tradition of Women's Autobiography from Antiquity to the Present.* Boston: Twayne, 1986. 148-67.
        A chapter entitled "Literary Autobiography Recast: The Oblique Heroism of Lillian Hellman" examines the memoirs in which her psychological sophistication and dramatic skills combine, emphasizing the personal and gradually discarding imitation of the progressive mode for the disjunctive one. From dissertation (S186).

S233   Luce, William. *Lillian: A One-Woman Play Based on the Autobiographical Works of Lillian Hellman.* New York: Dramatists Play Service, 1986.
        Of related interest, this script was based on Hellman's memoirs. Produced at the Barrymore Theatre, NYC, 16 Jan. 1986. Starred Zoe Caldwell.

S234   Parrish, Richard Dale. *Style in Lillian Hellman's Pentimento: The Rhetoric of Elusiveness.* Unpublished Dissertation (East Texas State University). DAI-A 46 (1986), 2285.
        Applies narrative discourse theories to *Pentimento*, identifying modern fiction techniques that characterize Hellman's style. Repeats Hellman's assertion that she did not wish to write autobiography, that she chose to write the memoirs with a feeling for fiction.

S235   Reynolds, R.C. *Stage Left: The Development of the American Social Drama in the Thirties.* Troy, NY: Whitson, 1986: 128-144.
        In a section entitled "Lillian Hellman: The Well-Made Melodrama," Reynolds analyzes *The Children's Hour*, *Days to Come*, and *The Little Foxes*, to show similarities to the works of Clifford Odets in the use of device and characterization, yet significant differences in social-critical stance and technique of writing.

S236   Sabinson, Eric Mitchell. *Script and Transcript: The Writings of Clifford Odets, Lillian Hellman and Arthur Miller in Relation to Their Testimony Before the U.S. House Committee on Un-American Activities.* Unpublished Dissertation (SUNY-Buffalo). DAI 47-A (1986), 2161.
        Examines the relationship of the three playwrights' work to their testimony. The writers' earlier plays are seen as rehearsals to the trial (Hellman's *The Autumn Garden* with its interrogation of faith), their later works as allegories responding to the experience (Hellman's *The Lark*, wherein Hellman as Joan of Arc, martyrs but defiantly creates herself).

S237   Taavila-Walters, Pia Seija. *Moral Questions in the Life and Work of Lillian Hellman.* Unpublished Dissertation (Michigan University Press). DAI 47-A: 2 (1986): 527.

Examines *The Children's Hour*, *Watch on the Rhine*, *The Little Foxes*, *The Autumn Garden*, and *Montserrat*, which best illustrated Hellman's ability to combine the worlds of moral vision and artistic endeavor.

S238   Wright, William. *Lillian Hellman: The Image, the Woman*. New York: Simon & Schuster, 1986. Sidgwick & Jackson, 1987. Ballantine Books, 1988.
A useful, unauthorized biography that debunks many myths with revealing details based on scores of interviews. Primary focus on Hellman's portrait. Includes a brief analysis of plays. Praises Hellman as a dramatist.

1987

S239   Erbin, Rudolf. "Mourning Becomes Regina: Lillian Hellman's Unfinished Trilogy." *Maske und Kothurn* 33 (1987): 125-32.
The Little Foxes and *Another Part of the Forest* are two parts of an unfinished trilogy in the Greek tradition. Erbin suggests that Hellman choose the form, since the moralism inherent in the Greek trilogy was a reflection of the prevailing mood in the 1930s, allowing Hellman the necessary scope to comment on America's social development; and because she could "rely on O'Neill's contemporary trilogy *Mourning Becomes Electra* as a source, as evidenced by the two family sagas' almost parallel plots, setting, and characters" (126).

S240   Griffin, Joseph. "Hellman, Williams, Hemingway and Cowley: Views and Interviews." *Canadian Review of American Studies* 18 (Winter 1978): 519-25.
Reviews Jackson R. Bryer's *Conversation with Lillian Hellman* along with three other books in the University Press of Mississippi series, though "Hellman's standing is not as high as that of the other three" (520).

S241   Holditch, W. Kenneth. "*Another Part of the Country*: Lillian Hellman as Southern Playwright." *The Southern Quarterly* 25 (Spring 1987): 11-35.
An in-depth analysis which examines the southern elements, motifs, and themes witnessed in Hellman's finest writings, particularly *The Little Foxes* and *Another Part of the Forest* and to a lesser extent in *The Autumn Garden* and *Toys in the Attic*.

S242   Johns, Ian. "On Stage Alone: Lillian. *Plays & Plays* 401 (Feb. 1987): 7-8.
An article regarding William Luce's *Lillian*, based on Hellman's memoirs, scheduled to open at the Fortune Theatre on February 6. The show was produced in October and November in a series of Sunday performances at the Lyric Theatre. Frances de la Tour, who stars in the one person show, says that there has been a tremendous response to the play, and that a tremendous attack against Hellman has resurfaced.

S243   Murphy, Brenda. *American Realism and American Drama*, 1880-1940. Cambridge: Cambridge University Press, 1987. 179.
While Hellman may give her audience an easy figure to condemn, she "make[s] a clear connection between the hateful aspects of the individuals and the hateful ideology they espouse, such as fascism or greedy capitalism."

S244   Pender, Thomas Murray. *Initial Critical Response to the Plays of Jean Anouilh on the New York Stage*. Unpublished Dissertation (University of Georgia). DAI-A 47 (1987), 1239.

Analyzes Anouilh's plays in terms of decisions made by translators, directors, and designers, and in American dramatic criticism. Includes a discussion of Hellman's *The Lark*.

S245   Waites Lamm, Kathleen Anne. *Lillian Hellman: Revisioning from Drama to Memoir*. Unpublished Dissertation (University of Nebraska-Lincoln). DAI-A 47 (1987), 2588.

Traces Hellman's literary development and the influences responsible for that development. She was steeped in the forms and views of traditional theatre, due to historical circumstances and the influence of Hammett. In the process, she discovered a form of writing that affirmed her female experience and prompted further inner exploration, the female-identified form of the autobiographical memoir.

1988

S246   Anderlini, Serena M. *Gender and Desire in Contemporary Drama: Lillian Hellman, Natalia Ginzburg, Franca Rame and Ntozake Shange*. Unpublished Dissertation (University of California, Riverside). DAI-A 19 (1988), 809.

Includes an examination of "the tinge of self-portraiture" in *The Little Foxes* and *Toys in the Attic*, which shows that Hellman was influenced by the mid-century antifeminist backlash. A Jewish-American writer, she used the literary form to conceal her Jewish and female identity from the public.

S247   Barranger, Milly S. "Lillian Hellman: Standing in the Minefields." *New Orleans Review* 15 (Spring 1988): 62-68.

Examines Hellman's career as a successful Broadway playwright, the use of her Southern heritage in the making of four major plays, and her leadership that cleared the path in profession theatre for women playwrights in particular.

S248   Feibleman, Peter S. *Lilly: Reminiscences of Lillian Hellman*. New York: William Morrow and Co., 1988. Rprt. Avon, 1990.

The novelist bases his reminiscence of Hellman on their 43-year relationship as friends and lovers. They met about 1940, when he was 10 and she in her mid-30s, became lovers in the early 60s after the death of Hammett, and remained significant others until she died in 1984. An appendix includes seven eulogies given at Hellman's graveside in Chilmark Cemetery on Martha's Vineyard.

S249   Rollyson, Carl. *Lillian Hellman: Her Legend and Her Legacy*. New York: St. Martin's Press, 1988.

An unauthorized biography based on extensive interviews. Rollyson argues convincingly that the strongwilled, self-centered, authoritarian playwright cleverly tailored her life and her writings to keep her legend intact. One interviewee recalls her "notoriety kick," in which "everything about her life became grander in the rewriting of it" (3) Another remarks, "She would lie about anything--a man, a woman, it could be anything--for what we used to call 'a pretty good story'" (4). Includes information culled from sources such as Hellman's FBI file and a CIA file of correspondence intercepted·in 1960s, revealing Hellman's affiliation with Communist party. In addition to the detailed account of Hellman's life, the book provides a substantial evaluation and background information on the plays.

S250   Warren, Ann L. *Word Play: The Lives and Work of Four Women Writers in Hollywood's Golden Age.* Unpublished Dissertation (University of Southern California). DAI 49:4 (1988): 821A.

Includes Hellman in an investigation of this unique area of employment for women during the 1930s and 1940s, high salaries which contributed to glamorous lifestyles, at a time when writers were politically active in one way or another.

1989

S251   Adams, Timothy Dow. "Lies Like Truth: Lillian Hellman's Autobiographies." In *Critical Essays on Lillian Hellman.* Ed. Mark W. Estrin. Boston: G.K. Hall, 1989. 194-216.

Examines Hellman's four autobiographies, examples of hybrid forms of life-writing styles that thwart·personal identity. Concluding that, "the act of repenting through mastery of the art of palimpsestic autobiography, ultimately produced a completed woman . . . " (214). Explores the veracity of "Julia."

S252   Adler, Jacob H. "The Dramaturgy of Blackmail in the Ibsenite Hellman." In *Critical Essays on Lillian Hellman.* Ed. Mark W. Estrin. Boston: G.K. Hall & Co., 1989. 31-42.

Compares the dramaturgical and philosophical purposes and effects of blackmail in the plays of Ibsen and Hellman; and concludes that Hellman deviates by linking blackmail to the notions of money and power.

S253   Adler, Jacob H. "Miss Hellman's Two Sisters." In *Critical Essays on Lillian Hellman.* Boston: G.K. Hall & Co., 1989: 43-49. Reprinted from *Educational Theatre Journal* 15 (May 1963). 112-17.

Compares *Toys in the Attic* to Chekhov's *The Three Sisters*, concluding that: while Hellman's well-made technique comes from Ibsen, the basic outline or source of her play comes Chekhov.

S254   Austin, Gayle. "The Exchange of Women and Male Homosocial Desire in Arthur Miller's *Death of a Salesman* and Lillian Hellman's *Another Part of the Forest.*" *Feminist Readings of Modern American Drama.* Ed. June Schlueter. Rutherford, NJ: Fairleigh Dickinson University Press, 1989. 54-66.

Analyzes the plays from a feminist perspective to show how the women are exchanged among the men and how they are represented as objects to be exchanged. In contrast to Miller's play, *Another Part of the Forest* "represents women in a very different way, as active subjects, making efforts to arrange their own exchange among men" (63).

S255   Austin, Gayle. *Feminist Theory and Post War American Drama.* Unpublished
        Dissertation (The City University of New York). DAI-A 19 (1989), 2023.
                Summarizes feminist theories from anthropology, psychology, literary
        criticism, and film theory; selects one theorist from each field to serve as an
        example of how feminism in that field can shed light on various plays. Discusses
        sixteen plays from the period 1945-1985. Includes Hellman in the canon of
        traditional playwrights.

S256   Estrin, Mark W., ed. *Critical Essays on Lillian Hellman.* Boston: G.K. Hall &
        Co., 1989.
                A comprehensive collection of scholarship, the twenty-three essays
        explore the "Hellman persona" as well a her plays and memoirs. A superb
        introduction by Estrin (1-27) serves as an important survey of Hellman's career
        and the critical reactions to it. The play section offers a reinterpretation of the
        dramatic canon.

S257   Felheim, Marvin. "*The Autumn Garden*: Mechanics and Dialectics." *Critical
        Essays on Lillian Hellman.* Boston: G.K. Hall & Co., 1989. 49-53. Reprinted
        from *Modern Drama* 3 (Sept. 1960): 191-95.
                Examines Hellman's move from the "well-made" play in the direction of
        Chekhov, the logical development of her lifelong study of Chekhov.

S258   Fleischer, Doris and Leonard Fleischer. "The Dramatic Adaptations of Lillian
        Hellman." *Critical Essays on Lillian Hellman.* Boston: G.K. Hall & Co., 1989.
        55-64.
                A detailed analysis of the four adaptations shows that Hellman's moral
        vision is harsh yet uncharacteristically hopeful. "For despite the corruption and
        cruelty, the opportunity for heroism and change remains. Self knowledge is
        possible . . ." (62).

S259   Newman, Robert P. *The Cold War Romance of Lillian Hellman and John Melby.*
        Chapel Hill: University of North Carolina Press, 1989.
                Tells the story of the Hellman-Melby romance that stated in 1944, and
        never really ended; the story of Hellman's appearance before the HUAC and of
        the interest of governmental agencies such as the FBI, the Passport Office and the
        State Department Security Office in Hellman's activities; as well as the story of
        Melby's dismissal from the State Department because of the Hellman relationship.
        The most sustained examination of Hellman's leftist involvements to date.
        Concludes Appendix 1, "Was Hellman a Communist?" in her defense (291-329).

S260   Patraka, Vivian M. "Lillian Hellman's *Watch on the Rhine*: Realism, Gender, and
        Historical Crisis." *Modern Drama* 32 (Mar. 1989): 128-145.
                Analyzes *Watch on the Rhine*, an exemplar of the general trend towards
        gendered inequality in response to "ungendered" historical crisis, as part of an
        ongoing feminist project to historicize gendered subjectivity as inscribed in plays
        and spectators. "In response to the urgent threat of fascism, Hellman sought to
        infuse anti-fascist polemic into the ahistorical structures of a naturalized and
        nostalgic version of gender relations" (129).

S261   Rapf, Joanna E. "A Larger Thing: John Michael Hayes and *The Children's Hour*." *Post Script: Essays in Film and the Humanities* 9 (Fall-Winter 1989-1990): 38-52.

Recounts the origins of *The Children's Hour* and comments on the first film adaptation, *These Three* (1936), before exploring the remake in 1962, *The Children's Hour* (script by John Michael Hayes) in which the comment on witch-hunting, intentional or not, is poignantly manifested.

S262   Towns, Saundra. *Lillian Hellman*. New York: Chelsea House Publishers, 1989.

Examines the Hellman's career, her early life, making it as a playwright, and her involvement in politics. Richly illustrated and written in a style especially for young adults. Part of American Women of Achievement series.

S263   Tufts, Carol Stongin. "Who's Lying? The Issue of Lesbianism in Lillian Hellman's *The Children's Hour*." *Minnesota Review* 53 (1989): 63-78.

Presents a convincing argument for lesbianism as the central issue. "Hellman's own need for acceptance into the world of men (and perhaps an uneasiness with the lesbian potential within herself) compels her to treat her female characters from a male point of view" (68).

S264   Wiles, Timothy J. "Lillian Hellman's American Political Theater: the Thirties and Beyond." *Critical Essays on Lillian Hellman*. Ed. Mark W. Estrin. Boston, MA: G.K. Hall & Co., 1989. 91-112.

Surveys the 1930s plays and includes the 1940s plays whose formative influence can be traced to political events, plays which demonstrate political art as a product of its age and a force of innovation, leading to "wider speculations about the genre (including her kinship with Brecht) and toward a more substantial evaluation of her current reputation as a feminist precursor" (92).

1990

S265   Austin, Gayle. *Feminist Theories for Dramatic Criticism*. Ann Arbor: University of Michigan Press, 1990. 51-55.

In a chapter entitled "Feminist Anthropology: The Exchange of Women," *Another Part of the Forest* is approached from a feminist perspective "[T]he female 'property' is allowed to act and speak for herself as a subject as we see her being exchange by the men on stage as if she were an object" (51). The black woman servant "underscores the particular intersection of race, gender, and property in the America of 1880" (51).

S266   Friedman, Ginger. *The Perfect Monologue*. New York: Bantam Books, 1990. 264-283.

Takes four scenes in *The Children's Hour*, creating monologues for Mrs. Mortar, age 45 to mid-60s; for Martha or Karen, age 20 to 40; for Martha, age 20 to 40; and for Mrs. Tilford, age 60 to 70. Includes performance advice.

S267   Georgoudaki, Ekaterini. "Women in Lillian Hellman's Plays, 1930-1950." In *Women and War: The Changing Status of American Women from the 1930s to the 1950s*. Eds. Maria Diedrich and Dorothea Fischer-Hornung. New York: Berg, 1990. 69-85.

Examines Hellman's approach to women, her concern with their psychological, financial, and other problems, as manifested in various female characters and situations. Analyzes how various stereotypes are presented and the restrictions that society has imposed on them. Points to Hellman's difficulties in developing solutions to the problems of her women in transition. (*The Children's Hour, Days to Come, The Little Foxes, Another Part of the Forest, Watch on the Rhine, The Searching Wind.*)

S268   Goodman, Charlotte. "The Fox's Cubs: Lillian Hellman, Arthur Miller, and Tennessee Williams." In *Modern American Drama: The Female Canon*. Ed. June Schleuter. Rutherford, NJ: Fairleigh Dickinson University Press, 1990. 130-42.

Explores the parallels between *The Little Foxes* and the plays by Miller and Williams that appear less than a decade later: *All My Sons, The Glass Menagerie*, and *A Streetcar Named Desire*. Confirms the relevance of Hellman's work to the younger American dramatists.

S269   Natalle, Elizabeth J. "Hellman, Lillian Florence." *Notable Women in the American Theatre: A Biographical Dictionary*. Eds. Alice M. Robinson, Vera Mowry Roberts, and Milly S, Barranger. Westport, CT: Greenwood Press, 1990. 409-15.

A biographical essay, including a critical overview of the plays and bibliographic sources.

S270   Weaks, Mary Louise. *Lillian Hellman. Mississippi Quarterly* 43 (Spring 1990): 258-62.

Reviews the two books, Robert P. Newman's, *The Cold War Romance of Lillian Hellman and John Melby* (S259) and Carl Rollyson's *Lillian Hellman: Her Legend and Her Legacy.*(S249).

1991

S271   Bailey, Lucille Marie. *Sex-Marked Language Differences: A Linguistic Analysis of Lexicon and Syntax in the Female and Male Dialogue in the Eight Original Plays of Lillian Hellman* . Unpublished Dissertation (Ball State University). DAI-A 52 (1991), 2124A.

Examines a randomly selected sample of 31,115 words from Hellman's original plays, using terms that are described by other researchers, especially Mary P. Hiatt, as belonging to generally feminine or masculine categories. Various categories indicate Hellman's use of these strategies to define personality.

S272   Salter, Susan. "Hellman, Lillian (Florence) 1906-1984." *Contemporary Authors*. New Revision Series, Vol. 33. Ed. James G. Lesniak. Detroit and London: Gale Research Inc., 1991. 206-210.

Comprehensive entry on the life and Hellman career by Susan Salter. Lists plays, screenplays, biographical and critical sources.

S273   King, Kimball. "Hellman, Lillian (Florence)." *International Dictionary of Theatre and Plays 2.* Playwrights volume. Ed. Mark Hawkins-Dady. Chicago and London: St. James Press, 1991. 464-67.
        A comprehensive biographical sketch which includes a critical overview of the plays.

S274   Lenker, Lagretta Tallent. "The Foxes in Hellman's Family Forest." In *The Aching Heart: Family Violence in Life and Literature.* Ed. Sara Munson Deats. New York: Plenum, 1991. 241-253.
        Gives a personal reading to the Hubbard saga which "chronicles the debilitating effects of family violence, especially spouse abuse, from the interwoven perspectives of husband-wife, brother-sister, and parent child" (242). (*Another Part of the Forest, The Little Foxes.*)

S275   Morris, Paula J. K. *Magnolias and Rattlesnakes: The Southern Lady in American Fiction.* Unpublished Dissertation (University of York, UK). DAI-A 51 (1991), 3074.
        Chapter 6 examines the ideal of the Southern lady in relation to Hellman's life and work, focusing on the autobiographical stories and the four Southern plays, *Another Part of the Forest, The Autumn Garden, Another Part of the Forest,* and *The Little Foxes.*

S276   Stubbs, Mary Frances. *Lorraine Hansberry and Lillian Hellman: A Comparison of Social and Political Issues in their Plays and Screen Adaptations.* Unpublished Dissertation (Indiana University). DAI-A 51 (1991), 3759.
        Analyzes *The Children's Hour* and *The Little Foxes* together with their film adaptations. Points out that the screen adaptations of *The Children's Hour,* *These Three* (1936) and *The Children's Hour* (1962), reflect different American political climates as well as disparate attitudes toward the original work and its contemporary relevance. Includes filmography and bibliographical references.

S277   Titus, Mary. "Murdering the Lesbian: Lillian Hellman's *The Children's Hour.*" *Tulsa Studies in Women's Literature* 10 (1991): 215-32.
        Hellman violently disposes of the lesbian in *The Children's Hour.* Insight into her complex response to contemporary sexual ideology is provided in "Julia." Hellman's interest in "establishing clear sexual identities coincided with her entrance into the male-dominated theatre world . . . By eliminating Martha Dobie, Hellman rather violently silenced any doubts about her own heterosexuality . . . doubts that perhaps she, too, possessed" (217).

1992

S278   Brown, Linda Ginter. *Toward a More Cohesive Self: Women in the Works of Lillian Hellman and Marsha Norman.* Unpublished Dissertation (Ohio State University). DAI-A 52 (1992), 2919.
        Chapter I, "The Mother Self," includes *Another Part of the Forest* and *The Little Foxes* in a focus on mother/daughter relationships. Chapter II, The (M)Other Self, includes an exploration of *The Children's Hour* and *Toys in the Attic*; although the mother is not physically present, she influences the daughter's

relation with the "idealized other." Chapter III, The Hungry Self, includes *Days to Come* in a discussion of the use of food to manifest the hunger for power and psychic cohesion in Cora Rodman. The basis of the work is drawn on the object-relations theory of Nancy Chodorow.

S279   Mobley, Maribeth L. *Fictions of Self in the Language of Lillian Hellman: An Analysis of the Autobiographical Works.* Unpublished Dissertation (University of South Florida). DAI-A 52 (1992), 2555.
        Traces the evolution in Hellman's awareness of the problematics of autobiography. In the writing of *An Unfinished Woman*, Hellman discovers that the objective truth she seeks is elusive, subject to imperfect memory and personal bias. In *Pentimento* she writes with full knowledge of the autobiographical self as a fictive construct. In *Scoundrel Time* she portrays her history of the McCarthy era as she wants it to be remembered, disregarding verifiable data in public records. And *Three* adds commentary to alter the past self. Though she had grappled to construct a unified self, her disjointed and conflicting narratives indicate an acceptance of the fragmented self.

S280   Paige, Linda Louise Rohrer. *The Other Side of the Looking Glass: A Feminist Perspective on Female Suicide in Ibsen's Hedda Gabler, Hellman's The Children's Hour, and Norman's 'night Mother.* Unpublished Dissertation (University of Tennessee). DAI-A 53 (1992), 1152.
        This study uncovers signs of female suicide, interpreting both method and meaning of the protagonist's death. Uses some theatre semiotics, explores relevant myths, analyzes key scenes, and identifies recurrent motifs of "housing" (especially "house" as the female body), "invalidism", "waiting", and "acting," all crucial to an understanding of the protagonist's motivation for self-destruction. Finds the suicides angry responses to patriarch as well as assertions of the heroine's will to control mind, body, and destiny.

S281   Reaves, Gerri. *Defining the Self in Twentieth Century American Autobiographical Writings: America As Paradigm.* Unpublished Dissertation (University of Miami). DAI-A 52 (1992), 1332.
        Includes Hellman in an examination of twentieth-century American autobiographies (Gertrude Stein, Lillian Hellman, Sam Shepard) which revise the teleology that comprises the given context of identity formation: inheritance, familial relations, genealogy, history, politics, and culture. In *Scoundrel Time*, her memoir of the McCarthy era, Hellman elevates a subjective accounting of the truth to the status of contemporary American history. As with each of the three authors considered, the work constitutes a private geography that structures the discourse and defines the autobiographical "I."

S282   Westbrook, Brett Elizabeth. *Lillian Hellman: Dramatist in Society.* Unpublished Dissertation (University of California). DAI-A 52 (1992), 2558.
        Reevaluates Hellman's position in the history of American drama and film by examining how her plays (the eight original) and movies politicize the everyday. The introduction addresses the inadequacies of previous Hellman criticism and the undue emphasis on her biography and dealings with HUAC.

1993

S283   Brantley, Will. *Feminine Sense in Southern Memoir: Smith, Glasgow, Welty, Hellman, Porter, and Hurston.* Jackson: University Press of Mississippi, 1993. 133-184.

Chapter 4 includes an exploration of the ethical and political positions outlined by Hellman in *Scoundrel Time.* Hellman was drawn to the important theme of the dangers of a passive collusion with evil. She used her self-writing to explore her own motives and vent scorn on those who, through passivity, ignorance or refusal to explore self, allowed evil to exist. Threads are evidenced in the plays: the scandal-mongering in *The Children's Hour*, the denunciations of those who remain passive in face of social and political threats in *Watch on the Rhine* and *The Searching Wind*, the doers and the bystanders in *The Little Foxes.* Her moral vision, however, expanded beyond the duality of active and passive doers of evil. In her adaptations she was drawn to characters who discovered personal dignity by remaining true to moral commitments. Hellman's translation of *The Lark* appeared three years after the HUAC hearing. In the play Joan's inquisitors merge with the "Inquisitor priests" denounced in *Scoundrel Time.*

S284   Fox, Larry Phillip. *A Comparative Analysis of Selected Dramatic Works and Their Twentieth-Century Operatic Adaptations.* Unpublished Dissertation (University of South Carolina). DAI 53 (1993), 115.

Includes a detailed comparison of Hellman's *The Little Foxes* and Blitzstein's *Regina*, a scene by scene analysis with emphasis on the techniques of condensation and expansion. Includes brief biographical material as well a production history and critical overview.

S285   Skantze, Pat. "Lillian Hellman 1905-1984." *Modern American Women Writers.* 1st Collier Books, ed. New York: Toronto: New York: Collier Books; Maxwell Macmillan Canada; Maxwell Macmillan International, 1993. 207-19.

An essay that combines a detailed account of the writer's life with an analysis of plays and memoirs, and a substantial bibliography.

1994

S286   Adler, Jacob H. Updated by Katherine Lederer. "Lillian Hellman." *Critical Survey of Drama* Rev. Ed. 3. Ed. Frank N. Magill. Englewood Cliffs, NJ: Salem Press, 1994. 1138-1149.

A comprehensive entry that includes biographical material, analyses of plays, and bibliographic information.

S287   Fallows, Randall Jonathan. *Dramatic Realities: The Creation and Reception of American Political and Fictional Dramas of the Late 1940s and their Influence on Gender Role Construction.* Unpublished Dissertation (University of California, San Diego). DAI 51 (1994), 1092.

Explores the influence of cold war political language on the formation of gender roles, in paradigmatic dramas of the late 1940s. Includes *Another Part of the Forest* which challenged the proper roles of responsible man and dutiful housewife.

S288   Foradori, Anne Bill. *Mark Blitzstein's Regina: A Pivotal Work in American Musical Theatre*. Unpublished Dissertation (Ohio State University). DAI 55 (1994), 1413.
         Examines *Regina*, its libretto and score, comparing and contrasting Hellman's *The Little Foxes* with the adaptation.

S289   King, Kimball. "Hellman, Lillian (Florence). *Contemporary Women Dramatists*. Ed. K.A. Berney. London: St. James Press, 1994. 93-96.
         A comprehensive overview of plays and contributions. Includes biographical and bibliographical information.

1995

S290   *Banned, Censored, Harassed and Jailed Writers Receive Grants: 48 writers from 23 countries recognized by Lillian Hellman/Dashiell Hammett Funds*. New York: Human Rights Watch Free Expression Project, 1995.
         Lists 1995 recipients with short biographies, and grants totaling approximately $175,000. Now in the sixth year, the trust set up by the Hellman and Hammett estates "to assist writers in financial need as a result of political persecution" (1).

S291   Beal, Suzanne Elaine. *"Mama Teach me that French." Mothers and Daughters in Twentieth Century Plays by American Women Playwrights*. Unpublished Dissertation (University of Maryland College Park). DAI 55 (1995), 3185.
         Explores mother-daughter relationships in plays written between 1909 and 1992. A chapter entitled "The Retreat from Feminism, 1930-1960 includes the works of Lillian Hellman wherein subtexts challenge hegemonic constructions of gender.

S292   Castor, Laura Virginia. *Historical Memory, Autobiography and Art: Redefining Identity Through the Writing and Theater of Isadora Duncan, Hallie Flanagan, and Lillian Hellman*. Unpublished Dissertation (University of Minnesota). DAI 55 (1995), 2107.
         Includes Hellman in an investigation of individual and cultural identity using theatre as a cultural microcosm. The study integrates literary and historical criticism, and American theatre history, with a discussion of autobiographical texts. The project also explores the politics of identity in terms of historical change.

S293   Foster, Karen K. *De-Tangling the Web: Mother-Daughter Relationships in the Plays of Marsha Norman, Lillian Hellman, Tina Howe, and Ntozake Shange*. Unpublished Dissertation (University of Nebraska-Lincoln). DAI 55 (1995), 3041.
         Uses psychoanalytic theories of Freud, Chodorow, Lacan, Kristeva, and Irigaray to explore the mother-daughter relationships in *The Little Foxes* and *Another Part of the Forest*, concluding that the plays reflect the semiotic in its relationship to the Symbolic order. Suggests that Hellman dealt artistically with her relationship to her mother in order to come to terms with the Symbolic order in which she was problematically enmeshed.

S294   Haedicke, Janet V. "Lillian Hellman." *American Playwrights 1880-1945*. Ed.
            William W. Demastes. Westport, CT: Greenwood Press, 1995. 132-144.
                 A contributing chapter which includes a biographical overview, a list of
            plays with production information, an assessment of the playwright's career, and
            bibliographic references.

S295   Johnston, Beverly Lynn Alexander. *Caught in the Flux of Change: The Southern
            Lady in Selected Plays and Films of the Twentieth Century*. Unpublished
            Dissertation (University of Georgia). DAI 55 (1995), 3041.
                 Includes *The Little Foxes* and *Another Part of the Forest* in a study of
            stereotyped southern women who are negatively cast in roles of debilitated victim
            or externally beautiful but internally wicked, as opposed to the cultivated manners
            of self-defined southern ladies.

S296   Martin, Annabel. *A Grammar of Happiness: A Filmic and Autobiographical
            Remapping of National Identity and Womanhood in the United States and Spain
            of the 1940s*. Unpublished Dissertation (University of Oregon). DAI-A 55:11
            (1995), 3502.
                 Brings a feminist perspective to a discussion of national identity and its
            relation to womanhood in a study that includes an analysis of Hellman's
            autobiographical and historical writing and how popular culture, Hollywood film
            narrative, and autobiographical writing demystify cultural identity.

S297   Scrimgeour, J.D. *Provisional Selves: Audience and the Autobiographical Act*.
            Unpublished Dissertation (Indiana University). DAI-A 55 (1995), 2375.
                 Includes Hellman in an investigation of how relationships between
            autobiographers and their reading publics influence the creation of self in
            autobiography. Argues that the autobiographical self is always provisional,
            contingent upon the distinct relation between autobiographer and audience at a
            particular moment.

S298   Turk, Ruth. *Lillian Hellman, Rebel Playwright*. Minneapolis: Lerner
            Publications, 1995.
                 A biography, richly illustrated, written for grade six and up. Listed under
            juvenile literature.

1996

S299   Mellen, Joan. *Hellman and Hammett*. New York: HarperCollins, 1996.
                 This book is the first to make use of Lillian Hellman's papers as well as
            those of Dashiell Hammett deposited with the Hellman archives at the Harry
            Ransom Humanities Research Center of the University of Texas in its telling of
            the Hellman-Hammett relationship.

Author Index

The following index lists all critics and scholars included in the secondary bibliographies. The references are keyed to the numbers ("R" = reviews; "S" = books, articles, sections) assigned to the entries.

General Index

The following index records page references as well as references keyed to the primary ("A" writings by Hellman; "P" = plays) bibliography and secondary ("R" = reviews; "S" = books, articles, sections) bibliographies.

About the Author

BARBARA LEE HORN is Associate Professor and Chair of the Department of Speech, Communication Sciences and Theatre at St. John's University in New York. Her publications include *The Age of Hair: Evolution and Impact of Broadway's First Rock Musical* (1991), *Joseph Papp: A Bio-Bibliography* (1992), *David Merrick: A Bio-Bibliography* (1992), *Colleen Dewhurst: A Bio-Bibliography* (1993), *Ellen Stewart and La Mama: A Bio-Bibliography* (1993), and *Maxwell Anderson: A Research and Production Sourcebook* (1996), all published by Greenwood Press.

ISBN 0-313-30264-2

90000>

EAN

9 780313 302640

HARDCOVER BAR CODE